Advance Praise

Grace Chang makes an enormous contribution by showing how immigrant women workers facilitate the operation of the global economy. These are histories at risk of invisibility.

—Saskia Sassen, author of *Guests and Aliens*

What a book for both scholars and activists! It offers a much needed understanding of the multi-faceted linkage between global and local issues in today's world. Grace Chang shows us how that linkage affects women with both clarity and passion.

—Elizabeth Martínez, author of *De Colores Means All of Us*

Disposable Domestics shows the underbelly of the dot.com economic boom—that is, the women who toil behind the scenes as caretakers and factory workers for wages that keep them mired in poverty. With great poignancy, Grace Chang traces how austerity programs imposed by the International Monetary Fund force poor women to emigrate to the United States, how they are vilified and exploited in their "host" country, and how they are fighting against tremendous odds to secure their basic rights. It is an essential book for those trying to connect the dots between global economic policies and women's labor.

—Medea Benjamin, Founding Director, Global Exchange

Grace Chang presents an eye-opening and path-breaking account of how so-called welfare reform in the United States, combined with racist anti-immigrant policies, has enabled Americans to take advantage of the labor of immigrant women. Chang demolishes the myth that immigrant women are "welfare queens" and "baby machines." In this book, she documents the essential role that immigrant women play in the U.S. economy as workers who clean houses, offices, and hotel rooms and also take care of our elderly and children. *Disposable Domestics* should be read by anyone wanting to understand the realities of how the U.S. political and economic system is treating immigrant women at the beginning of the twenty-first century.

—Evelyn Nakano Glenn, University of California at Berkeley

Disposable Domestics is a compelling book that is all too rare these days, combining academic research and theory, political conviction, and moral outrage.

—Kitty Calavita, University of California at Irvine

With patience and clarity, Grace Chang shows us that the work of immigrant women is an indispensable feature of global capitalism. Their blood and sweat has been rewarded only by increasing government regulation, domestic violence, and cultural commodification. Feminists and labor organizers beware! *Disposable Domestics* names the hot-button social justice issue of this decade.

—Karin Aguilar-San Juan, editor of *The State of Asian America*

In her illuminating book, Grace Chang shows us clearly how global capital and international policy are linked with domestic policy to trap immigrant women in their paradoxical position as the most valuable and the most vulnerable workers in the United States today, whether they are domestics and nannies in their homes, farm workers who put food on their tables, or factory workers who benefit both the U.S. and their homeland economies. Chang's book exposes the hypocrisy, cruelty, and insanity of anti-immigrant policies and attitudes that persist toward those whose labor benefits others so much more than themselves. Chang also offers an inspiring account of how immigrant women and immigrant advocates are organizing to fight for justice. I hope everyone will read this important book.

—Elaine Kim, University of California at Berkeley

Disposable Domestics is especially timely given the globalization of the economy and the growing number of immigrant women working for wages in the United States. The analysis provided in this book is critical both for understanding the plight of immigrant women workers and for designing strategies for change.

—Mimi Abramovitz, author of *Regulating the Lives of Women*

DISPOSABLE
DOMESTICS

Immigrant Women Workers in the Global Economy

GRACE CHANG
Foreword by Mimi Abramovitz

South End Press
Cambridge, Massachusetts

Some material in this volume was previously published in *Radical America* 26: 2 (October 1996) and in Evelyn Nakano Glenn, Grace Chang, and Linda Rennie Forcey, eds., *Mothering: Ideology, Experience, and Agency* (New York: Routledge, 1994).

Library of Congress Cataloging-in-Publication Data

Chang, Grace.
Disposable domestics : immigrant women workers in the global economy / Grace Chang.
p. cm
Includes bibliographical references and index.
ISBN 0-89608-617-8 (paper) — ISBN 0-89608-618-6 (cloth)
1. Women alien labor—United States. 2. Women domestics—United States. 3. Alien labor, Asian—United States. 4. Alien labor, Latin American—United States. I. Title.

HD6095 .C48 2000
331.4' 8164046' 086910973—dc21   99-462383

South End Press, 7 Brookline Street, #1, Cambridge, MA 02139
    05 04 03 02 01 00   1 2 3 4 5 6
PRINTED IN CANADA

Table of Contents

Acknowledgments

I owe many thanks to the countless people who contributed to the development of this book. I especially wish to thank the women I interviewed, who took precious time to share with me their insights and experiences as careworkers, organizers, and mothers. I regret that I have had to change their names for confidentiality in most cases. I hope that the use of pseudonyms has served not to render these women invisible but to allow them to speak more freely about their work and life struggles. I hope that I have done justice to their remarkable stories and that their stories will in turn serve to do justice.

Of those workers, advocates, and organizers who need not remain anonymous, I want to thank the following people for making time in their busy schedules to share their expertise with me and to facilitate interviews with other workers and organizers: Susan Drake, Stephen Rosenbaum, Pauline Gee, Vibiana Andrade, Maria Griffith-Cañas and SEIU Local 250 members, William Tamayo, Donya Fernandez, Cathleen Yasuda, Luisa Blue, Josie Camacho, Mayee Crispin, Ninotchka Rosca, Carole Salmon, Felicita Villasin, Miriam Ching Louie, Linda Burnham, Emma Harris, Steve Williams, Ilana Berger, Michelle Yu, Cristina Riegos, Muneer Ahmad, Amy Schur, Muzzafar Chishti, James Elmendorf, Wei-ling Huber, David Rolf, Rudy Barragan, Cathi Tactaquin, Sasha Kokha, Monica Hernandez and the members of Mujeres Unidas y Activas, Victor Narro, Libertad Rivera, and the members of the Domestic Workers Association.

I owe special thanks to two of my academic mentors, Evelyn Nakano Glenn and Percy Hintzen, not only for their influence on my ideas and nurturance of my critical thinking, but for their continual support and encouragement to finish my dissertation and Ph.D. I have also benefitted from working with Raka Ray, Beatriz Manz,

Jean Molesky, Julia Curry Rodriguez, Elaine Kim, and Sau-ling Wong while at Berkeley. I am indebted to my colleagues Arlene Keizer, Eithne Lubheid, and José Palafox, who have provided thoughtful editing and comments on all or parts of the book manuscript at various stages.

I also appreciate the contributions of all of the editors I have had the good fortune of working with at South End, including Cynthia Peters, Sonia Shah, and especially Lynn Lu and Anthony Arnove in their faithful performances of "good cop" and "bad cop," which facilitated my finally letting go of the manuscript.

I have much love and gratitude for the many people who have made up my and my family's life support system over the years—a small army of bad ass women and a few good men: Patricia Castillo, Vivian Chang, Pamela Chiang, Malkia Cyril, Nicole Davis, Amy Reyes-Drackert, Dana Ginn-Paredes, Dawn Phillips, the women warriors at Hand to Hand, David Bacon, Dug Calderon, my brother Philip Chang, Lance Lee, José Novoa, and Nathaniel Silva. Included in these ranks are my fellow radical-not-soccer-Moms, from whom I have drawn strength and inspiration time and again: Alana Althouse, Rachel Chapman, Nancy Chu, Maria Corral-Ribordy, Tracie Elliot, Marilyn Isaac, Gail Mandella, Melinda Micco, Michelle Nardone, and Mari Rose Taruc. Jose Guzmán and Mary Carbonara kept me and my sons on our toes; Sharon Braz and her staff helped me to keep my family "intact," sheltered, and fed; Christa Donaldson and Ginny Howe kept me "well-adjusted"; and Megan Micco and Suzy Garren provided such loving and brilliant care for my children. I thank my sister and mother, Primalia and Janet Chang, for their support over the long haul. I am also grateful to all of the teachers and careworkers who have enabled me to survive as a single mother and sustain my family throughout these years.

Finally, I thank my sons Lucas and Ricky for humoring, challenging, and inspiring me while I wrote this first book and hope that their recent remarks bear out in the future: When Ricky asked, "Are you done with your book now?" his older brother Lucas said, "Yeah, but that's only this book."

Foreword

by Mimi Abramovitz

Many of us have heard at least one news story about sweatshop workers, home-care attendants, mail-order brides, and foreign nannies—mostly immigrant women who have come to the United States to work. But what do we really know about the lives of the women (and men) who take these jobs or why they come here? Grace Chang—a writer, single mother, activist—begins to answer these questions, focusing on the role of government policy itself. *Disposable Domestics* is especially timely given the globalization of the economy and the growing number of immigrant women working for wages in the United States. The analysis provided in this book is critical both for understanding the plight of immigrant women workers and for designing strategies for change.

The temptation when writing a book such as this is to "put a human face" on the issues by dwelling mainly on the stories of hardship faced by poor immigrant women and/or their political struggles against the odds. While Chang recounts the lives of individual women and their collective actions, the strength of this book lies in Chang's gendered analysis of how government policies regulate the lives of women in the increasingly global labor market. In a series of fascinating, convincing, and easy-to-read essays, *Disposable Domestics* also conveys Chang's underlying message—that the dynamics of immigration are less a matter of individual choice and more a product of the interests of First World nations whose economic investment policies often bring harm to Third World people and places. While this critique of immigration as voluntaristic may not be altogether new, its focus on low-income women and government policy yields important new understandings and interpretations.

Disposable Domestics extends existing studies of the ways in which government policy shapes women's work and family life. First and foremost, Chang highlights how government policies in the US—both structural adjustment policies and domestic social welfare policies—interact to shape the lives of immigrant women. Second, she focuses on low-income women who immigrate to the United States, a group that both immigration and welfare state researchers often overlook. Chang assures us that the unique experiences of poor Latina and Asian women are no longer lost in the shuffle. Third, Chang uses a gender lens. In addition to writing "about" women, Chang follows the important feminist tradition that elevates gender to an analytic variable. Among other things, this leads Chang to recognize that when investigating the lives of women, one must look at work and family life or, more broadly speaking, at the dynamics of economic production and social reproduction. And like increasing numbers of feminists, Chang's gender lens filters in race and class. Finally, Chang shows that the hardship suffered by many has mobilized some immigrant women to become activists on their own behalf.

Chang takes on the argument of immigration as voluntaristic when she describes the way in which structural adjustment policies imposed by First World on Third World nations have helped to create "disposable domestics." Unlike many observers and scholars, Chang disputes the idea that individuals "decide" to leave the Third World simply to either escape grinding poverty or political persecution or to benefit from the economic opportunity and democracy promised in the First World. Chang joins those who fault First World economic development policies for forcing people to leave home. In contrast to the popular belief that economic development policies create jobs and reduce emigration, Chang finds that in many instances, structural adjustment policies create the conditions—austerity, poverty, and unemployment—that make it necessary for people to search for jobs elsewhere. To the extent that the profits of First World banks and corporations depend on debt reduction and the

extraction of resources (both capital and human), government policies eventually force Third World individuals "to follow their country's wealth" to the First World. Because the low-paid jobs in the
First World pay more than work in their own countries, Third
World nations have no choice but to "surrender their citizens, especially women," to First World companies and countries. They "surrender" them because both family members and the national
economy rely heavily on the dollars the women send back. As long
as First World imperialism creates the poverty that causes Third
World women to "want" to leave home, Chang concludes that the
"decision" to emigrate cannot be regarded as a "free" one.

Chang's argument against the voluntaristic interpretation of immigration extends from structural adjustment policies imposed on
Third World economies to First World domestic policies. Nearly every chapter in this book depicts how the increasingly restrictive immigration and welfare policies in the United States since the
mid-1980s have channeled thousands of new arrivals into the growing number of low-paid jobs in the rapidly expanding service sector
of the US economy. Typically reserved for women, many of these
jobs—especially in the nation's cities—are part of the infrastructure
needed to operate the global economic system—be it manufacturing, import-export trade, or international finance. Among other important points, Chang's discussion exposes the historic relationship
between the denial of access to cash benefits, enforced work, and
low wages.

The 1986 Immigration Reform and Control Act (IRCA), for example, retained the 1882 public-charge rule that prevents aliens
from applying for immigration visas if they are likely to become a
public charge. Immigrants must prove that they can support themselves without receipt of public aid. IRCA also bars legalization applicants from most federal assistance programs for five years from the
time they apply for temporary residency and denies legal status to
undocumented women who apply for public assistance for themselves or their citizen children.

The 1996 federal welfare "reform" similarly denied benefits to
immigrants and other poor women. It banned state and local gov-

ernments from providing all but emergency services to undocumented immigrants and to some legal immigrants and denied aid to children born to any women on welfare. Along with the fear of jeopardizing legalization, these punitive provisions have kept immigrant women away from public assistance and turned them, especially immigrant women of color, into a super-exploitable, low-wage workforce to staff the nation's nursing homes, ever-increasing sweatshops, and middle-class households.

Other punitive features of welfare reform have also thrown poor women off welfare. The five-year lifetime limit on welfare eligibility, the new tougher work rules, the workfare program (which requires welfare recipients to work off their benefit in public or private sector jobs), the child exclusion legislation (which denies aid to children born to women on welfare), and a host of punitive sanctions have channeled thousands of women of all races and nationalities into service, manufacturing, and private household employment.

The use of immigration and welfare reform to deny cash aid, combined with fears of deportation and other features of the immigrant experience, forces poor Third World women to take virtually any job regardless of its wages and working conditions. In addition to channeling women into low-paid and often unsafe employment, the policies help to press wages down for all low-wage workers. Flooding the low-wage labor markets with additional workers increases the number of people competing for jobs. This makes it easier for employers to pay less and harder for unions to negotiate good contracts.

The historic use of US welfare policy to increase the supply of low-wage women workers only reinforces Chang's point. From 1940–60, Chang reminds us, welfare's "employable mother" rule drove women, especially poor African-American mothers in the South, into low-paid domestic and agricultural work, as did the suitable home rules that penalized single motherhood. In fact, the practice of limiting welfare benefits and supplying employers with cheap labor dates back to colonial times when town governments established the principle that the value of cash benefits must always fall below the lowest prevailing wage—so that only the most desperate people would choose welfare over work.

The current effort to deny benefits to immigrant women and to restrict eligibility for all recipients continues this harsh tradition. The tradition persists, in part, because access to a viable alternative to market wages (for example, adequate welfare, food stamps, unemployment benefits) has the potential to enable women to avoid taking the worst jobs. Limited as it is, the economic security provided by cash benefits can, at times, embolden women (and men) to join a union, to strike, or to otherwise fight back. To the extent that economic assistance provides poor women with some autonomy, independent entry into the mainstream culture, and the wherewithal to escape abusive relationships, the availability of cash benefits can also undermine patriarchal power relations. Given the welfare state's potential challenges to the imperatives of capital and patriarchy, it is no wonder that its benefits have always remained so low!

Chang's examination of the relationship between social welfare provision and the labor market needs of US corporations benefits from her gendered analysis. Many welfare state theorists have established that when the profit-driven market economy failed to produce the income and jobs needed to sustain the average family, the government stepped in to mediate the tension between the limits of economic production and the requirements of social reproduction. That is, the provision of cash assistance—however reluctant and meager—helped to ensure that families deprived of adequate market income could continue to form and to sustain their members.

Using a gender lens, feminists have pointed out that this dynamic placed the welfare state in a specific relationship to families and women. For one, the tasks of social reproduction—family formation, caretaking, and maintenance—take place largely in the home. Second, given the gender division of labor, the actual work of social reproduction still falls largely to women in the home. Third, the work of social production not only serves the needs of family members but also those of the wider society, for it ensures employers a regular supply of healthy, educated, and properly socialized workers. Finally, when women go to work outside the home, they need government-supported child care, family leave, and other services if they are to balance home and work responsibilities.

Drawing on this contextual framework, Chang finds that when it comes to immigrant households, the United States uses domestic polices to avoid, rather than to support, the cost of social reproduction. That is, the powers that be seek to extract labor from immigrant workers without incurring the costs of family formation and maintenance. It is one thing to admit adults "whose reproduction and training costs have already been borne by their home country.... It is another to absorb the costs for their children, who will not be productive workers for many years."

Chang's gender lens also reveals that once immigration to the United States included large numbers of women, the means used to avert the costs of biological and social reproduction changed dramatically. When men predominated among immigrants, the government tried to lower the costs of family formation and maintenance by preventing the men from marrying and settling down in the US. To this end, the immigration office issued temporary work visas and prevented wives from accompanying their husbands to the United States. The medical community tolerated doctors and hospitals that sterilized immigrant women without their consent, while the media demonized the male immigrants by arguing that they "stole" jobs from "native" workers.

As First World investment and development policies dislocated more women and "sent" them to the United States in search of work, the target of the anti-immigration arguments shifted from restricting family formation and maligning male job seekers to attacking the welfare state's support of immigrant families. The desire to minimize the cost of family maintenance and enforcing work among poor immigrant women was fueled in the early 1980s by the rise of conservatism, which favored reducing the role of government spending, and by the fact that the children born in the United States to female immigrants became citizens who were entitled to a host of public benefits and services.

Unable to prevent family formation by immigrant women, US immigration and welfare policies simultaneously minimized the cost of maintaining immigrant households *and* increased the supply of cheap female labor to US firms employing workers in secondary labor market jobs. In the early 1980s, the anti-immigrant rhetoric began to condemn "high birth rates and consumption of public services," implicitly maligning women as mothers and social program recipients. If male immigrants "stole" jobs from "native" workers, female immigrants drained the public purse by applying for welfare, sending their children to public schools, and overusing the health-care system.

The 1994 Proposition 187 campaign in California sought to deny the children of immigrant women access to public schools, hospitals, and cash benefits. The 1996 welfare reform stigmatized single motherhood and penalized childbearing among poor women to reduce the costs of family support. In addition to the denial of benefits to children born to women on welfare, Congress created the "illegitimacy" bonus of $20 to $25 billion per year for three years to be shared by the five states that lower their nonmarital birthrates the most (not just among women on welfare)—without increasing their statewide abortion rates above 1995 levels. Welfare reform also earmarked $250 million in matching funds for states that run "abstinence-only" programs in the public schools—programs that stress postponing sex until marriage and that prohibit sex education. New Medicaid rules and other restrictive policies either eliminated or significantly reduced government responsibility for paying for the health, education, housing, and training of immigrant women and their families.

Finally, Chang's feminism is a broad one that by definition includes the impact of race and class as well as gender. She concludes that in addition to concerns about loss of jobs and high welfare state costs, public hostility to immigrants reflects fears about threats to the "purity" of the race and/or the dominance of the mainstream culture. In the early 20th century, President Theodore Roosevelt chastised native-born American women for having too few children. Reflecting the period's xenophobia, he told them that their low birthrates would lead to an overabundance of the foreign-born population and otherwise endanger the purity of the native-born racial stock.

Today's opponents of immigration argue that the growing number of immigrants on US soil—many more of whom are persons of color than at the turn of the 20th century—threatens to turn America into a multicultural society. Given the demand for cheap female labor, the government is not about to ban immigration. However, fears about the cost and cultural impact of immigration help to explain both the government's resistance to family formation and settlement by immigrant workers, as well as the popularity of Americanization, English-only, parenting, and other resocialization programs mounted by the government over the years. Whatever benefits these programs yielded, they also encouraged immigrant families to give up their traditional culture in favor of white middle-class norms. The burden of the conversion still falls on immigrant women who are expected to socialize their children to the "American Way."

Nor does Chang dodge the troublesome tensions between women from different classes. While feminists and students of immigration and women's studies often evade the issue, Chang makes it clear that the policies that harm poor and working-class women often benefit their white middle- and upper-class counterparts as well as business firms and the state. For example, many white middle- and upper-class individuals either demonized poor immigrants and women of color as "bad mothers" and "welfare queens" or sat by silently as others used these negative stereotypes to build support for "reforming" welfare. At the same time, these affluent families frequently hired poor immigrants and poor women of color to care for their children and parents at home or in an institutional setting. Likewise for employers who hired former welfare recipients to work in their restaurants, hospitals, shops, and offices.

Chang believes that the middle-class household's need for the services of poor women and poor women's need for the job may stem, at least in part, from restrictive domestic policies: social program cutbacks and the overall lack of family support available to all working women in the United States. However, the outcomes vary widely by class. The career advancement of many middle- and upper-class women depends heavily on the availability of immigrant women to clean their homes and to care for their dependents. The labor of poor women also allows middle- and upper-class wives to add significantly to the household income. The increased income, combined with reduced gender conflicts over housework, helps to preserve these families as traditional two-parent households favored by the social conservatives.

Meanwhile, lacking access to welfare state benefits, the requisites of economic survival effectively force poor women to work long hours (often for low pay) in the homes of the affluent. The income helps. But the job heightens the stress for poor women who work, who worry about the supervision of their own children—due largely to the lack of affordable quality child care. The economic coercion built into US public policy leaves poor immigrant women, many of whom are single mothers, with little or no time to tend to their own homes, to care for their own children or parents, or to pursue the education or training that might lift them out of poverty.

Both welfare and immigration policies also contain the racially coded messages that imply that it is okay, or even beneficial, for government programs to force immigrant women to forgo full-time mothering in favor of employment. Indeed, many social conservatives regard single mothers, by definition, as ineffective and irresponsible adults whose parenting may even bring harm to their children. These advocates of "family values" support tax and spending policies that encourage white and middle-class women to stay home, while forcing poor women to work outside the home. Indeed, they regard the latter as better suited for low-paid labor than for mothering. Some social conservatives now call for removing poor children, especially children on welfare, from their mothers' care, placing them in foster care and group homes, if not orphanages.

Chang makes it very clear throughout this book that both immigration and welfare policies have placed Congress and the White House squarely on the side of corporations seeking to increase their profits on the backs of poor women and children. Despite this strong critique, Chang does not end on a pessimistic note. First, she believes that government policy should recognize and reward women for the service they provide through both their productive and reproductive labor. Access to such resources would not only ease the economic hardship faced by poor immigrant women, but would also provide them with a degree, however limited, of autonomy and control over their lives. Chang also reports that poor women are not taking the pain and the punishment lying down. While many immigrants internalize the popular but negative stereotypes of themselves as "invaders and parasites," a growing number of women are working for personal and social change. Despite its low pay, employment has led immigrant women to become more comfortable participating in wider society. Joining a long tradition of activism among poor and working-class women in the United States and throughout the world, large numbers of immigrant women have become more involved in their own community affairs, joined mainstream unions, participated in living-wage campaigns, created community-based organizations, and otherwise found individual and collective ways to fight back. Like the women who preceded them, they understand that neither social conditions nor social policy can change for the better unless pressed from below.

Introduction

> Instead of Mandela's New World, our politicians and their media flunkies busily and viciously strive to resurrect an Old World in which there will be no safety, no asylum, for anybody but themselves. These men, direct descendants of other men who came to America never asking anybody's permission to arrive or to invade or to conquer or to exterminate or to enslave or to betray or to exploit and discriminate against those who preceded them and those who, willingly or not, came after them—these men now contrive a so-called immigration crisis and they invent and then promulgate pathological idiot terms like "illegal aliens."
>
> —June Jordan, "We Are All Refugees," 1994[1]

In 1994, during one of the worst, but certainly not unprecedented, systematic attacks on immigrants to the United States, immigrants and their allies began sporting T-shirts bearing the face of an indigenous man and the slogan, "Who's the illegal alien, *Pilgrim?*" reflecting indignation at the ignorant and malicious anti-immigrant sentiments of the day. Specifically, this was in direct response to a campaign that had been brewing for years in policy circles and "citizen" groups, culminating in California's Proposition 187. The initiative proposed to bar undocumented children from public schools and turn away undocumented students from state colleges and universities. It also proposed to deny the undocumented an array of public benefits and social services, including prenatal and preventive health care, such as immunizations.

While the overt purpose of this voter initiative was to curtail immigration, ostensibly by restricting the use of public benefits and social services by undocumented immigrants, the real agenda behind it was to criminalize immigrants for presumably entering the country "illegally" and stealing resources from "true" United States citizens. More to the point, Proposition 187 came out of and was aimed at perpetuating the myth that all immigrants are "illegal," at worst, and, at best, the cause of our society's and economy's ills.

Throughout US history, immigration has been viewed and intentionally constructed as plague, infection, or infestation and immigrants as disease (social and physical), varmints, or invaders. If we look at contemporary popular films, few themes seem to tap the fears or thrill the American imagination more than that of the timeless space alien invading the United States, and statespeople have snatched up this popular image to rouse public support for xenophobic policies. Ironically, in every popular "alien invasion" movie, only the United States is hit by invaders, and so it is in the public imagination about invasions by intraterrestrial aliens. The common perception mirrors popular media in Americans' adamantly held conviction that Third World emigrants only have interest in landing in or taking over the United States, forgoing all other territories on earth, presumably because the United States is the most civilized society with the most coveted resources.[2]

In stark contrast to these American fantasies, less than two percent of the world's migration actually ends in the United States, and migration by people within the Third World is far more common than the movement of Third World citizens to the First World.[3] Furthermore, neither America's natural resources nor its social service system, which is in fact one of the stingiest among industrialized nations, is the attraction. The attraction is jobs. These jobs, however hazardous and low paying, are still preferable to the poverty most migrants are escaping in their home countries, often the result of First World imperialism. As the National Network for Immigrant and Refugee Rights outlines in its 1994 "Declaration on Immigrants and the Environment," First World imperialism and development policy in the Third World have resulted in resource depletion, debt, and poverty for many people in these nations. The extraction of resources by the United States and other First World nations forces many people in the Third World to migrate to follow their countries' wealth.[4]

Moreover, the "draw" of the United States is more accurately described as a calculated pull by the United States and other First World countries on the Third World's most valuable remaining resource: human labor. This "pull" or extraction is often facilitated by a desperate "push" or expulsion of people by sending countries, which are also often the result of First World economic and military interventions.

This argument is not to be confused with one of the most popular theories used to explain the causes of migration, the "push-pull" theory, proposing that factors such as high unemployment in sending countries act as a "push" and perceived opportunities in receiving countries serve to "pull" migrants from the Third World to the First World. In *The Mobility of Labor and Capital,* Saskia Sassen exposes the limitations of this theory, which does not serve to explain, for example, situations in which economic "development" in some of the largest sending countries does not actually deter emigration. Sassen suggests instead that migration is rooted in the creation of linkages between sending and receiving countries through foreign investment and military interventions by First World countries in the Third World. For example, the establishment of an off-shore plant from the United States in a "developing" country brings not only goods and information about life in the United States but often creates social networks making migration more feasible. Sassen also points to the disappearance of traditional manufacturing jobs, their replacement with high-tech industries, and the expansion of the service sector in response to the demands of this new, high-income workforce—a ready market for immigrant women seeking work.

Extending Sassen's analysis, I argue that First World countries routinely make deliberate economic interventions to facilitate their continued extraction of Third World resources, including and especially people. Like Sassen, I suggest that immigration from the Third World into the United States doesn't just happen in response to a set of factors but is carefully orchestrated—that is, desired, planned, compelled, managed, accelerated, slowed, and periodically stopped—by the direct actions of US interests, including the government as state and as employer, private employers, and corporations. For example, austerity programs imposed on Mexico and other nations effectively create situations of debt bondage such that these indebted nations must surrender their citizens, especially women, as migrant laborers to First World nations in the desperate effort to keep up with debt payments and to sustain their remaining citizens through these overseas workers' remittances. As President Carlos Salinas de Gortari of Mexico declared to US audiences during the North American Free Trade Agreement negotiations in 1991, Mexico would either export its people or its products to the United States, although the latter was preferable.[5]

In the past, public opinion and the rhetoric surrounding immigration have emphasized the charge that male migrant laborers steal jobs from "native" workers. In the last decade, however, this concern has been largely drowned out by cries that immigrants impose a heavy welfare burden on "natives." A 1986 CBS/*New York Times* poll found that 47 percent of Americans believed that "most immigrants wind up on welfare." In a review of studies on the economic impacts of immigration to the United States, Annie Nakao reported for the *San Francisco Examiner*, "What is generally accepted is that immigrants do not take jobs from natives."[6] While the abundance of studies examining how immigrants affect the US economy disagree on many points, most recent studies imply that Americans should be more worried about protecting public revenues than about their jobs.

This new emphasis on the alleged depletion of public revenues by immigrants signals an implicit shift in the main target of anti-immigrant attacks. Men as job stealers are no longer seen as the major "immigrant problem." Instead, the new menace is immigrant women who are portrayed as idle, welfare-dependent mothers and inordinate breeders of dependents. Thus, a legislative analyst on California Governor Pete Wilson's staff reported that Latinas have an AFDC (Aid to Families with Dependent Children) dependency rate 23 percent higher than the rate for all other women.[7] Such "findings" are almost always coupled with statements about higher birthrates among immigrant women and the threat they pose to controlling population growth.[8]

Perhaps this new rhetoric, identifying immigrant women, and particularly Latinas, as the major threat to American public resources, reflects a growing awareness of changes in the composition and nature of Mexican migration to the United States in the last two decades. Wayne Cornelius of the Center for US-Mexican Studies reports that in the 1970s and through the 1980s, there was a shift in Mexican migration from that dominated by "lone male" (single or unaccompanied by dependents), seasonally employed, and highly mobile migrant laborers to a *de facto* permanent Mexican immigrant population including more women, children, and entire families.[9] There has been more migration by whole families, more family reunification, and more migration by single women.[10] Cornelius explains that Mexico's economic crisis has driven more women to migrate to the United States, where there is "an abundance of new employment opportunities for which women are the preferred labor source," including child care, cleaning, and laundry work.[11]

Cornelius's analysis of 1988 US Census Bureau data suggests that, as a result of this expanded female migration, women may now represent the majority of "settled" undocumented Mexican immigrants.[12] In her study of undocumented Mexican immigrant communities, Pierrette Hondagneu-Sotelo reports that women tend to advocate and mobilize families toward permanent settlement in the United States. She suggests that US xenophobia has come to focus on women because they are perceived as the leaders of this threatening demographic trend.[13]

The popular media illustrate quite vividly this shift in the target of anti-immigrant attacks. While perhaps the general message projected by the media is that immigrants threaten to overwhelm the United States, the focus on immigrants' alleged high rates of birth and consumption of public resources is clearly not gender neutral. Since women are seen as responsible for reproduction and consumption, they are blamed for the strains thought to be imposed by immigrants on public resources. The media not only "reflect" these public perceptions but promote this imagery to advance restriction-ist policy. With the new focus on curtailing immigration and immi-grant consumption of public goods, we have seen women in "starring roles" in media images put forth to reinforce this agenda.

For example, in January 1994, the network television program *60 Minutes* showed droves of pregnant Mexican women crossing the border into the United States. This footage was followed by inter-view clips suggesting that these women were coming to the country to have their babies and soak up social services for themselves and their children. Medi-Cal fraud investigators and social service work-ers implied that the abuse of social services by undocumented immi-grants is widespread. Brian Bilbray, then–San Diego county supervisor, now a US representative, conjectured to countless view-ers: "I mean, we have 4,800 people last year come to this county from a foreign country, illegally, to give birth to their child; 41 per-cent of them immediately went on welfare."[14]

Similarly, in a June 1994 issue of *Reader's Digest,* Randy Fitzgerald reported that an "investigation into the exploitation of our welfare and social service system by illegal immigrants ... reveals a pattern of abuse, fraud, and official complacency costing tax payers billions each year." Fitzgerald wrote that pregnant Mexican women commonly float across the Rio Grande in inner tubes within sight of the US Bor-der Patrol. Once here, he suggested, they gain easy access to medical care and a range of benefits and services for their babies, including welfare, food stamps, nutrition programs, and public housing.[15]

It was these images that informed—or, rather, misinformed—the creation and adoption of Proposition 187 in November 1994. Civil rights and immigrant rights groups questioned the measure's constitutionality and a temporary injunction was placed on the mea-sure. Federal District Court Judge Pfaelzer finally ruled in 1998 that much of the proposition was unconstitutional because it was super-seded by federal law or court precedent. Subsequently, however, then-Governor Wilson filed an appeal of this decision, passing the issue on as his personal legacy to his successor, Gray Davis. In a skillful political maneuver, Davis chose to turn the issue over to ar-bitration.[16] After months of mediation, Davis announced in July

1999 that his office had reached an agreement with civil rights groups to drop the state's appeal of the ruling by Judge Pfaelzer. The agreement was almost identical to Pfaelzer's 1998 ruling, overturning most of the provisions and leaving intact only those imposing state criminal penalties for making, distributing, and using false immigration documents.[17]

According to reports collected by the National Immigration Forum and other immigrant advocacy groups, Proposition 187 had many tragic consequences despite the injunction and Judge Pfaelzer's ruling. For example, in the month following its passage, a twelve-year-old boy and an elderly woman died because they were afraid they would be deported if they sought treatment.[18] Not surprisingly, such accounts were not featured in the newspapers or television news.[19]

It is in the context of such media hype around immigrant welfare "abuse" and omissions about real tragedies that draconian populist initiatives such as Proposition 187 and similar federal policy proposals have emerged, with the intent to control and punish immigrant women and their children. The myths of immigrant women as brood mares and welfare cheats were the centerpieces of the anti-immigrant hysteria that propelled the passage of Proposition 187, and they continue to fuel the ongoing attacks on immigrant women and women of color through measures such as the Personal Responsibility Act (PRA), which was proposed the following year. In immigration policy circles, the PRA was called a federal Proposition 187 because it barred state and local governments from providing all but emergency services to undocumented immigrants and prohibited several classes of people—including documented immigrants, unwed teen mothers, and children born to mothers already on welfare—from receiving public benefits.

In August 1996, Congress passed and President Clinton signed into law the Personal Responsibility and Work Opportunity Reconciliation Act, ending the federal government's 61-year commitment to providing cash assistance to poor families with children. The welfare reform law, grossly misnamed the Personal Responsibility Act and otherwise known by critics as "welfare deform," served in a perverse way to fulfill Clinton's promise to "end welfare as we know it." The PRA eliminated several entitlement programs and transformed them into block grants to the states, resulting in drastically reduced funding for these programs and, more importantly, the end of the principle of guaranteed cash assistance for poor children in effect under federal law since the New Deal.[20] Specifically, it brought an end to the Aid to Families with Dependent Children (AFDC) program, which, although decidedly inadequate, had provided the only existing semblance of a "safety net" for poor families headed by single women since its establishment under the Social Security Act of 1935.[21]

Under the PRA, AFDC was replaced by the Temporary Aid to Needy Families (TANF) block grants to states, with a definitive focus on the *temporary* provision of aid and emphasis on work requirements. TANF places a five-year lifetime limit on receipt of federal welfare benefits and requires adult recipients to engage in work activities or lose their benefits. The PRA gave states discretion to exempt up to 20 percent of their TANF caseloads from work activities, but states must meet overall work requirements for recipients or their block grants are reduced. TANF restrictions also limit what types of work activities count toward a state's participation rates.[22]

Although the PRA was not explicitly immigration policy, it was clear that it was largely aimed at immigration "reform" and budget cuts on the backs of immigrants. Almost half of the projected $54 billion savings through the PRA, about $24 billion, was achieved by continued restrictions on the receipt of any aid except emergency assistance by undocumented immigrants, and by new restrictions on the receipt of food stamps and Supplemental Security Income (SSI) by documented immigrants. At the same time that this so-called welfare reform was being instituted with devastating impacts for low-income immigrants, immigration law was being formulated toward the same ends in the form of the Illegal Immigration Reform and Immigrant Responsibility Act (IIRIRA) of 1996. Passed one month after the PRA, IIRIRA essentially reinforced the restrictions on immigrant welfare use embodied in Proposition 187 and the PRA.[23] Thus, when Governor Davis was asked whether 187 was officially struck down by the July 1999 agreement, he was able to respond from a position of great political safety and comfort, "Yes, but it is supplanted by federal legislation that is faithful to the will of the voters who passed 187 and [that] will require the state to deny virtually all of the benefits that would be denied under the terms of 187."[24]

The attack from all fronts on immigrant rights and entitlements through IIRIRA, the PRA, and Proposition 187 and its look-alike legislation opened the way for a return to racist, nativist, and patriarchal practices abolished long ago. For example, one provision of the PRA denies aid to children unless paternity is established, even when the mother complies with the District Attorney's invasive and degrading inquiries. As welfare scholar Gwendolyn Mink says, the PRA is "the most aggressive invasion of women's rights in this century."[25] Mink says that the law did not erode all women's rights equally, however, but "hardens legal differences among women based on their marital, maternal, class, and racial statuses."[26]

> While middle-class women may choose to participate in the labor market, poor single mothers are forced by law to do so.... While middle-class women may choose to bear children, poor single mothers may be punished by government for making that choice.... While middle-class women enjoy still-strong rights to sexual and reproductive privacy, poor single mothers are compelled by government to reveal the details of intimate relationships in exchange for survival.... And while middle-class mothers may choose their children's fathers by marrying them or permitting them to develop relationships with children—or not—poor single mothers are required by law to make room for biological fathers in their families.[27]

For poor immigrant women, the picture is even more grim as IIRIRA also reduced judicial discretion in immigration matters, resulting in the automatic deportation of immigrants convicted of even minor crimes. Within this web of immigration and welfare "reform" laws, Ana Flores, a permanent resident from Guatemala with two US-citizen daughters aged eight and nine, is now facing deportation for defending herself against her abusive husband in 1998. Prior to 1996, Flores might have benefitted from a process in which she could claim hardship or argue that the deportation is "unjustifiably cruel," and an immigration judge could have stopped the deportation. IIRIRA eliminated that process; the PRA left her few options if she is able to remain in the country as a single mother; and the atmosphere created around Proposition 187 most likely discouraged her from seeking those options or any assistance when she was being battered in the first place.[28] In conjunction, IIRIRA, the PRA, and the aftermath of Proposition 187 served to reinstitute many of the worst measures aimed at regulating poor women of color and immigrant women, as well as their labor and reproduction.

Women migrants pose a distinct set of challenges to lawmakers and "reformers." The current American obsession with alleged "welfare abuse" by immigrant women and their supposed hyperfertility are actually age-old "social problems." This rediscovery of women of color and immigrant women as laborers, potential consumers, and reproducers only revisits dilemmas that have historically concerned the state and "reformers": While immigrant women's labor is desired, their reproduction—whether biological or social—is not. Biological reproduction is deemed undesirable because it entails the United States having to provide basic needs for raising and training the children of immigrants. Although immigrant children may ultimately be useful as labor, as well, they are nevertheless not able to serve as laborers immediately like their parents, whose reproduction and training costs have already been borne by their home countries. As Rubén Solís of the Southwest Workers' Project points out:

> It takes about $45,000 to raise a child with all the human and social services needed, including education, to get them to eighteen years old, or productive age. The US doesn't pay one cent to produce those workers who come at a productive age to join the workforce. So the United States saves $45,000 per worker. Many of the workers pay income taxes and social security.[29]

Immigrants' social reproduction is perhaps even more threatening, since it implies a transformation of "American" culture, departing from dominant white European culture and the dominance of Western civilization.

Throughout US history, immigration and welfare law have been formulated to address these "problems," and the "solutions" have followed certain predictable models. First, the migration and settlement of women have been directly prohibited in order to prevent the reproduction and formation of immigrant families.[30] In addition, women of color and immigrant women have historically been subjected to enforced sterilization and contraceptive testing to effectively limit their reproduction.[31] Second, temporary or "guest" worker laws have provided for the importation of male migrant contract laborers but prohibited their remaining in the country beyond their contracts. These laws have operated in conjunction with miscegenation laws restricting the intermarriage of nonwhites with white citizens. Third, "reform" programs, often under the guise of "Americanization," have been created to rid immigrants of their backward ways and inculcate proper "American" values and habits. Often these have encompassed training or work-relief programs to prepare immigrant women and children for their ultimate roles in US industrial society as menial, low-wage workers. Finally, immigrants have been refused the rights and benefits accorded to citizen workers and thus coerced into low-wage work. Moreover, those viewed as unable to work or potentially welfare dependent have been excluded outright.

All of these policies are aimed at the same objective: to capture the labor of immigrant men and women separate from their human needs or those of their dependents. In essence, the goal of these laws and "reforms" is to extract the benefits of immigrants' labor while minimizing or eliminating any obligations or costs, whether social or fiscal, to the "host" US society and state. While it is easier to extract cheap labor from independent men through temporary worker programs by recruiting single men, ensuring that they remain single, and ultimately ousting them once they have served their purpose, it is more difficult to accomplish this extraction from women who bear and care for children. Instead, the state utilizes other methods, such as the "Americanization" programs, imposing cultural "rehabilitation" at the same time that work is required of the participants.[32]

Some form of each of the methods described above has been used and is currently in use to deal with the dilemma of capturing immigrant women's labor while limiting their social and biological reproduction. In some cases, these methods operate in much the same way that they always have; in other cases, it is less explicit. It can be argued, for example, that even though we no longer see the direct exclusion of women, and sterilization programs aimed at immigrant women and women of color are more covert now, restriction of these women's reproduction is accomplished through measures like Proposition 187 and the immigration law of 1996. The unspoken (or sometimes explicit) rationale of these measures is that denying basic needs will make it so difficult for immigrants to raise a family that they will leave or be discouraged from having children. As anthropologist Leo Chavez points out,

> [D]enying immigrants social services would clearly make immigrant families' lives more difficult.... [I]f the families of immigrant workers decide to return to Mexico or other family members back home stay put, then we will have reduced the costs associated with immigrant labor while maintaining, and even increasing, the profits of that labor.[33]

Moreover, several proposals have been made in Congress that children born to immigrants should not receive citizenship automatically (as they have for centuries past); they would receive citizenship only if their parents are "legal" immigrants.[34]

This book can be read as a series of essays discussing contemporary continuity of historical policies and ideologies used to maintain immigrant women as super-exploitable, low-wage labor. In this book, I focus on how migrant women workers are effectively imported into the United States from the Third World and subsequently channeled into the service sector, specifically in care work or paid reproductive labor. I examine both their roles as care workers in institutional and private household settings and as providers of unpaid reproductive labor in their own families—that is, as mothers and heads of household. Finally, I analyze the relationship between these roles and how immigrant women's needs and responsibilities within their families are used to constrain their positions in the out-side labor market. I argue that immigrant women in each of these roles have become the primary focus of recent public scrutiny and media distortion, and the main targets of immigration regulation and labor control.

I aim to redress the popular myths casting immigrant women as brood mares who come to the United States to have babies, collect welfare, and overburden the environment, public hospitals, and schools. These constructions of immigrant women as "welfare queens" and "baby machines" have been used to advance brutal welfare policies denying immigrants access to benefits and services. These policies in turn allow the state to fulfill a dual agenda. First, they force many undocumented, as well as "legal," immigrant women to take and remain in low-wage jobs for lack of critically needed government assistance. Second, they allow the state to mini-mize its costs for providing basic needs and rights to these immi-grant women workers. Ultimately, both private employers and the state capture a pool of cheap labor—cheap because women are cheated of fair wages, because they are denied the rights and benefits of citizen workers, and because they have already been raised and trained in their home countries.

Ironically, these women's labor—caring for the young, elderly, sick, and disabled—makes possible the maintenance and reproduc-tion of the American labor force at virtually no cost to the US gov-ernment. At the same time, this labor is extracted in such a way as to make immigrant women's sustenance of their own families nearly impossible. Indeed, employers and the state capitalize on immigrant women's vulnerability as mothers and heads of household to com-pel these women to take jobs in the desperate effort to provide for their families. In short, I examine the actual root causes—indeed, the engineering—of Third World women's labor migration to the United States, and their coercion into service work. I also analyze the racialized images of these women used to rationalize immigration and welfare policies and the exploitative labor systems that they support.

Chapter 1 examines the historical and contemporary uses of im-agery portraying immigrants as invaders and parasites to rationalize policies excluding immigrants or maximizing the use of their labor while minimizing the costs of their maintenance. I examine the sources of these images among the media, academic institutions, statespeople, and right-wing "citizen" groups. Specifically, I look at the ironic contradiction between the construction of immigrants as resource depletors and their very exploitation as resources.

Chapter 1 also discusses the question of whether migrant women themselves are exposed to and adopt anti-immigrant or antipoor rhetoric. In this chapter, I explore how the transmittal of these ideologies may be accomplished largely through the media and through government policies structured differently for immigrants and refugees. Finally, I look at how these pervasive myths of immigrant welfare abuse function to reinforce divisions among racial and ethnic groups in the United States, including migrants and people of color, and to limit public support within these groups for government assistance programs.

Chapter 2 deals with the Immigration Reform and Control Act (IRCA) of 1986, which had two contradictory goals: first, to offer undocumented immigrants who had already lived and worked in the country the chance to "legalize," and second, to curtail immigration, ostensibly through penalizing those employing undocumented immigrants, limiting immigrant use of public assistance for five years after entry, and excluding immigrants deemed likely to become "welfare dependent." This last component of IRCA was essentially an extension of the old public charge laws, dating back to 1882, excluding those "likely to become a public charge" from entering the country.

In chapter 2, I argue that the images of Latina immigrant women as welfare abusers and as inordinate breeders of dependents are deliberately propagated by the state and by capital to serve a dual function. First, they provide the ideological justification for denying aid to immigrant women, on the rationale that they are criminals and potential public burdens. Second, this denial of aid provides an effective means of coercing immigrant women into low-wage service work. This chapter examines contemporary and historical uses of welfare policies to coerce immigrant women and women of color into work as domestic servants and caregivers while simultaneously preventing them from providing adequate care or sustenance for their own families.

Chapter 3 examines a second way in which the state functions to capture and maintain this labor force for US employers: through the direct recruitment of migrant laborers specifically identified as temporary workers and through policies restricting the rights of these workers, thus preventing them from becoming potential new citizens. In this chapter, I compare recent guestworker proposals in the agricultural, nursing, and service industries to the Bracero program of the 1940s to 1960s. Through the Bracero program, workers were imported from Mexico, initially in response to the wartime demands of southwestern agricultural employers. The Bracero program is generally seen as having established the precedent in US immigration policy for the nonimmigrant, temporary worker visa. Those entering under this type of visa are presumed to be residing in the United States temporarily, not intending to stay or settle. This type of worker is seen as offering the advantage of imposing few costs to either the employer or "host" society.

In chapter 3, I also look at the use of abusive workplace policies, such as English-only rules, not only as racist, anti-immigrant attacks but as antilabor tactics. While such policies are rationalized as promoting "Americanization" or assimilation of immigrant workers, their use in attempting to oust certain targeted groups of immigrants belies this rationale. I argue that these policies are instituted precisely to construct immigrants as "unassimilable," not worthy of citizenship, but useful only as temporary, indeed disposable, workers. Accordingly, they function as highly effective antilabor measures, applied selectively to remove particular immigrant groups if and when they are identified as "troublemakers" or deemed no longer useful as laborers.

In chapter 4, I attempt to put the phenomena of labor migration and importation of women from the Third World in the context of the growth of global capitalism. Specifically, I analyze the use of structural adjustment policies, or SAPs, by which First World nations attach preconditions to their loans to Third World nations. These include requiring debtor nations to cut social spending and wages, to open their markets to foreign investment, and to privatize state enterprises. SAPs wreak havoc on the lives of women, especially in Third World nations, often making it impossible for them to sustain their families.

I argue that the simultaneous dismantling of social service systems in the Third World and the First World is no coincidence. Instead, I suggest that First World agencies deliberately engineer the destruction of Third World social services via SAPs to render Third World debtor countries ultimately vulnerable to their First World creditors. This facilitates the commodification of Third World women for labor export as it becomes impossible for women to sustain their families at home under the devastation of SAPs and they are forced to migrate, often to work as domestic servants in the First World. Their role as commodities (or, at best, mercenaries) in this global exchange is explicit, as they are both prodded to migrate and lauded for doing so by statesmen calling them the new "heroes" of their countries.

The denial of all forms of aid to immigrants in "host" countries such as the United States seals the fate of these women, making them more receptive to scorned, low-paid service jobs once they arrive. The demise of social supports in the First World has created both an expanded demand for care workers and a lack of alternatives to this low-wage work. Thus, the demolition of social supports in the Third World through SAPs is not only parallel to the dismantling of the welfare state in the United States and elsewhere, but serves to reinforce the channeling of immigrant women workers into service work as the only viable choice. These women's vulnerability is further exacerbated in a global market and political structure that enables both sending and "host" countries' governments and private employers to avoid ultimate responsibility for "overseas" workers.

In chapter 5, I discuss collaborations between the Immigration and Naturalization Service (INS) and other government agencies, particularly social service agencies, as well as corporations, to regulate and control immigrant labor. By attempting to pit immigrant workers and welfare workers against each other, these collaborations serve to control low-wage and unpaid workers in general. In this chapter, I compare the plights of immigrant workers and workfare workers. Both groups are identified as "employable" yet are defined not as workers or employees but "charity" cases and criminals. Employers, including private household or corporate employers and city or state governments, rationalize denying these workers fair wages, benefits, and rights on the basis of the same racist ideology. Identifying these workers as the beneficiaries of charity, training, or even punishment, and thus seeing the work itself as fair reward or just penalty, employers absolve themselves from responsibility for providing any further compensation.

In the context of welfare "deform," as immigrants and welfare recipients are rapidly being denied or cut off from benefits without viable jobs being created, the stage is set for competition between all low- and no-wage workers. Government and private employers utilize increasingly sophisticated antilabor tactics to coordinate their assaults on these workers, all under the guise of workplace enforcement of immigration law and instituting welfare-to-work programs. Low-wage, welfare, and unionized workers have begun to recognize these common challenges, to forge alliances against these collaborative attacks, and to resist being pitted against each other.

In chapter 6, I discuss the ongoing threats to immigrants in several domains, including increased border militarization, the growth of citizen vigilante groups, and the continued, ever more sophisticated tactics and frequently collaborative efforts among government agencies to erode worker and human rights of immigrants. Chapter 6 also examines the dangers of rhetoric framed to appeal to and divide different segments of the immigrant rights and labor communities. In the face of these challenges, immigrant workers, and low- and no-wage contingent workers across the spectrum are developing new messages and radical, alternative strategies. This chapter examines the central and leading roles that immigrant women and men are playing in both mainstream and nontraditional labor organizing, and the particular strategies and strengths that they bring to these movements.

1   June Jordan, *Affirmative Acts: Political Essays* (New York: Anchor Books, 1998), p. 93.

2   For example, in the 1996 film *Independence Day*, the president of the United States reads the mind of a captured alien and reports: "They're like locusts. They're moving from planet to planet, their whole civilization. After they've consumed every natural resource, they move on. And we're next."

3   Interview with Cathi Tactaquin, executive director of National Network for Immigrant and Refugee Rights (NNIRR), January 15, 1999.

4   NNIRR, "Declaration on Immigrants and the Environment," *Network News* 7: 1 (July–August 1994), pp. 4–5.

5   Saskia Sassen, *The Mobility of Labor and Capital: A Study in International Investment and Labor Flow* (New York: Cambridge University Press, 1990). Wayne Cornelius, "Impacts of North American Free Trade on Mexican Labor Migration," paper presented for US congressional staff at the Symposium on North American Free Trade: Prospects and Analysis, Center for US-Mexican Studies, UC San Diego, May 4, 1991.

6   Annie Nakao, "Assessing the Cost of Immigration," *San Francisco Examiner,* December 1, 1991, pp. B-1, B-3.

7   Nakao, "Assessing the Cost of Immigration."

8   Nakao, "Assessing the Cost of Immigration."

9   Wayne Cornelius, "From Sojourners to Settlers: The Changing Profile of Mexican Migration to the US" (San Diego: Center for US-Mexican Studies, UC San Diego, August 15, 1990), p. 17; Jorge Bustamante, Raul Hinojosa, and Clark Reynolds, eds., *US-Mexico Relations: Labor Market Interdependence* (Stanford, CA: Stanford University Press, 1991).

10   Cornelius, "From Sojourners to Settlers," p. 18.

11   Cornelius says there has been rapid expansion in jobs for which undocumented Mexican women are the "preferred" labor source. In the San Francisco Bay area, there is a "booming market" for these women in child care, house and office cleaning, and laundry work. In the border cities of San Diego and El Paso, domestic work has become institutionalized as the exclusive work of undocumented female immigrants. Also, Mexican immigrant women still dominate the garment firms, semiconductor manufacturing firms, fruit and vegetable canneries, and packing houses of California (Cornelius, "From Sojourners to Settlers," pp. 19–20).

12   Cornelius, "From Sojourners to Settlers," p. 17.

13   Pierrette M. Hondagneu, "Gender and the Politics of Mexican Undocumented Immigrant Settlement," Ph.D. dissertation, University of California (1990), p. 249. See also Pierrette Hondagneu-Sotelo, *Gendered Transitions: Mexican Experiences of Immigration* (Berkeley, CA: University of California Press, 1994).

14   "Born in the USA," *60 Minutes,* prod. Jim Jackson, January 23, 1994. Brian Bilbray is now a US representative (Republican–San Diego).

15   Randy Fitzgerald, "Welfare for Illegal Aliens?" *Reader's Digest* 144: 866 (June 1994), pp. 35–40.

16   The promoters of Proposition 187 are preparing once again to put a similar initiative on California's November 2000 ballot, which would bar the legislature from approving new laws providing benefits to undocumented immigrants and require law enforcement to check the citizenship of every person arrested ("Proposition 187 Look-Alike Planned for Ballot," *San Francisco Chronicle,* January 13, 1999, p. A-3).

17   *Immigration News Briefs* 2: 7, July 31, 1999, citing *Los Angeles Times,* July 29, 1999, and July 30, 1999; Josh Richman and Jack Chang, "Davis Drops Appeal on 187," *Oakland Tribune,* July 30, 1999, p. 1.

18   National Immigration Forum, "Memorandum Re: Proposition 187, One Month Later," December 5, 1994; see also New York Association for New Americans (NYANA), "The Spirit of Prop. 187 Comes to New York," *Torch,* April 8, 1995, pp. 1–3.

19   See also Coalition for Humane Immigrant Rights of Los Angeles, "Hate Unleashed: Los Angeles in the Aftermath of 187," November 1995.

20   Coalition for Immigrant and Refugee Rights and Services, "Welfare Reform—House Passes Personal Responsibility Act," *Eye on Immigration Policy* 1: 1 (May 2, 1995): 3.

21   Nancy Naples, "From Maximum Feasible Participation to Disenfranchisement," *Social Justice* 25: 1 (Spring 1998), p. 50.

22   For example, under TANF only one year of vocational education can count toward a state's work participation rate (Equal Rights Advocates, "From War on Poverty to War on Welfare: The Impact of Welfare Reform on the Lives of Immigrant Women," April 1999, p. 3).

23   See Leo Chavez, *Shadowed Lives: Undocumented Immigrants in American Society* (Fort Worth, Texas: Harcourt Brace College Publishers, 1998), p. 190, for more on attempts to institute more drastic measures, such as denying undocumented children access to public schools, in IIRIRA.

24   *Immigration News Briefs* 2: 7, July 31, 1999.

25   Gwendolyn Mink, "Feminists, Welfare Reform and Welfare Justice," *Social Justice* 25: 1 (Spring 1998), pp. 146–157.

26   Mink, "Feminists, Welfare Reform and Welfare Justice," p. 147.

27   Mink, "Feminists, Welfare Reform and Welfare Justice," p. 147.

28   Anthony Lewis, "The Mills of Cruelty," *New York Times,* December 14, 1999, p. A-31.

29   Interview with Rubén Solís of Southwest Workers' Project, in *New World Border,* prod. Casey Peek and Jose Palafox, Rollin' Deep Productions, 1997, videocassette. Second edition forthcoming, available from the National Network for Immigrant and Refugee Rights, 310 8th Street, Suite 307, Oakland, CA 94607; (510) 465-1984.

30   See Evelyn Nakano Glenn, *Issei, Nisei, Warbride: Three Generations of Japanese American Women in Domestic Service* (Philadelphia: Temple University Press, 1986), pp. 196–200, on Chinese bachelor societies and measures aimed at preventing family formation among Chinese and Japanese immigrants. See also Maxine Baca Zinn, "Family, Feminism, and Race in America," *Gender and Society* 4 (1990), pp. 68–82, and Bonnie Thornton Dill, "Our Mothers' Grief: Racial-Ethnic Women and the Maintenance of Families," *Journal of Family History* 13 (1988), pp. 415–431.

31   See Carlos G. Velez-Ibanez, "Se Me Acabo la Cancion: An Ethnography of Non-Consenting Sterilizations Among Mexican Women in Los Angeles," *Mexican Women in the United States: Struggles Past and Present,* eds. M. Mora and A. Del Castillo (Los Angeles: Chicano Studies Research Center, UCLA, 1980); Linda Gordon, *Women's Body, Women's Right: Birth Control in America* (New York: Penguin Books, 1990); Rosalind Petchesky, "'Reproductive Choice' in the Contemporary United States: A Social Analysis of Female Sterilization," *And the Poor Get Children: Radical Perspectives on Population,* ed. Karen Michaelson (New York: Monthly Review Press, 1981); Angela Davis, "Racism, Birth Control and Reproductive Rights," *Women, Race and Class* (New York: Vintage Books, 1981).

32   See George Sanchez, "'Go After the Women': Americanization and the Mexican Immigrant Woman, 1915–1929," in Ellen Dubois and Vicki Ruiz, eds., *Unequal Sisters* (New York: Routledge, 1990), pp. 250–263. See also Sarah Deutsch, *No Separate Refuge: Culture, Class and Gender on an Anglo-Hispanic Frontier in the American Southwest* (New York: Oxford University Press, 1987).

33   Chavez, *Shadowed Lives,* p. 194.

34   Chavez, *Shadowed Lives,* p. 190.

Breeding Ignorance, Breeding Hatred

Alien Acts

People who have recently immigrated to New York have been among our most valuable resources throughout the city's history, and it is only right that we give them back their share of what they have contributed to us…. Please use this manual in a spirit of generosity and fairness. No one wants New Yorkers to be overly dependent on government services, but neither do we want them to go unassisted when they need and deserve our help.

—Mayor David Dinkins, opening message
of "Immigrant Entitlements Made (Relatively) Simple,"
a manual for New York City social service workers, 1990[1]

Our life has always been difficult…. [W]e are like ET [extraterrestrial] aliens…. [I]f we are ET beings, then why should we have to pay taxes? I ask you, how much do we contribute to this country and how much do we lose? Then you may ask, why are we here in this country? But that is a different story.

—Maria Olea, *Mujeres Unidas y Activas* (MUA),
a Latina immigrant domestic workers' support
and advocacy group, 1993[2]

At first glance, New York's former mayor's message seems to present an unusually generous position regarding the extension of aid to immigrants, particularly in the context of recent public opinion and policy. But upon closer inspection, perhaps it is not so magnanimous. In fact, it may only reflect a long-standing tradition among politicians of singing the praises of immigrants as indispensable resources while treating them instead as disposable workers. Maria Olea's unsentimental statement, in contrast, represents her clear understanding that immigrant women workers are viewed as aliens, not just in terms of immigration law but in a broader sense, in public opinion casting them as the ultimate outsiders and invaders. Her statement also confronts this construction of immigrant women workers as aliens and parasites, asserting instead their large contribution of labor to the country and the great personal costs and losses suffered in providing this labor.

Olea challenges the more common perception among the US public that immigrants take more than they give to the country, threatening everything from air quality to the reign of "Western civilization" in the United States. For example, organizations such as Zero Population Growth suggest that America has outgrown its natural resources and cannot support more people without destroying the environment.[3] Glenn Spencer of Voices of Citizens Together, a "citizens" group backing Proposition 187, claimed that illegal immigration is "part of a reconquest of the American Southwest by foreign Hispanics."[4] Linda Hayes, media director for the southern California Proposition 187 campaign, similarly warned that if Mexicans continued to "flood" the state, a "Mexico-controlled California could vote to establish Spanish as the sole language of California ... and there could be a statewide vote to ... annex California to Mexico."[5]

In recent years the immigration debate has been dominated by questions concerning resources. What public benefits should be extended to immigrants? Are there enough natural resources to support immigrants and "citizens"? While in the past discussions of the "costs and benefits" of immigrants emphasized the charge that male migrant laborers displace "native" workers, this concern has been largely drowned out in the last decade by cries that immigrants, especially undocumented immigrants, deplete US public resources.

The sophisticated language of "limited resources" and "legal entitlement" in which the immigration debate has been framed serves to lend legitimacy to anti-immigrant attacks. As Eisenstadt and Thorup suggest in *Caring Capacity versus Carrying Capacity,* their study examining community conflicts in response to Mexican immigration to San Diego's North County:

> [U]nlike past years when unabashed racism and hostility against immigrants were common, the debate has recently assumed a more sophisticated form.... [By] and large the immigration policy battleground has moved from the city streets ... into the meeting rooms where government budgets are written and school board policies enacted.[6]

A large cast of actors has participated in the public debate on whether immigrants contribute to or deplete more from public resources and US society. This chapter presents a brief outline of this rhetoric and imagery portraying immigrants as undeserving resource depletors, and its uses in promoting anti-immigrant policies historically and today.

In his examination of popular fiction and films depicting disaster in Los Angeles in *Ecology of Fear: Los Angeles and the Imagination of Disaster,* Mike Davis, a professor of urban theory, observes that nine major story types emerge. For example, while the theme of "hordes" enjoyed greatest popularity during the 1900s to 1940s, the story of "alien invasions" dominated the 1980s to 1990s. Davis comments:

> The abiding hysteria of Los Angeles disaster fiction, and perhaps of all disaster fiction, ... is rooted in racial anxiety.... [W]hite fear of the dark races lies at the heart of such visions.... And it is this obsession, far more than anxieties about earthquakes or nuclear weapons, that leads us back to ... the deepest animating fear of our culture.[7]

Davis traces the impeccably timed appearance of novels about "floods" of barbaric Irish and Chinese at the turn of the century, just as government concern about controlling these foreign "hordes" and populist anti-immigrant movements were mounting. For example, tales of Chinese invaders are depicted in the trilogy *The Yellow Danger* (1899), *The Yellow Wave* (1905), and *The Dragon* (1913), in which the Chinese are ultimately contained and, in the last book, wiped out by the bubonic plague. In Jack London's 1906 short story "The Unparalleled Invasion," he solves the "Chinese problem" with germ warfare, finishing off any survivors by massacre, and the white race succeeds in recolonizing China, following a "democratic American program." It is fascinating that in each of these stories, the American victors use disease to fend off the invaders, choosing to fight plague with plague. Ironically, in the Jack London story, he writes that as peace is restored, "all nations solemnly pledge themselves never to use against one another the laboratory methods of warfare they had employed in the invasion of China."[8]

The timing of these books' appearances with the simultaneous rise of anti-Chinese populist movements and legislation cannot be overlooked. Beginning in the 1850s, the Chinese had been recruited to work in the dangerous and undesirable jobs in the American west, most notably in constructing the transcontinental railroad. While they were always strictly segregated and denied rights enabling them to participate in US society as citizens, landowners, or business proprietors, they became the targets of the most vehement discriminatory laws and hate violence beginning in the 1870s, when the railroad was completed, their usefulness had presumably been exhausted, and the country was in economic recession. White labor-led populist groups pushed for anti-Chinese legislation, culminating in the 1882 Chinese Exclusion Act, prohibiting the entry of "Chinese of the laboring class." The act was extended twice, in 1892 and 1902, just as Chinese invasion fiction was abundant and enjoying great readership.

Davis goes on to analyze popular film and fiction of the 1980s and 1990s, commenting that the boom in imagined aliens during this period coincided with the growing presence and visibility of Central American, East Asian, and Mexican immigrants in the Los Angeles area. Davis says, "[I]mmigration and invasion, in a paranoid register, became synonyms," with the widespread image of alien impregnation both representing and playing into white fears of changing demographics.[9] The popular 1988 film and subsequent television series of 1989–90, *Alien Nation,* depicts precisely this equation of space invaders and illegal immigrants.

In *Alien Nation,* the "newcomers," a group of humanoids who have been genetically engineered for hard labor and are ideally suited for work in toxic industries, have rebelled against their slave masters when they arrive in Los Angeles aboard their slave spaceship. They are initially quarantined in camps and then resettled in a downtown Los Angeles barrio remarkably similar to the Central American neighborhood of MacArthur Park. Created for menial and dangerous labor as they have been, they settle in comfortably to this work and the "poverty, alienation, and addiction of the urban class," depicted in each episode.[10]

Ironically, Peter Brimelow, one of the most vehement contemporary anti-immigrant writers, chose to name his 1995 book, an extremely influential best-seller, *Alien Nation.* Unfortunately, Brimelow presented his book as a scholarly work, immodestly titling the first part as "Truth," and it has been largely received as such, despite the inordinate amount of time he spends rationalizing why the citizenship endowed by the blessed birth of his son in the United States to him and his wife, neither of whom are US citizens by birth, is entirely different from any other child's citizenship by birth to non-US citizens or foreigners, particularly "illegal immigrants."[11] Brimelow shamelessly makes one unsubstantiated assertion after another, including the claim that many modern American intellectuals are "just unable to handle a plain historical fact: that the American nation has always had a specific ethnic core. And that core has been white."[12] Moreover, he says,

> The mass immigration so thoughtlessly triggered in 1965 risks making America an *alien nation*—not merely in the sense that the number of aliens in the nation [is] rising to levels last seen in the nineteenth century; ... but, ultimately, in the sense that Americans will no longer share in common what Abraham Lincoln called ... "the mystic chords of memory, stretching from every battle-field and patriot grave."[13]

Brimelow's chords of memory obviously fail him, or perhaps he is in need of a US history lesson to learn that the specific purpose and ultimate result of bringing in large numbers of both white and nonwhite immigrants to the United States in the 19th century was for their labor, which brought this country to its industrial strength and stature in the world. Immigrants are being imported today in huge numbers for their labor in the service industries, again allowing the elite to carry on the American tradition of privilege, as one of the richest countries in the world. Brimelow is unaware that, as a colonial power, the United States (much like his own country of origin, Britain) has always been multiracial, though people of color have been stratified by class, segregated by race, relegated to the periphery, and often rendered invisible to the white "core" throughout history.

It does not take Brimelow long to begin spewing forth the predictable "statistics" and horror stories about treacherous "illegal immigrants." Immediately after referring to the glorious arrival of his son for the third time, on page four, he launches into an all-out attack on "illegal immigrants" and their offspring. Brimelow declares that while his son was born after he and his wife had applied for and been granted legal permission to live in the United States, the arrival of others is not so holy. "There are currently an estimated 3.5 to 4 million foreigners who have just arrived and settled here in defiance of American law. When these illegal immigrants have children in the United States, why, those children are automatically American citizens, too."[14]

Brimelow obtained this information, an "unofficial preliminary estimate as of April 1993," through an interview with an unidentified "Bureau of the Census spokesman." He adds that two-thirds of the births in Los Angeles County hospitals are to illegal immigrant mothers, and that one survey found that 15 percent of "new Hispanic mothers" in California border hospitals said they "had crossed the border specifically to give birth," of whom a quarter said that "their motive was to ensure US citizenship for their child."[15]

However, as I will discuss extensively in the following chapters, immigrant women use social services and public benefits at extremely low rates, even when they or their dependents are legally entitled and desperately need these forms of assistance. One particularly useful study by Wendy Walker-Moffat of the School of Social Welfare at the University of California at Berkeley in 1994 examined the fertility rates and public-service usage rates among Mexican women who had migrated to the United States between 1987 and 1990.[16] Using 1990 California Census data, Walker-Moffat found that the average Mexican-born woman in her sample had 1.5 children, a fertility rate that is lower than US citizens as a whole, than US-born Latinas, and—most significantly—than the "replacement level rate" or 2.1 births per female of childbearing years necessary for the population to remain constant.[17] Walker-Moffat also found that use of Medi-Cal and Aid to Families with Dependent Children (AFDC) and attendance at public schools by the women in her sample were extremely low, in contrast to the public perception and media hype at that time.[18]

Walker-Moffat suggested that many of the studies frequently cited in media reports on immigration and used as the basis for Wilson's 1994–95 California state budget were seriously flawed in a number of ways.[19] It was common practice for hospital personnel to assume that any Spanish-speaking woman or woman with a Spanish surname was Mexican, an immigrant, and undocumented. When women were hesitant to report their immigration status because they feared deportation or problems obtaining permanent residency, hospital personnel were again likely to identify them as undocumented. Walker-Moffat said that hospitals had a vested interest in classifying any indigent patients served as undocumented in order to receive partial reimbursement from the state (since this was prior to Proposition 187).[20]

I would venture to guess that Brimelow's numbers from studies on "new Hispanic mothers" may have suffered from the same methodological flaws of the "official" studies cited by Wilson and others. Nevertheless, Brimelow uses these numbers to sound alarms of a nationwide invasion by border births. He follows this by chastising the "typical American editor" for lopsided coverage of immigration, insisting that the media focuses on success stories such as immigrants-become-Harvard-valedictorians to the neglect of tales of immigrants-become-terrorists-and-mass-murderers.[21] Thus, Brimelow would like to see news coverage of immigration in nothing short of Hollywood style, something of which there has never been any great shortage.

Politics and the Professors

Brimelow is certainly not alone in using sensationalist and sentimentalized rhetoric toward anti-immigrant ends. Lawmakers, academics of all kinds, and environmental—even self-identified immigrant rights—activists have each added their own unique contributions to the cauldron. Indeed, academics can be credited with helping to bring the hysteria directed at immigrants, people of color, and "other" suspects to historic heights. Periodically, with great predictability, scholars undertake studies with the purpose of determining the "net effect" of immigration on the American economy and society, most often to promote prescriptions of what types of immigration should be encouraged and what rights or benefits immigrants should or should not be able to receive. The notion that immigrants pose a burden on "native" citizens has held fast in public perceptions, despite study after study's consistent finding that immigrants contribute a great deal more than they "cost" this country. In particular, the perception that immigrants drain the public coffers by heavy dependence on public assistance and social services persists. A 1993 *Newsweek* poll found that 59 percent of Americans say that "many immigrants wind up on welfare."[22] This myth of immigrant welfare dependency endures precisely because it is perpetuated by scholars and utilized by policy makers to advance popular restrictive immigration and welfare policies.[23]

Undocumented Studies

In 1985, the Undocumented Workers Policy Research Project compiled an extensive review of studies on alien access to and use of public services.[24] An overwhelming majority of the studies cited in the review reported findings of low utilization of public services by immigrants. One of the few exceptions was, not surprisingly, a 1982 monograph by Roger Conner, leader of the Federation of American Immigration Reform (FAIR), a restrictionist group. Conner attacks studies reporting low service use by "illegal" immigrants, faulting their samples as small and "unrepresentative," and portrays "illegals" instead as urban, educated, permanent, and "more aggressive" in dealing with the government than ever before. He points to studies citing the receipt of AFDC and unemployment benefits by "illegals" and argues that high utilization of such services is one more reason to restrict illegal immigration.[25] At the time, Conner was actually exceptional in these findings and in his use of them to advocate restricting immigration. In retrospect, it is clear that he was paving the way for the initiative that his organization sponsored twelve years later, Proposition 187.

In the pre-187 era, it was more in vogue for scholars to take a different twist on immigration policy recommendations entirely, citing the economic pluses brought by tax-paying immigrants to call for expanding immigration while reducing aid to immigrants. Several prominent scholars pointed to the economic advantage of savings because of immigrants' low utilization of public services, particularly with the added insurance of closing immigrants' access to such benefits. Julian Simon, professor of business administration at the University of Maryland, was one of the major proponents of such recommendations. In his study *The Economic Consequences of Immigration,* Simon says that "illegal" immigrants provide the greatest economic bonus because they use practically no welfare services, while about three quarters pay Social Security and income taxes.[26] He devotes much of the rest of the study to the question of whether legal immigrants also offer such bonuses or impose a welfare burden upon "natives." His analysis of 1976 Census Bureau data on welfare use and taxes shows that legal immigrants actually use less than their share of medical care, unemployment insurance, food programs, AFDC, retirement programs, and educational programs.[27]

Simon explains that legal immigrants typically arrive in the prime of their working lives with relatively few children, and thus are not in great need of aid.[28] He reports, however, that even compared to "natives" of the same ages and educational backgrounds, these immigrants do not use a disproportionate share of services. Furthermore, the average immigrant family pays more taxes than its "native" counterpart.[29] Simon concludes happily, "[M]ore immigrants mean a lighter rather than a heavier burden upon natives because immigrants are ... net contributors to the [welfare] system.... So, perhaps ironically, the very phenomenon that causes many natives to object to immigration turns out, upon investigation, to be a strong argument for increased immigration."[30]

Many other writers employed similar reasoning to advance proposals that were pro-immigration, though not necessarily pro-immigrant. Stephen Moore, then-director of the American Immigration Institute, takes a similar approach to refugee policy in an article shamelessly titled "Flee Market—More Refugees at Lower Cost." He summons all of the available evidence on refugees' diminishing use of social services and plummeting rates of unemployment in the period after arrival in the United States to document the "rapid socioeconomic transition" of refugees. No sooner has he rejoiced in this finding than he tempers it with this statement: "Still, beneath this good news is a stubbornly persistent high rate of dependency [on public aid] for some recent refugee groups."[31] He claims that "well-intentioned" public aid programs hurt refugees by encouraging welfare dependency and delaying entry into the labor force.[32] Thus, Moore recommends that the United States terminate federal grant programs aiding refugees in resettlement and replace them with low-interest loans for all "able-bodied" new refugees.[33] Moore says that one of the outstanding benefits of such a loan program is that it will help to counter hostility toward refugees and generate public support for opening up refugee admissions.[34]

Simon points to the same advantage in his recommendations on welfare programs for immigrants: "Tighten up procedures preventing immigrants from taking illegal advantage of welfare services, to prevent hostility to immigration as well as to reduce costs."[35] Thus, Simon and other authors arrive at the same prescription: We should expand immigration, but ensure that we continue to maximize the "cost-efficiency" (read: exploitability) of immigrants by denying them state aid of any form.

Simon remarked in *Fortune* magazine that immigrants are a "windfall for any society."[36] He told the *Washington Times*, "If you consider immigrants like any other investment, they provide a fantastic return on investment."[37] Clearly, the message is that we should extend a hearty welcome to potential laboring and tax-paying immigrants but extend no such welcome, nor any offer of aid, to those without such profit potential. This view of immigrants as commodities or "investments" completely neglects the fact that many immigrants exist as members of families, including those who are not young people in the "prime of their working lives," ready and eager for employment and unlimited contribution to the public revenues. They include the elderly, the disabled, children, and those, usually women, who must care for these other family members. For many, the situation is further complicated if there are both undocumented persons and documented persons or citizens who are legally entitled to public benefits and services in the family. A look at family profiles of undocumented persons in Texas reveals that about 40 percent of households surveyed included US-born people, while more than 30 percent had US-born citizen children.[38]

Just prior to the introduction of Proposition 187, scholars and activists seemed to have tired of the cost-benefit debate, recognizing that even the "best" finding can be put to ill use: to advocate pro-immigration policy that is effectively anti-immigrant. Advocacy groups for immigrants seemed to reach a consensus that this analysis missed the point that immigrants have human and workers' rights. Moreover, some immigrant advocates had succumbed to sacrificing undocumented immigrants for those with "legal" status. Frank Sharry, executive director of the National Immigration Forum, issued a statement signaling that anti-immigrant forces had succeeded in dividing immigrants and allies along artificial and immoral lines.[39] Immigrant rights advocates began to urge those involved in these debates to go beyond the cost-benefit approach and to pursue these issues from a human and worker rights perspective. But no sooner had this shift begun than the most vehement resurgence of the cost-benefit mentality and the immigrants-as-parasites myths began to sweep California in the fever of Proposition 187.

In a 1994 report that was widely quoted throughout the 187 debate, economist Donald Huddle claimed that immigrants cost the United States $42 billion more than they contribute in taxes.[40] Several sources, including the bipartisan Urban Institute, disputed these findings, pointing out major flaws in Huddle's method. For example, he had counted the 2.7 million immigrants legalized under the 1986 law twice when deriving the cost of immigrants in the country. He had also assumed that all immigrants entering the United States in 1994 and thereafter will pay no taxes, including income and sales taxes. After correcting for Huddle's errors, the Urban Institute found that immigrants actually contribute a net surplus of $27.4 billion a year.[41] Although the Huddle Report was largely discredited, lawmakers and the media continued to quote it widely. Predictably, this policy skirmish over the Huddle Report coincided with California voters adopting Proposition 187 and the subsequent, seamless introduction of the Personal Responsibility Act (PRA).

The Invisible Woman

What am I, a man or a resource?

—Ralph Ellison, *The Invisible Man*[42]

We believe that we do the worst jobs. If we immigrants left, who would do these jobs? Since Washington, abuses have increased, without regard for whether we are undocumented.... Here they blame us for everything—even for the environment. But we don't have factories. We don't throw things into the sea.

—Nohemy Ortiz, *Mujeres Unidas y Activas*[43]

Interesting bedfellows have been made in the name of keeping immigrants out of the United States. One alliance in particular merits closer examination: the love affair between immigration restrictionists and mainstream environmentalists, particularly those concerned with "population control." Alongside the charges that immigrants deplete the public coffers, environmental groups commonly advance the claim that immigrants overburden or pose a threat to US natural resources or the environment at large. The most recent example of the efforts of such an alliance was the proposal of the Sierra Club, dubbed Alternative A, advocating the reduction of immigration as a component of a "comprehensive population policy for the United States." The initiative was put forth by some membership of the Sierra Club and backed by right-wing, white-supremacist, anti-immigrant groups, such as the Pioneer Fund, FAIR, and Population-Environment Balance (PEB).[44]

Although the proposition was ultimately defeated, popular initiatives like Alternative A reflect a frightening trend. US consumers are buying the products of racist, nativist groups such as the Pioneer Fund, FAIR, and PEB: the rhetoric that immigrants and their offspring pose a threat to the environment and quality of life of American "citizens." Such propaganda reflects a fundamental ignorance about both the processes of immigration and environmental degradation. As the National Network for Immigrant and Refugee Rights outlines in its 1994 "Declaration on Immigrants and the Environment," First World imperialism and development policy in the Third World have resulted in resource depletion, debt, and poverty for many people in these nations. The extraction of resources by the United States and other First World nations forces many people in the Third World to migrate to follow their countries' wealth. Thus, rather than see immigration as a cause of environmental degradation in the United States, we should see it as a consequence of the exploitation of Third World resources and people upon which US wealth has been built.[45]

A country's population and immigration patterns do influence the rate of environmental degradation, but they have much less impact than do consumption patterns of wealthier segments of the population and especially the production practices of industries. At the root of US and global environmental problems are the overconsumption habits of privileged citizens of the United States and First World. While the United States represents only 5 percent of the world's population, it uses a disproportionate amount of the world's nonrenewable resources and other commodities. Of course, along with this gross overconsumption of resources comes a corresponding disproportionate production of waste.[46]

It must be understood that people of color and immigrants in the United States tend not to be in the high-income segments responsible for overconsumption, or in decision-making positions responsible for promoting harmful industrial practices. Moreover, they have been the primary victims rather than the perpetrators of environmental degradation in their workplaces and homes. In the US, three out of every five blacks and Latinos live in areas with uncontrolled toxic waste sites, which are deliberately placed in these communities because these groups have little power to fight them.[47] At work, these groups are commonly exposed to a wide variety of health threats, from pesticides in agricultural fields to toxic chemicals in factories or service workplaces.[48]

The rhetoric about immigrant women as resource depletors and threats to the environment is almost always coupled with claims that immigrant groups have abnormally high fertility rates. Mexican women's fertility has consumed the attention of researchers and politicians in recent anti-immigrant campaigns, just as those of racial and ethnic groups who were the targets of exclusion did before them. Immigration restrictionists warn that immigrants threaten to overwhelm the country not only by their increased presence through migration but also through rapid reproduction. Such arguments echo the age-old claims of excessive fertility among black women, used to advocate welfare cuts or restrictions on welfare for black mothers.[49] Just as black women have babies in order to suck up welfare, we are told, immigrant women come to the United States to have babies and consume all of the natural resources in sight.

A central principle that many welfare rights and immigrant rights scholars and advocates have worked to bring into these debates is that people do not have babies and do not migrate to get prenatal care or collect welfare for their families. In 1994, 79 scholars of poverty, labor markets, and family structures issued a press release stating that there was no evidence that women's childbearing decisions were linked to the availability of welfare.[50] Also, the states with the most restrictive welfare systems do not have fewer nonmarital pregancies, and some states with the lowest benefits have very high nonmarital birth rates.[51]

Driving behind an ABC Diaper Service truck emblazoned with the slogan, "A clean environment is as easy as ABC," I was reminded recently of the dilemma confronting me and many mothers of babies in diapers: cloth or disposable? The American public has nearly exhausted itself in trying to assess the pros and cons of cloth versus disposable diapering, comparing the damage done to the environment through the use of detergents and water-laundering cloth diapers with the irrevocable pile-up of nonbiodegradable diapers disposed in landfills. When my second son was born in 1992, it appeared that some sources had resolved the debate as a "wash," asserting that in ecological terms, both options were equally bad.

What has rarely been figured into these analyses is labor—not labor costs, but costs to laborers in the business of diapering inside and outside the home, who are primarily women. The conventional wisdom in middle-class mothering circles is that using a diaper service is the better option. The reasoning goes that then you can be environmentally correct (for those who still subscribe to that school), and it's even cheaper than disposable diapers. Few stop to ask why using a diaper service is cheaper. The answer is simple: As in most service work in the United States, the workers in diaper services are predominantly working-class women of color who are poorly paid to deal quite literally with other people's shit (and toxic detergents) all day.[52]

Moreover, many "working" mothers ask their children's in-home caregivers to respect their "choice" of cloth diapering, and thus pass on this oppressive work to other women while they go "to work." The cloth or disposable diaper debate is a common dilemma encountered by many Americans in their daily lives, and it provides a striking illustration of how immigrant and women-of-color workers are dehumanized, indeed rendered invisible, in the name of environmentalism and even feminism for a privileged few. The efforts of primarily white, middle-class professional women to "have it all," including careers, leisure, and the ability to claim environmental correctness, are secured by exploiting immigrant women and women of color as cheap laborers.

Ironically, these immigrant and women-of-color service workers are not paid even as much as lip service for their contributions to environmental protection, while their employers (whether corporate or private household) can market or congratulate themselves for "doing their parts" for the environment. Employers profit and benefit tremendously from workers suffering the consequences of a privileged few's choices "for the protection of the environment," but not for the protection of people. "Environmental" solutions such as these, achieved through the exploitation of one group of people by another and thus through the reproduction of social inequalities of nationality, race, gender, and class, should truly give us pause. So-called environmentalists' charges that immigrants pose a threat to the environment add gross insult to injury.

Reproducing Racism

Just prior to the introduction of Proposition 187, I set out to explore whether the images of immigrant women as welfare abusers and breeders of public burdens were being consumed by immigrants themselves. I interviewed women, all working in housecleaning or child care, who had migrated to the United States as either "immigrants" or "refugees."[53] In US immigration law, a distinction is made between "economic immigrants," or those who presumably come to this country only to seek economic opportunities, and "political refugees," or those seen as forced to leave their countries to escape political or religious persecution or repression.[54] This is largely a false distinction, as the US government has had a hand in creating the economic and political crises that force many immigrants or refugees to leave their home countries. Moreover, a discriminatory two-tiered system of access to public assistance and social services has been built around this distinction, restricting access for so-called economic immigrants while favoring and extending more open access to these benefits for refugees.[55]

These differential policies for immigrants and refugees have had predictable outcomes in terms of participation rates—that is, low utilization of public aid and social services by immigrants and higher usage by refugees. As I will discuss in chapter 3, immigrants, especially those legalizing through the amnesty program, use these programs at very low rates, in part because of the widespread perception that such use will threaten their chances to gain legal status. In contrast, refugees use these programs and job-training and resettlement-assistance programs at higher rates, probably because it is formally legal for them to do so and thus doesn't pose a threat to their immigration status.[56] One study by Shiori Ui based on interviews with Cambodian refugee women in Stockton, California, showed that most of the women received some sort of refugee assistance to supplement earnings through petty trading.[57]

These patterns raise the question of how immigrant and refugee women's participation in government programs, constrained by their different statuses vis-à-vis the state, bring about different experiences that might in turn affect these women's conceptualizations of entitlement (that is, right) and entitlements (that is, government programs). In other words, how do state designations of refugee and immigrant women as "worthy" or "undeserving" of government assistance lead these women to view the receipt of welfare differently? And how do these designations affect refugee and immigrant women's support for government assistance in general?

What I encountered most consistently among the women I interviewed, regardless of their immigration status and access to or experience with government assistance programs, was the belief that immigrants and black Americans abuse welfare. Although none of the Latina immigrant women I interviewed had received any kind of government assistance, two were convinced that many immigrants abuse welfare. While each rejected the myth that *all* Latino immigrants come here for welfare and pointed out that the American public mistakenly lumps together all Latinos, each indicated that she believed that there was some truth in the perception that immigrants abuse the system. In fact, Xochitl even suggested that the reason she did not receive welfare was that she had not immigrated here with that intention:

> Yes, I've heard of all the facilities that the welfare gives to single mothers, that schools give to students. Yes, I've heard about all those things, but I'm never really interested to get involved with those things because—probably because I didn't come with that idea, just to come to receive help for free.[58]

Xochitl had come from Mexico City to the United States four years ago for a vacation and overstayed her tourist visa. Xochitl, who has a bachelor of science degree from a prominent Mexican university, worked as a live-in baby-sitter for the first year here, and has since worked cleaning houses.

Xochitl suggested that perhaps other Mexican immigrants who come to the United States only to use welfare are the cause of this stereotype:

> A lot of people think that we came here just to see what we could get from this government.... Of course, if they think that, it's because many of our own community have come here and they have done things like that, but that doesn't mean that all of us are the same.

In response to my asking if she had heard about the cuts proposed by then-Governor Wilson (as precursors to 187), she said, "I think it's not fair for all—in some cases it's really necessary to help people, but on the other hand, I've seen people who came here to have babies, just to have that welfare." When I asked if she knew anyone personally who had come here for this purpose, Xochitl said that she had met one person, but explained that she thought that the woman had come in part because of the "culture in Mexico, [where] to be a single mother is not permitted, is not allowed, in some families." When I asked if she knew other women with a similar history, she said she didn't know any personally, but that that woman had said she knew many others like her. Xochitl then suggested that many women from Central America, especially, came to the United States for this purpose.

Veronica also believed that abuses of the welfare system by immigrants were common:

> I think that, sometimes I do understand United States's point, because they try to give help, but it's a lot of people try to take advantage of that, abuse that.... So, sometimes I do understand why they want to do all those cuts, because, you know, it's kind of bad and eventually people feel angry about us.[59]

Veronica came to the United States from Venezuela without a visa in 1988 and has worked in a baby-sitting, housecleaning, packing and shipping, and office management. She also holds a bachelor's degree from a Venezuelan university. Veronica's statement suggests that fear of indiscriminate backlash against Latinas or immigrants explains, at least in part, her tendency to believe these myths or to voice sympathy for the proposed cuts. Both Veronica and Xochitl expressed almost a defensive pride about not receiving any benefits, yet both voiced anger at people's assumptions that all Latino immigrants receive welfare.

Similarly, Tecle and Winta, refugees from Eritrea, reported that they knew of many refugees coming from other states to California because of the higher welfare benefits offered there. Tecle left Eritrea during the revolution there and arrived in the United States just before Eritrea achieved independence from Ethiopia. She left with her two children to join her husband, who had lived here for almost 13 years prior. Tecle was a primary school teacher for twenty years in Eritrea and now works in child care and teaches part-time. Winta left Eritrea during the war in the late 1970s, first went to Italy, then Texas in 1981, and arrived in California in 1987. She had worked as a cashier in a gas station and as a caregiver for a family, and now works in a day-care center in Oakland. I interviewed these two women together. The following is part of our conversation:

> Winta: You know, in Texas land, where I go, everybody is working.... It is not like California. Everybody is working, including everybody, the woman and the man. It's not like here.
>
> Grace: What do you think is different here?
>
> Winta: Here has—everybody has to get the welfare.
>
> Tecle: Yeah, I know every—so many people come from another state here, because they know about the welfare. Yeah, I know Eritreans and some people who come from Sudan [a common transitional point for those leaving Eritrea] to another state. When they hear about California, they come from that state to California, especially if they have children—they have six, seven children—they can live with that welfare.
>
> Grace: You know people from ... which state?
>
> Winta: I don't know, but we know that they come here.
>
> Tecle: They come like that.

Winta: We hear it on the news.[60]

Tecle insisted that widespread immigrant abuse of welfare explained why California's governor planned to cut the programs. While the women expressed strong beliefs that these abusers or abuses existed in significant numbers, and suggested that they "knew" of these cases first hand, when I asked them for further details, they indicated that they were actually only personally familiar with one case, or heard of such cases from the newspaper, radio, or television.

A similar pattern emerged among the Southeast Asian refugee women I interviewed. Chi-lan left Vietnam with her daughter, Lan, in 1990 to join her husband, who had been here since 1970, after spending almost ten years in a re-education camp in Vietnam. Chi-lan worked as an accountant in Vietnam, and works now as a baby-sitter for a family while taking ESL classes some evenings. Lan was 21 years old, lived with her parents, attended a community college full time, and worked part time in a jewelry factory. Lan described a large number of Asian "financial-aid cheaters," whom she saw as abusing the system by going to school "just in order to get that money [financial aid or welfare]" while "[t]hey not learning anything ... just be in the class and do whatever the teacher say is fine with them."[61]

Chi-lan reported having benefitted from government assistance programs and, in contrast to her daughter, relatively positive experiences with social service workers.[62] Thus, Chi-lan expressed support for government assistance programs, further suggesting that such a wealthy country should provide assistance to poor people. She cautioned, however, that it was critical for institutions to help people to find jobs so that they could leave welfare as soon as possible.

> It's very good when we come here the first time. Because we don't have jobs. But when you live a long time here, you know that is a tax of everybody.... I think we have welfare and social—and any high country, we have to help the poor. But we have to encourage them to get out. We all in that situation when we came. But when we can do it we have to go out, and somebody or some center help them get out—as soon as possible.

At the same time Chi-lan cautioned that people should not become dependent on welfare, she and Lan pointed out the extreme hardship—and even the irrationality—of leaving welfare, only to take on innumerable expenses such as medical care against low wages.[63]

Yuet, another woman who had left Vietnam with her husband and three children in 1996, expressed similar views. Her daughters attended prestigious state universities after transferring from community college. Yuet teaches at a private day-care center and also takes child development classes at a nearby state college. She did not work outside the home in Vietnam. When Yuet's family first arrived in the United States, they received AFDC for her son and food stamps for their first two years here. Although Yuet expressed that she felt "very ashamed" to receive these benefits, she said that these programs were very helpful to her family, because they enabled both her and her husband to go to school during their first years here:

> We got AFDC and it helped a lot when we first came here, because my son still young, you know.... We didn't have to worry about financial problems, so it was very relaxing to go to school and don't worry about our financial problems, but we always thought about getting out of that system as soon as we can do it.... I feel really uncomfortable, you know, but we really need that system when we first came here, because we didn't take anything with us. We didn't have any money, and this is like a booster, you know, just like a start—really useful.[64]

Yuet also expressed concerns about widespread welfare abuse, and emphasized her view that this drained other people's resources, rather than the government's. Yuet's expressions of embarrassment about receiving welfare are particularly noteworthy, since they reflect the successful operation of a welfare system designed to be as humiliating and punitive to recipients as possible, ostensibly to motivate people to leave welfare quickly.[65]

Yuet's and Chi-lan's statements encompass some contradictions: While each expressed general support for government programs and recognition of their value to society and as a rational choice for individuals, each also believed that there was rampant welfare abuse and dependency.[66] At least one possible explanation is that Yuet's and Chi-lan's views reflect their having enjoyed protected or favored status as refugees deserving of US residence and its benefits. First, they had been given access to income supports, training, and job placement services, making it possible for them to attain better jobs than their immigrant counterparts. Second, by their accounts, they had not encountered many of the harsh realities of the market. Neither spoke of the hardships or barriers of unemployment or discrimination that the Latina immigrants I interviewed were quick to point out. Both were employed full time in long-term jobs and reported that child-care jobs were extremely easy to find. In contrast, the Latina immigrant women reported great difficulty in finding full-time work or enough jobs that could be strung together to offer sufficient, stable hours.

In their studies about Central American immigrant women and Cambodian refugee women, Salzinger and Ui suggest that:

> Today, American foreign policy determines not only who enters the country, but their access to welfare and social service programs after arrival. Thus, the relationship of new immigrant groups to the emerging service economy is fundamentally mediated by their relationship to the state and by their ability or inability to improve their market situation through the use of state services.[67]

Salzinger and Ui explain that refugee status provided the Cambodian women in their study with access to extrafamilial resources, such as state services, while the Central American women were not "shielded from the market by the presence of the state" and thus developed "occupational strategies around the service economy"—or, more simply, took service jobs.

Extending Salzinger and Ui's thesis, I ask whether those who enjoy or do not enjoy this protected status vis-à-vis the state also have different conceptions of the state and its proper role. In addition, I ask how dominant images of people of color around work and welfare influenced these women's attitudes about welfare. Two sets of myths have been propagated in tandem to reduce public support for state programs such as welfare, social services, and affirmative action. The "black culture of poverty" myth—encompassing images of black Americans as lazy, lacking ambition, motivation, or intelligence, and caught in an intergenerational cycle of welfare dependency—is utilized to argue that state programs will be useless in mitigating against cultural flaws of black Americans.[68] The Asian "model minority" myth—incorporating images of Asian Americans as hard working, ambitious, intelligent, education oriented, and self-sufficient—is invoked to argue that state programs are unnecessary, since inherent cultural assets of Asian Americans have enabled them to succeed without them.

Immigrant and refugee women in the United States are undoubtedly exposed to this rhetoric. We can see how Asian "model minority" rhetoric could influence attitudes about welfare within Asian refugee communities in a number of ways. Numerous accounts point to the "success" stories of Southeast Asian refugees, documenting their amazing transitions from high unemployment rates upon arrival to self-sufficiency and incomes higher than the median for US-born families. For example, the following explanation by Leo Cherne of the International Rescue Commission is typical: "Starting from scratch, refugees have to be more inventive and more determined.... They have to be more frugal and work harder."[69] This statement certainly deploys Asian "model minority" rhetoric, and we can speculate that this type of propaganda could have a significant influence on refugees' attitudes toward welfare. They might adopt the belief that Southeast Asian refugees are indeed today's model minorities, who are worth the initial "investment" of state aid. Thus, they might view welfare receipt relatively unburdened by the stigmatization heaped on African-American women. Or, if they are able to "succeed" without receiving government assistance for long, they might adopt the view that these programs are unnecessary or should be limited to transitional, temporary measures. Finally, they might accept prevailing attitudes that those who receive government supports long-term are inherently inferior, need to exercise greater thrift, work harder, etc.

Perhaps not surprisingly, both the Asian "model minority" myth and the "black culture of poverty" myth seemed to be deeply ingrained in the minds of women who have been in this country, including those who have been here for as few as four years. Consumption of these images by immigrant and refugee women leads some to accept antiwelfare and antipoor rhetoric and to embrace ideas that individual effort and ability determine economic success. It also leads some to disassociate themselves from the racial or ethnic group or from people of color in general.

Yuet and Chi-lan both seem to have absorbed, wholesale, the dominant negative images of black Americans as welfare abusers and positive images of Asian Americans as "model minorities." When I asked Chi-lan what she thought the stereotypes of Asians were, she offered the following portrait:

> We work hard ... and we spend small—little bit money to be better. But everybody in America, they spend a lot for everything, for their enjoy. And they don't work hard, too. So they think, why we come here a short time but we have car, we have everything. And we push our children to be better, so they good in school, so they don't like.

When Chi-lan expressed her view that people should try to leave welfare as soon as possible, I asked her if she thought that most Americans would agree. She hesitated and then said in a low voice: "Black Americans don't think so." Later, I asked whether this might be different if there were more jobs available for black Americans. She responded:

> I don't know.... Maybe they don't want to go? Or they—I don't know why, but I say, I see they stay home, all of them, almost all of them. But somebody, some black very smart and they have a high, high situation social. Very good, but I don't know.

I wondered how and when Chi-lan was able to see black Americans staying home and in what context she actually had contact with black Americans. Yuet's comments were helpful here, indicating that her main contact with "black" people was with Eritrean refugees at a job training program for refugee women. Yuet suggested that Eritreans were the most likely to be welfare dependent:

I think that people from Eritrea, they stay on welfare longer.... Because I see that they have many children. Each family has many children, so it is difficult for them to get out of the welfare. Yes, because I met at [the job training program], some Eritrean women, they don't want to get a job.

When I asked her why she thought Eritreans participated in the training program, she replied: "Because they have to—if not, they will lose their GA [General Assistance] or something. They cannot stay at home and receive the welfare.... And I think that Asian people, they like working."

Ironically, these women's ideas about black Americans were based on their limited experience with African refugees, who themselves did not identify as blacks or African Americans. Tecle's comments, denouncing and actively disassociating herself from black Americans, make this clear and offer another measure of how powerful the myths of black Americans as "welfare queens" are in our society. I stumbled onto Tecle's strong antiblack sentiments when I asked her whether she thought the typical American could distinguish African refugees from black Americans:

Tecle: No. They don't say anything about that. Generally, they [whites] do not respect for the black people, but the blacks are not good for them.

Grace: What do you mean?

Tecle: The blacks, when they are speaking with the whites, they are not respect. When I see black Americans, they don't speak with respect for whites. So we are with them also, we have no respect for them. (She laughs.)

Grace: What do you mean?

Tecle: White Americans are better, I think. I don't know, but when I see them speaking, they respect people. Not the blacks.

Tecle's experience with black Americans has been as an ESL teacher in her children's school and in their neighborhood in Oakland. Interestingly, she did not see these racial relations in terms of discrimination against blacks but rather mutual hostility between black and whites—a conflict in which she allied herself with whites.

Yuet's observations were perhaps the most astonishing representation of the power of US rhetoric casting immigrants as those who are rightfully denied access to the benefits of citizenship. When I had finished my interview questions, she offered that she had something to add. She said that in Vietnam, the Chinese are the minority, and she described them as a "good" minority because they "never caused problems," they "just worked and contributed" to society, and were never a "burden" to anyone. She said that they were only interested in business, did not "interfere" with politics, and built their own schools and hospitals, which the Vietnamese could use if they wished. She suggested that there was no resentment toward the Chinese in Vietnam because there were no social services or welfare that they were receiving. She emphasized several times that they "only worked and contributed."

Yuet's views may resemble very closely the view many Americans hold about the proper role and conduct of immigrants and people of color in American society. Essentially, she says that what constitutes a good minority is a group that contributes labor and capital without any expectations of enjoying the same privileges as the dominant group, and without imposing a "burden" by using social services. Moreover, the ideal minority shares its resources with the larger public but does not expect this to be reciprocated. Nor does the ideal minority meddle in the body politic to gain such privileges or resources. Ironically, her vision of the "model minority" is in fact embodied in the situations of the undocumented and many legal immigrants in the United States today.

At the outset of these interviews, I had anticipated that Latina immigrants might feel a sense of entitlement to social services and benefits based on, if nothing else, claims to proper compensation beyond the low wages that they typically receive for service work. At the very least, I expected that many of these women might assert the injustice of having taxes and other costs extracted from them in the workplace, while having no access to services or benefits normally afforded to workers. I predicted that refugee women, in contrast, might develop views closer to the American public at large, seeing their receipt of government assistance as acceptable, at least as a temporary or transitional measure.

While the views of the refugee women fulfilled my predictions quite closely, the degree to which both the immigrant and refugee women expressed antiwelfare ideologies and repeated the myths of immigrants and blacks as welfare abusers was disturbing. I am not suggesting that the women I interviewed were dupes who passively accepted the dominant rhetoric they were fed.[70] My point is more that this rhetoric is so pervasive that the women I interviewed seemed to have largely incorporated it into their stated views on the proper role of the state and their beliefs about newcomers' and people of color's work and welfare practices. The general opposition to government assistance programs voiced by all of these women stands as testimony to the power of myths and imagery, and to the effectiveness of immigration and welfare law systems maneuvered to divide people against each other.

In *From Mammy to Miss America and Beyond: Cultural Images and the Shaping of US Social Policy,* sociologist K. Sue Jewell argues that the privileged classes use mass media to put forth images of African Americans as sexually and financially irresponsible so they can justify the denial of aid to African-American single mothers as the "undeserving" poor:[71]

> The fact that the materially privileged have successfully proliferated these myths over a period of more than 100 years has enabled them to maintain a monopoly on power and wealth. Equally important, these media-created images facilitate the efforts of policy makers, who represent the interests of the nation's elite, to formulate policy and pass legislation which is in the interests of those in power and to the detriment of the country's poor, many of whom are African-American women and children.[72]

That US media, acting on behalf of and through the support of capital and the state, have disseminated these myths as assaults on black women is perhaps not news. What is of greater concern is that such imagery has been extended to other racial and ethnic groups, such as Latinas, and that these images are even infiltrating the very communities against which these attacks are being leveled. That is, these myths serve to perpetuate misunderstanding and reinforce divisions among racial and ethnic groups that might otherwise forge alliances around their common plights as low-wage workers, migrants, and second-class citizens.

When these notions are consumed by immigrants, a tragic result is that people are deterred from seeking aid or services even when they and their dependents need and are entitled to them. Moreover, immigrant workers are unlikely to support these programs as taxpaying residents or as taxpaying, voting citizens. The proliferation of myths about immigrants and people of color as welfare abusers, and the operation of a two-tiered welfare system for refugees and immigrants, work together all too successfully to limit public support for entitlement programs and to instead reinforce conflicts among people of color and the working class. Thus, anti-immigrant and antipoor rhetoric serve not only to perpetuate a racialized class system, but to reproduce the very racism and classism on which the system rests. As members of the Milwaukee County Welfare Rights Organization articulate in *Welfare Mothers Speak Out:*

> [M]yths are used to hide the reality of welfare. All of them are contradicted by the facts. Yet they are used to capture the minds of the overburdened taxpayer, the low-income laborer, and even their target, the welfare recipient.[73]

1   New York Department of City Planning, Office of Immigrant Affairs, "Immigrant Entitlements Made (Relatively) Simple," Pamphlet 90-14, January 1990.

2   Statement of Maria Olea at the general meeting of the Coalition for Immigrant and Refugee Rights and Services, San Francisco, CA, March 4, 1993.

3   Sharon Begley, "America's Changing Face," *Newsweek*, September 10, 1990, p. 48.

4   Leo Chavez, *Shadowed Lives: Undocumented Immigrants in American Society* (Fort Worth, Texas: Harcourt Brace College Publishers, 1998), p. 192.

5   Chavez, *Shadowed Lives*, p. 192.

6   Todd A. Eisenstadt and Cathryn L. Thorup, *Caring Capacity versus Carrying Capacity: Community Response to Mexican Immigration in San Diego's North County*, Monograph Series 39 (San Diego: Center for US-Mexican Studies, UC San Diego, 1994), p. 7.

7   Mike Davis, *Ecology of Fear: Los Angeles and the Imagination of Disaster* (New York: Henry Holt, 1998), pp. 280–82.

8   Davis, *Ecology of Fear*, pp. 289–90.

9   Davis, *Ecology of Fear*, p. 340.

10   Davis, *Ecology of Fear*, pp. 341–42.

11   Peter Brimelow, *Alien Nation: Common Sense About America's Immigration Disaster* (New York: Random House, 1995), p. 4.

12   Brimelow, *Alien Nation*, p. 10.

13   Brimelow, *Alien Nation*, p. xix.

14   Brimelow, *Alien Nation*, p. 4.

15   Brimelow, *Alien Nation*, p. 4, citing Judith T. Fullerton, *Access to Prenatal Care for Hispanic Women of San Diego County*, Latina/Latino Research Program, California Policy Seminar (Berkeley, CA: Regents of the University of California, 1993).

16   Presentation by Wendy Walker-Moffat at "Tempest in the Melting Pot: An Assessment of the Anti-Immigrant Campaign" forum, UC Berkeley, April 13, 1994; see also Wendy Walker-Moffat, "Recent Mexican Immigrant Women to the United States: Fertility Rates and Use of Public Services," School of Social Welfare, UC Berkeley, prepared for California assembly member Grace Napolitano, chair of the Assembly Select Committee on Statewide Immigration Impact, June 1994.

17   Walker-Moffat, "Recent Mexican Immigrant Women to the US," pp. 4, 22.

18   Walker-Moffat, "Recent Mexican Immigrant Women to the US," pp. 26–27.

19   Specifically, Walker-Moffat critiqued three studies: the November 1993 report "The Net Costs of Immigration to California," by Donald Huddle; the August 1992 report "A Fiscal Impact Analysis of Undocumented Immigrants Residing in San Diego County," by Louis Rea and Richard Parker, prepared by the Auditor General's Office; and the November 1994 report "The Impact of Undocumented Persons and Other Immigrants on

Costs, Revenues and Services in Los Angeles County," prepared by the Los Angeles County Internal Services Department.

20   Walker-Moffat, "Recent Mexican Immigrant Women to the US," p. 8.

21   Walker-Moffat, "Recent Mexican Immigrant Women to the US," p. 6.

22   Tom Morganthau, "America: Still a Melting Pot?," *Newsweek*, August 9, 1993, p. 18.

23   See also Bill Ong Hing, "Don't Give Me Your Tired, Your Poor: Conflicted Immigrant Stories and Welfare Reform," *Harvard Civil Rights–Civil Liberties Law Review* 33 (Winter 1998), on myths of elderly Asian immigrants and refugees as welare abusers (see especially pp. 159, 166).

24   Undocumented Workers Policy Research Project, "The Use of Public Services by Undocumented Aliens in Texas," No. 60 (Austin, Texas: Lyndon B. Johnson School of Public Affairs, 1984), pp. 250–55. See also Kevin McCarthy and R. Valdez, "Current and Future Effects of Mexican Immigration in California," Report No. 3365 (Santa Monica, CA: The Rand Corporation, November 1985); Thomas J. Espenshade and Charles A. Calhoun, "An Analysis of Public Opinion Toward Undocumented Immigration," *Population Research and Policy Review* 12: 3 (1993), p. 189.

25   Undocumented Workers Policy Research Project, "The Use of Public Services," p. 251.

26   Julian Simon, *The Economic Consequences of Immigration* (Cambridge, MA: Blackwell, 1989), p. 125.

27   Simon, *Economic Consequences of Immigration,* p. 106.

28   Simon, *Economic Consequences of Immigration,* pp. 106, 110.

29   Simon, *Economic Consequences of Immigration,* pp. 106, 115.

30   Simon, *Economic Consequences of Immigration,* p. 124.

31   Stephen Moore, "Flee Market—More Refugees at Lower Cost," *Policy Review* (Spring 1990), p. 66.

32   Moore, "Flee Market," p. 64.

33   Moore, "Flee Market," p. 68.

34   Moore, "Flee Market," p. 67.

35   Simon, *Economic Consequences of Immigration,* p. 319.

36   Julian Simon, "Lots More Immigration Would Be a Windfall," *Fortune,* March 26, 1990.

37   Karen Riley, "Economic Pluses Usually Arrive with Immigrants, Professor Says," *Washington Times,* March 30, 1990, p. C-1.

38   Undocumented Workers Policy Research Project, "The Use of Public Services," p. 22.

39   For example, Frank Sharry, executive director of the National Immigration Forum, put forth official statements such as "legal immigration is not the same as illegal immigration" and "the American people want the federal government to take decisive and effective action to control illegal immigration." National Immigration Forum memoranda "Local Lobby Days to Defend Immigration" and "What's Wrong with the House

   Immigration Bill (HR 2202)," November 1995.
40   Michael Fix and Jeffrey Passel, "Immigration and Immigrants: Setting the Record Straight," Urban Institute, May 1994.
41   Fix and Passel, "Immigration and Immigrants." See also Jeffrey S. Passel and Rebecca L. Clark, "How Much Do Immigrants Really Cost? A Reappraisal of Huddle's 'The Cost of immigrants,'" Urban Institute, February 1994.
42   Ralph Ellison, *Invisible Man* (New York: Random House, 1995).
43   Statement of Nohemy Ortiz, CIRRS general meeting, March 4, 1993. "Washington" refers to the controversy surrounding the disclosure that Zoë Baird, nominated for attorney general in 1993, had employed two undocumented immigrants, one as a nanny and the other as a driver. Ultimately, Baird lost the nomination because of the scandal.
44   Cathi Tactaquin, "The Greening of the Anti-Immigrant Agenda: Stopping Immigration to 'Save the Environment,'" *Network News*, National Network for Immigrant and Refugee Rights (NNIRR), Spring 1998, p. 6.
45   NNIRR, "Declaration on Immigrants and the Environment," *Network News* 7: 1 (July–August 1994), pp. 4–5.
46   NNIRR, "Declaration on Immigrants and the Environment"; see also Greta Gaard and Lori Gruen, "Ecofeminism: Toward Global Justice and Planetary Health," *Society and Nature* 2: 1, p. 3.
47   Cynthia Hamilton, "Women, Home and Community: The Struggle in an Urban Environment," in *Reweaving the World*, eds. Irene Diamond and Gloria Orenstein (San Francisco: Sierra Club Books, 1990), p. 215.
48   See also Tactaquin in *Network News* (Spring 1998), and Peter Reich, "Environmental Metaphor in the Alien Benefits Debate," *UCLA Law Review* 42 (August 1995), p. 1577.
49   Dorothy Roberts, *Killing the Black Body: Race, Reproduction, and the Meaning of Liberty* (New York: Vintage Books, 1999), p. 217.
50   "Researchers Dispute Contention That Welfare Is a Major Cause of Out-of-Wedlock Births," June 23, 1994, press release by Sheldon Danziger, director of the Research and Training Program on Poverty, the Underclass and Public Policy at the School of Social Work at the University of Michigan, Ann Arbor, cited in Mimi Abramovitz, *Regulating the Lives of Women: Social Welfare Policy from Colonial Times to the Present* (Boston: South End Press, rev. ed. 1996), p. 365.
51   Abramovitz, *Regulating the Lives of Women*, p. 365.
52   See Evelyn Nakano Glenn, "From Servitude to Service Work: Historical Continuities in the Racial Division of Paid Reproductive Labor," *Signs: Journal of Women in Culture and Society* 18: 1 (1992), pp. 1–43, for a discussion of the historical concentration of women of color in paid reproductive labor or service work in the US. I thank Jean Molesky for pointing out, in a discussion of the informal sector, that diaper service workers are primarily women of color and immigrant women.

53 I have changed these names to ensure the confidentiality of my participants.

54 Included in the category of "immigrants" are those who come to the United States seeking to reunite with families, provided there is no public cost for this reunification.

55 For example, the conservative think tank the Heritage Foundation reports that each refugee is entitled to about $5,000 in resettlement aid for readjustment costs such as English language training, job placement, and medical checkups. See Moore, "Flee Market," p. 66.

56 A report by Stephen Moore, director of the conservative American Immigration Institute, claims that 25 percent of all refugees are dependent on some form of public assistance. This figure is likely inflated because Moore uses it to advocate the replacement of these assistance programs with loans. See Moore, "Flee Market," p. 67.

57 Moreover, Ui found that some were even recruited to work in social service agencies, to act as liaisons to their communities. Shiori Ui, "Unlikely Heroes: The Evolution of Female Leadership in a Cambodian Ethnic Enclave," in Michael Burawoy, *Ethnography Unbound* (Berkeley, CA: University of California Press, 1991), pp. 161–177.

58 Interview with Xochitl, Albany, California, March 1994.

59 Interview with Veronica, Albany, California, March 1994.

60 Joint interview with Winta and Tecle, Albany, California, April 1994.

61 Joint interview with Chi-lan and Lan, Berkeley, California, March 1994.

62 The most common forms of cash assistance received by the refugee women I interviewed included General Assistance (GA), Refugee Assistance (RA), and Aid to Families with Dependent Children (AFDC). GA is a county-administered loan program, which then offered up to $5,000 a year for individuals over 18 years of age. RA is also administered by the county and at that time provided an average grant of $300 per month for up to eight months. The grant level is not based on the number of dependents per family but on a calculation of need based on income balanced against expenses such as rent. Participants could apply for GA after eight months if they were eligible. Those who were eligible for AFDC participated in that program instead of RA. The AFDC program provided an average grant of $300 per child under 18 years of age. This information was conveyed to me by one of the directors of Caregivers, a refugee women's assistance program that provided training and placement services for women to secure child-care employment.

63 Chi-lan said: "Because, you know, when we have welfare, we have Medicare—easier than you go to work with $5 an hour. Easier because you go to work with $5 an hour, you have to pay tax—15 percent—and you don't have Medicare. Very difficult ... Like me now, I work, my husband work, my daughter work part-time. But I have to share costs [for] Medicare." Lan added: "You want to work for $5 an hour, you have to pay tax and pay rent, all kinds of things ... So, it costs more than just staying home, and you receive from [the government], you receive money, Medicare, and sometimes housing, too."

64   Interview with Yuet, Berkeley, California, April 1994.

65   This should be viewed in the context of studies suggesting that refugees (in this case, Laotian) received better treatment in social service offices than citizen welfare recipients. Thanks to Mary Kelsey, Ph.D. candidate in UC Berkeley's Sociology Department, for this information.

66   There are a number of other possible explanations for these women's contradictory views: First, the more privileged economic backgrounds of these women in their countries of origin may have predisposed them to classism, which they then carried over into US society. Moreover, they may have been trying to distinguish themselves from the alleged welfare or "financial-aid cheaters," implying that they too could just live off the system and other taxpayers, but they were above this.

67   Leslie Salzinger and Shiori Ui, "Introduction to Part 3," in Burawoy, *Ethnography Unbound,* p. 136.

68   In chapter 2, I discuss how these myths about African Americans' welfare dependency are being extended to Latinas/Latinos.

69   See the 1988 survey by the Federal Office of Refugee Resettlement, and Leo Cherne's statement, both cited in Moore, "Flee Market," p. 66.

70   These preliminary observations raise complex issues that merit further investigation. For example, it would be important to understand the degree to which these women's views are a product of their class backgrounds in their home countries, the existence of state supports in those countries, and a variety of other factors. Moreover, these women may have perceived me as being a member of dominant society, or at least not sympathetic to their situations or experiences, and responded accordingly, presenting what they believed I wanted to hear.

71   K. Sue Jewell, *From Mammy to Miss America and Beyond: Cultural Images and the Shaping of US Social Policy* (New York: Routledge, 1993).

72   Jewell, *From Mammy to Miss America and Beyond,* p. 152.

73   See "Welfare Mythology," in Milwaukee County Welfare Rights Organization, *Welfare Mothers Speak Out* (New York: W.W. Norton, 1972).

Undocumented Latinas

The New Employable Mother

The nomination of Zoë Baird for US Attorney General in 1993 forced a confession that provoked a public uproar: Baird admitted to employing two undocumented Peruvian immigrants, as a baby-sitter and a driver, in clear violation of the immigration law prohibiting the hiring of "illegal" aliens. Responses to Baird's disclosure indicate that her "crime" is a pervasive phenomenon.[1] Deborah Sontag reported in the *New York Times* that two-career, middle-class families employing so-called illegal immigrants to do child care and domestic work is so common that employment agencies routinely recommend undocumented immigrants to their clients. As the director of one Manhattan nanny agency said, "It's just a reality of life that without the illegal girls, there wouldn't be any nannies, and the mommies would have to stay home and mind their own kids."[2] Another agency's director said bluntly, "It all comes down to money.... The reason that people hire immigrants without papers is that they're looking to save. If they want legal, they can get it, but it costs."[3] According to a survey of 18 New York agencies, "illegal" workers earned as little as $175 a week and "legal" workers as much as $600.[4]

Thus, the uproar surrounding Baird was not so much a response to the discovery that some people flouted the law by employing undocumented workers. This was hardly news. Rather, the public outcry was a reflection of resentment that this practice was so easily accessible to the more privileged classes while other working-class working mothers struggled to find any child care. As one critic of Baird commented, "I don't think it's fair. I raised my kids while I was working. I worked days. My husband worked nights at the post office. Our in-laws filled in when they had to."[5] Another woman pointed out: "Average working mothers don't make nearly what she makes, and yet we are obligated to follow the law."[6]

What was conspicuously absent from most of the commentary on the Baird controversy was concern for the plight of the undocumented workers themselves. Two other news stories involving immigrant women working in private households appeared in a California newspaper the same time Baird's situation was making headlines across the nation; yet these stories did not receive comparable attention. The first of these involved Claudia Garate, who immigrated from Chile at age 19 in order to take a job as an au pair for a professional couple. Garate testified before the state Labor Commissioner in Sonoma County that she slept on the floor and worked on call twenty-four hours a day, seven days a week as a maid, baby-sitter, cook, and gardener for $50 a month. Garate's employers held on to her visa and passport and withheld her pay for 13 months, claiming they would deposit it in a bank account for her. The second case involved Maria de Jesus Ramos Hernandez, who left her three children in Mexico to work as a housekeeper in California. Once here, her employer repeatedly raped her, telling her that he had paid her way here and would have her jailed if she did not submit to him.[7]

Evidence indicates that while Garate's and Hernandez's cases may have been extreme, abuse of undocumented women working in private households is not uncommon. Lina Avidan, then–program director for the San Francisco–based Coalition for Immigrant and Refugee Rights and Services (CIRRS), said, "I have clients who work … seven days a week, doing child care from 6 a.m. to 10 p.m. [for] $200 a month. Clearly, they are working in the homes of the wealthy and they're not even getting minimum wage."[8] A 1991 CIRRS survey of Chinese, Filipina, and Latina undocumented women in the San Francisco Bay area revealed that the majority (58 percent) of the employed undocumented Latinas surveyed held jobs in housecleaning and in-home care of children or the elderly, while the remainder worked in service jobs or factories. They were usually earning between $250 and $500 per month. Forty percent of these women were supporting between one and three people on these wages, while 38 percent were supporting between four and six.[9] Members of *Mujeres Unidas y Activas* (MUA), a support group for Latina immigrant domestic workers, report that they commonly endure conditions approaching slavery or indentured servitude.[10]

These statements are echoed by immigrant domestic workers in Los Angeles, years after the Zoë Baird episode has passed. Patricia Tejada fled from El Salvador in 1988 because of the war, leaving her three children and husband behind. She worked as a baby-sitter and housekeeper for the next four years in Los Angeles to try to save enough money to bring her family to join her. She recalls spending many nights crying, wondering how her children were and whether they were safe. Throughout those years, she often became very attached to the children she cared for, only to find that she would be dismissed coldly and abruptly when her services were no longer necessary: "We love the children, but the employers just need us. When they don't, they say, 'We don't need you anymore,' " she says with a wave of her hand.[11]

Another woman, Amalia Hernandez, who fled El Salvador with her four cousins, found her first job working in Los Angeles as a live-in nanny caring for a newborn infant. Although Amalia had been offered $80 per week, she was paid $50 instead to work from 6 a.m. until midnight, most days. In her next job, she was supposed to be paid $100 per week, but was told by her employer for a year and a half that her salary was being saved for her. When she asked for her pay, the employer told his wife to throw her out. Amalia left the house with only one month's pay and a bunch of "hand-me-down" clothes. Although she tried to take the employer to small claims court, the employer won the case by insisting that Amalia was a very bad worker and threatening in the courtroom that she would call the INS to deport her. Amalia recalls that she hardly spoke any English at the time and was frightened by her employer's threats.

She describes her current employment situation as tolerable: She takes care of three children, ages four, two, and two months. In a typical day, she begins at 6 a.m. preparing breakfast, gives the children lunch for school, brings the four-year-old to preschool for half a day, cleans the house, does laundry, and cooks dinner. Essentially, she works around the clock every day while "the lady stays home all day and gets angry if I sit down." Suffering from an injury sustained on the job, Amalia is in constant pain carrying the baby around, up and down the stairs all day. She wishes she could go to the doctor for the injury but is afraid she will lose her job if she takes time off to do so. She is paid $275 per week and has random times off, given at her employer's whim.[12]

Taken together, these accounts indicate that middle-class households often make exploitative use of immigrant women to do child care and domestic work. They also suggest the advances of many middle-class white women in the workforce have been largely predicated on the exploitation of poor, immigrant women. While middle- and upper-class women entrust their children and homes to undocumented immigrant women, the immigrant women often must leave their own children to work. Some leave their children with family in their home countries, hoping to earn enough to return or send money back to them.[13] Thus, middle- and upper-class women are readily able to find "affordable" care for their children at the expense of poor immigrant women and their children. The employment of undocumented women in dead-end, low-wage, temporary service jobs makes it possible for middle- and upper-class women to pursue salaried jobs and not have to contend with the "second shift" when they come home.

A predictable outgrowth of the Baird controversy has been the proposal that the existing Immigration Reform and Control Act (IRCA) be changed so that household employers are exempted from the prohibition against hiring "illegal" immigrants, or that household workers are given special visas.[14] If the law were changed to meet this "popular demand," it would only serve to legitimize the exploitation of thousands of undocumented immigrants. These proposals raise the specter of a counterpart in private household work to some of the most brutally exploited contract laborers used in agriculture: "disposable nannies" who may be dumped once babies become older or newer immigrants can be found who are willing to work for even lower wages.

The Immigration and Naturalization Service (INS), through its execution of IRCA, has continued to fulfill the historical role of the state in using immigration and welfare policies to maintain women of color as a super-exploitable, low-wage labor force.[15] A historical example is the use of "employable mother" rules by many states from the 1940s through 1960s to deny black mothers benefits, thereby coercing them to perform agricultural and domestic work. In implementing current immigration policy, the INS has continued this pattern. The INS's execution of IRCA, denying legalization to undocumented women whose citizen children have received public assistance, channels these women into and maintains them in the secondary labor force, private household work, and institutional service work.

The Immigration Reform and Control Act of 1986: A Compromise

The Immigration Reform and Control Act of 1986 emerged after nearly a decade of debate in Congress and in the public domain about what impact immigration, particularly "illegal" immigration, had on the US economy. The act had two main objectives that were contradictory: to reduce the number of undocumented immigrants and to provide rights and the chance to legalize to those undocumented immigrants who had already lived and worked in the country. Unable to reconcile these conflicting impulses, Congress incorporated a number of provisions into the law as concessions to various interest groups. First, to discourage illegal immigration, the law established employer sanctions against those who knowingly employed undocumented immigrants. Second, to provide rights and protections to undocumented persons, the amnesty program offered those who could prove they had lived in the country "illegally" since at least 1982 the chance to apply for temporary resident status. Finally, in response to the concerns of growers about how the law might affect the availability of agricultural labor, Congress created three special classes of those who could enter the country or gain residency as agricultural workers.[16]

Some of the most heated debate surrounding IRCA centered around the issue of whether immigrants generally contribute to or deplete from the public coffers. This debate led lawmakers to include in IRCA provisions governing whether those perceived as potentially welfare dependent should be able to gain residency and whether "legalized persons" should be allowed to receive certain entitlements. The virtual hysteria that has arisen around protecting public revenues and guarding against the growth of a population of welfare dependents undoubtedly influenced the inclusion of two provisions of IRCA, the public-charge exclusion and the five-year bar, to restrict aliens' access to social services and public benefits. Clearly, these restrictions were formulated with the immediate goal of limiting welfare expenditures; but, in executing IRCA, the INS went even further, utilizing an interpretation of the law that effectively denied amnesty to those seen as potential welfare abusers— that is, undocumented women with children. To illustrate how the INS's interpretation of the law was more restrictive than intended by Congress, I will review how these provisions were originally formulated.

The Five-Year Bar from Federal Assistance

The amnesty program represented a recognition, at least on the part of some lawmakers, that thousands of undocumented aliens had lived in the United States, worked, and contributed to the American economy for years without ever enjoying the rights of those recognized as full, "legitimate" members of the society.[17] The remarks of one representative suggest that some lawmakers hoped to bring relief to the undocumented through IRCA: "We will be bringing people out of a shadow economy, people will be paying taxes, people will be coming out into the sunshine, there will not be the abuse of workers, employers will not be able to provide poor-quality jobs for people, they will not be able to oppress people."[18] Of course, not all lawmakers had such generous intentions in mind in formulating IRCA. Many were more concerned with protecting public resources for "native" Americans than with protecting the rights of the undocumented. The perception of immigrants as welfare burdens fueled fears that the amnesty program would create a tremendous, immediate strain on social service funds.[19] In direct response to these concerns, Congress included in IRCA a provision barring legalization applicants from most federal assistance programs, including AFDC, food stamps, and certain forms of Medicaid. The bar period extends for five years from the time someone applies for temporary residency.[20]

The Public-Charge Ground of Exclusion and the Special Rule

In addition to the five-year bar, a provision of immigration law dating back to 1882 was retained in IRCA to guard against the expected welfare drain by newly legalized aliens. This provision, excluding those "likely to become a public charge," is used to identify those who might be unable to support themselves because of some physical or mental limitation.[21] Prior to IRCA, all aliens applying for an immigrant visa were subject to a test to determine whether they were likely to be able to earn a living in the United States. This test considers factors such as the applicant's age, health, past and current income, education, and job skills. Past receipt of public benefits is considered a significant but not determinative factor. The traditional test gives applicants one way of overcoming the public-charge ground of exclusion, even if they have received public benefits, if they can show that they are currently employed or able to provide for themselves and their families.[22]

Under IRCA, Congress established a "special rule" providing a second test for legalization applicants unable to pass the traditional test.[23] This test examines the alien's recent past and requires the applicant to have a history of employment that demonstrates self-support without receipt of public cash assistance.[24] This history of employment need not be continuous, thus allowing for periods of unemployment and seasonal or migrant labor.[25] Congressional testimony indicates that Congress created the "special rule" with the intent of liberalizing the public-charge standard or providing a second means of overcoming this standard.[26] Specifically, it was made with the recognition that many of the undocumented are "working poor," unlikely to become dependent on public benefits despite their low incomes.[27]

The amnesty, five-year bar, and public-charge provisions of IRCA were formulated in the face of a wide spectrum of views on what rights and benefits should be extended to immigrants. IRCA represented an uneasy compromise of these views and the task of implementing IRCA was left to the discretion of the INS. In executing IRCA, the INS has applied more restrictive interpretations of the law. For example, Congress intended to open eligibility for legalization to large numbers of people, including those who were low-income, with the "special rule."[28] But the INS did not utilize the "special rule" properly and instead implemented its own interpretations of the law, which were not consistent with Congress's liberalizing intent. The result of this practice was that many undocumented women who had received public assistance for their children were wrongfully denied amnesty.

The Case of *Zambrano v. INS*

The INS's implementation of IRCA, particularly its application of the law to undocumented women, has been challenged in the case *Zambrano v. INS*. The class-action suit was filed in the Ninth Circuit in April 1988 on behalf of a group of plaintiffs who were mostly women with dependents and the class they represent.[29] The complaint against the INS, filed by California Rural Legal Assistance (CRLA), the National Immigration Law Center (NILC), and San Mateo County Legal Aid (SMCLA), co-counsel for the plaintiffs, made two claims: that the INS's practices contradicted the congressional intent in passing IRCA and that these practices discriminated against and imposed extreme hardship on undocumented women with children.[30] In August 1988, the NILC and SMCLA withdrew from the case and the Mexican American Legal Defense and Education Foundation (MALDEF) joined CRLA as co-counsel. The declarations of two of the plaintiffs, Marta Zambrano and Maria C., illustrate how the INS's execution of the amnesty and public-charge provisions of IRCA adversely affected undocumented women with children and obstructed their chances of obtaining better working and living conditions.[31]

Marta Zambrano, whose name the case assumed, was a Mexican citizen who had lived continuously in the United States since 1979. Marta had four children with US citizenship, ages eight, six, four, and three, at the time of her declaration in 1988. Between 1979 and 1983, she worked in a factory, picked cauliflower, and did many kinds of work in the fields, even while she had two small children. She only began receiving AFDC for her children in 1983, when she became pregnant with her third child and her common-law husband left her because she refused to have an abortion.[32]

Marta first heard about the amnesty program in 1986 on the radio and through friends. She went to a program at her church for information and was told that she could not receive AFDC for her children if she wanted to legalize. She also heard on the radio and from her friends that people who received welfare were not eligible for legalization. Convinced that she would not qualify, Zambrano did not pursue an amnesty application. Only at the urging of an attorney did she file her application on May 4, 1988, the latest possible date. In June 1988, she was interviewed by the INS and informed that her application was denied because her children had received AFDC.[33]

Marta received AFDC for her US-citizen children because their natural fathers contributed no support to the family. Since 1986, Marta sought work but was refused in many instances because she did not have work authorization, which she could only obtain through legalization. Potential employers turned Marta away from work in the fields and as a dishwasher and housecleaner. Even when Marta obtained part-time work, she did not earn enough money to cover living expenses and child care.[34]

Anna R. was less fortunate than Marta Zambrano in that she never even applied for amnesty. She was a citizen of El Salvador and had lived in California since 1981. She had four children, two of whom were US citizens. Shortly after IRCA was passed, Anna began preparing to apply for amnesty by gathering necessary documents. In January 1988, Anna was abandoned by the father of her children. At that time she was unable to find full-time employment without work authorization and applied for AFDC for her children, who had US citizenship. She also began working as a housekeeper, one day per week for three different employers. She earned about $400 per month and received no support from her children's father.[35]

Anna heard from the radio, television, and her relatives that receiving welfare would disqualify her from legalization. Thus she did not apply before the May 4, 1988, deadline, as she had intended to since 1986. Had she been informed that the receipt of AFDC by her US-citizen children should not disqualify her from legalization, she would have applied and would otherwise have been eligible.[36]

The other plaintiffs reported similar circumstances and obstacles to legalization. Each of the women had children, some or all of whom were US citizens. Those who received AFDC payments had received them only for US-citizen children, who were fully entitled to these benefits. Most of the women had some work history and, if unemployed at the time of applying for amnesty, would have presumably returned to the workforce when their family circumstances and child-care needs allowed. Some were employed at the time, but their incomes were insufficient to provide for them and their dependents without supplementary AFDC benefits. One received Supplemental Security Income (SSI) payments on behalf of her child, who had cerebral palsy.[37]

These women represent an entire class of people adversely affected by the improper INS practices. The plaintiffs contended that they are among the many thousands of undocumented persons to whom Congress intended to offer an opportunity to become citizens.[38] Yet they have been impeded from obtaining legal status and its benefits (such as work authorization) either through outright denial by the INS or because they were discouraged from applying based on information about the INS's improper practices. The complaint against the INS presented two claims, only the first of which has been addressed by the Court.

First Claim: The INS Has Violated IRCA

The complaint filed against the INS in April 1988 alleged that INS policies and procedures were "in contradiction of the plain meaning of IRCA and Congressional intent."[39] The INS applied its own "Proof of Financial Responsibility" (PFR) regulations, which the plaintiffs maintained were more restrictive than intended in the liberalized standards created under IRCA.[40] The PFR regulations attributed public benefits received by an amnesty applicant's dependents to the applicant. As revealed in the declarations of the plaintiffs, this included AFDC received by children who were fully entitled to these benefits as US citizens. The INS's use of these regulations resulted in the denial of amnesty to applicants who would otherwise have been eligible under IRCA's liberalized standards, such as the "special rule."[41]

The US District Court for the Eastern District of California addressed the first claim in the *Zambrano* case on July 31, 1989. After a thorough review of the INS regulations, the IRCA statute, and the legislative history surrounding its passage, Judge Edward Garcia issued a partial summary judgment and a permanent injunction on the INS regulations. The INS was ordered to reopen the cases of those who had been adversely affected by the regulations. This included two classes of people: first, those who filed applications on time but were denied as "likely to become a public charge" under the invalidated regulations, and second, those who were eligible for legalization but had not applied because they were discouraged by information about the INS's prior practices.[42] The INS was ordered to accept amnesty applications until December 31, 1989, for this second class of people.[43]

The INS appealed the July 1989 decision on a number of grounds.[44] The INS first appealed it in the Ninth Circuit Court of Appeals.[45] In February 1992, the court ruled against the INS, and the INS subsequently filed a writ of certiorari to the US Supreme Court in November 1992.[46] If the Supreme Court does take up the case, it could remand it to the lower courts to decide the remaining issues, such as the second claim made against the INS.

Second Claim: The INS's Regulations Discriminate on the Basis of Sex

A second claim made against the INS was the charge that the INS regulations are discriminatory on the basis of sex and thus violate the equal protection clause.[47] The complaint asserted that the effect of the INS's regulations and procedures was that "legalization under IRCA [was] not made available or [was] made available on an unequal basis [with men] to substantial numbers of women."[48] Certainly, the declarations of the plaintiffs indicated that the INS's practices resulted in the wrongful denial of amnesty to many women whose children received AFDC or other benefits. Moreover, it was estimated that at least 4,000 potential women applicants chose not to apply for amnesty in California alone because they were discouraged by information about the INS's regulations.[49]

Diane Bessette, who acted as a legalization counselor for Catholic Community Services in Sacramento, has called attention to a third group of women for whom the INS regulations have posed inhumane choices. These women have managed to qualify for temporary resident status but must again overcome the INS's public-charge exclusion practices when they apply for permanent residency. Under the five-year bar, a legalization applicant must not receive certain public benefits after applying for temporary residency to maintain his or her application in good standing. He or she must choose between continuing to receive public assistance for his or her dependents or losing this means of support to complete the legalization process.[50] Because many single women with children cannot survive without the assistance, Bessette points out, many will be forced to forego adjusting to permanent residency.[51] In other words, these women face a double bind. Without legal status and its concomitant work authorization, they cannot find employment at adequate wages. Without adequate wages, they must provide for their children by some means, but they sacrifice the chance to gain legal status for themselves if they receive aid for their children as supplements to these wages.

One woman who made a declaration in the *Zambrano* case revealed that she became homeless because she gave up public assistance to apply for amnesty.[52] Others who "choose" illegal status or are denied amnesty will most likely suffer unemployment or employment in exploitative circumstances because they lack work authorization.[53] Rather than bringing these women "out of the shadows," the law has served to condemn them and their children to marginal working and living conditions. Perhaps one of the gravest consequences of the INS regulations has been to perpetuate the feminization of poverty among undocumented immigrants.

A number of recent studies indicate that undocumented persons, particularly women, have become or remain part of an underclass despite the generous potentials of the amnesty program.[54] First, undocumented women have been confined to employment in the secondary sector and often remain in highly exploitative work conditions for fear of losing their chances to legalize. The CIRRS survey revealed that undocumented women suffer many forms of worker exploitation, including not being paid for work, being paid lower wages than documented coworkers, and sexual harassment. In 1991, the US Labor Department investigated abuses in the garment industry, such as runaway shops and shops that didn't pay employees for months at a time. The Department estimated that 337 employees were owed $87,330 by 18 El Paso garment industry employers. The study reported that these abuses were prevalent in the industry because its workers, mostly poor Latinas in the process of applying for legal residency, were too frightened of deportation to complain. Spokespersons for the International Ladies Garment Workers' Union in New York and a group called *La Mujer Obrera* ("The Working Woman") in Texas emphasized that the abuses are related specifically to women's pending amnesty applications. Women who are applying for amnesty continue working for employers who pay late or not at all because they fear their employers will rescind the certification of steady employment necessary to complete their applications.[55]

Second, these women earn incomes far below the poverty level; yet they underutilize public assistance and social services to which they or their children are fully entitled, fearing that they will jeopardize their legalization applications. A study conducted in 1989 by the Comprehensive Adult Student Assessment System (CASAS) found that newly legalized persons used services and benefits at very low rates, "probably lower than for the [California] population as a whole." Two factors need to be considered to see how the improper INS regulations may have affected these rates: first, the family profiles of the respondents, and, second, the proper IRCA regulations regarding amnesty applicants' rights to public assistance and services. Of those who participated in the survey, approximately 43 percent of the families had at least one child born in the US. This implies that for almost half of the survey participants, at least one family member should not have been restricted by his/her immigration status, by IRCA's five-year bar, or by public-charge concerns. AFDC, the program that raised complications most often in the *Zambrano* case, is restricted by the five-year bar for legalization applicants and is a cash assistance program. Therefore, it is only available to the citizen children of newly legalized persons, but receipt of these benefits should only be attributed to the children themselves, not their parents. Yet fewer than one percent (0.9 percent) of families that entered the country prior to 1982 reported receiving AFDC benefits at the time of the survey.

CASAS tried to uncover reasons for these low usage rates with one item in the survey, asking: "Within the last five years, have you ever needed assistance but been reluctant to apply for it for any reason? If yes, why?" Eighty-seven percent of the respondents said they had not needed or had never been reluctant to apply for assistance. Given the level of confusion about the public-charge provision, one can speculate that some of these respondents simply may not have wished to reveal having ever needed assistance. The second largest group of respondents (8 percent) reported that they had needed assistance but feared jeopardizing their amnesty applications.[56]

Moreover, these studies indicate that the INS has contributed to both of these patterns by its improper practices and its failure to publicize the proper regulations regarding amnesty and the public-charge exclusion. The INS failed to publicize accurate information about the amended regulations, even after they were permanently enjoined under the 1989 order. While the INS claimed that "clarification memos" were issued in 1987 and 1988, the court rejected these claims, pointing out that they were never disseminated to the public.[57]

It should be noted that two of the studies cited here were conducted after the August 1988 order in *Zambrano* had already placed a temporary injunction on the improper INS regulations. Yet the responses of those surveyed indicate that widespread fear and misinformation about how use of public assistance would affect their amnesty applications persists. The evidence clearly refutes the myth of undocumented Latinas as nonworking welfare dependents or public resource depletors. Instead, it suggests that the INS's practices have locked countless undocumented women and their dependents into an underclass, without access to legal recourse for workplace abuses or relief from poverty that legalization might afford them.

The evidence certainly supports the second claim made in *Zambrano v. INS* that the INS has "acted knowing and intending that the direct effect of their actions is to exclude or burden substantial numbers of women."[58] For several reasons, the plaintiffs' attorneys did not have the opportunity to pursue this second claim. Earlier, they attempted to show that a large percentage of those persons who have been denied under the improper regulations are single women with children, but the INS refused to comply with discovery orders that would allow them to compile statistics demonstrating this pattern.[59] Stephen Rosenbaum of CRLA, co-counsel for the plaintiffs, commented that sexual discrimination is extremely difficult to prove; the INS's noncompliance with the discovery orders certainly contributed to this difficulty. Rosenbaum also said that the plaintiffs did not pursue this claim because the first claim, charging the INS's statutory violations, was deemed stronger.[60]

Nevertheless, the evidence clearly suggests that the INS's practices discriminate largely against women. In fact, one could argue that the second claim could be expanded to charge that the INS's actions constitute not only sexual but racial discrimination as well. Through these actions, the INS has performed its historical role in regulating the labor of immigrant women for local business interests in manufacturing and agriculture and for middle-class households seeking child care and domestic workers.[61] Thus, it could be established that the INS indeed acted "knowing and intending" that the effects of its practices would be to exclude many women so that they would need to seek or remain in low-wage employment.

The Historical Precedent for the INS's Actions

In *Regulating the Poor: The Functions of Public Welfare*, Frances Fox Piven and Richard Cloward argue that poverty policy and practice have historically been coupled with labor practice to accommodate local employers' demands for low-wage labor. That is, poverty policy has been designed and implemented to serve two basic functions. In times of economic contraction, welfare can be expanded to quell or prevent civil unrest by unemployed masses. Or, in times of relative economic and political stability, welfare can be contracted to expel people from the rolls, thus ensuring their availability to perform low-wage labor according to local needs. Piven and Cloward aptly describe this second function as "enforcing" low-wage work for impoverished people considered to be "able bodied," regardless of age or sex.[62]

Socialist feminist Mimi Abramovitz refines Piven and Cloward's thesis with regard to women in her book *Regulating the Lives of Women*. Abramovitz proposes that the welfare state mediates the conflicting demands of capitalism for women to provide two functions: to remain in the home to reproduce and maintain the labor force, and to undertake traditionally "female" low-wage work in the paid labor force. Abramovitz argues that the state resolves this conflict by encouraging and subsidizing some women to remain home and nurture the current and future workforce while forcing others into low-wage work.[63] This division is achieved through patriarchal poverty policies or practices predicated on racist assumptions that some women (that is, white women) are fit to be mothers and homemakers and thus "deserve" subsidies allowing them to remain in the home. Other women (that is, women of color and immigrant women) are deemed "unfit" nurturers—indeed, are thought to be undesirable reproducers—and thus are viewed as better suited to fulfill the demands for certain kinds of market labor.

Building on this analysis, sociologist Evelyn Nakano Glenn has formulated a model of the racial division of reproductive labor that is helpful in explaining such phenomena.[64] Glenn argues that women of color have historically relieved privileged white women of much of the burden of reproductive labor by performing both private household and institutional service work. Moreover, she argues, women of color's performance of reproductive labor for others frees dominant-group women to pursue leisure or employment, thus making possible the privilege and "liberation" of white women.[65]

Drawing on Glenn's model, I propose that in some cases the state channels women of color into service work to "support" or completely assume the reproductive functions of privileged white women. The state thereby captures the labor of subordinate-group women for dominant-group women, benefitting middle-class households (both women and their partners in traditional nuclear families) and capital. The interests of each of these parties is served through the transferral of the burden of reproductive labor from white women to subordinate women by ameliorating or eliminating conflicts over housework, thus helping to preserve the traditional nuclear family, or allowing middle- and upper-class women to contribute significantly to two-income families.

In the following section, I will trace how welfare policy has been applied differentially for white women and women of color to enforce different kinds of labor for each group of women. This will allow us to analyze how the state has mediated the tension between the demand for women's reproductive labor and women's low-wage labor in the paid work force historically and in the contemporary period.

Regulating the Labor of White Women and Women of Color

The Mothers' Pension program, the first program of public assistance to dependent children, was created to support women at home as the proper guardians of their children and the "stable" home life necessary to cultivate good citizens.[66] The founders of the Mothers' Pension program never claimed that this good home life was to be extended to all women and children; nor were all women thought to be able to maintain good homes for children. The creators envisioned limiting this support to a privileged group of mothers. The White House Conference that convened in 1909 to outline the program produced two principles. First, a select group of families would be removed from the class of paupers and from the stringent provisions of the Poor Law. Second, the state would provide assistance to enable these women to keep their children in their own homes rather than in institutions, so they could nurture them into productive citizens. In return, these mothers were to demonstrate that they were proper and competent custodians of their children and that they could maintain "suitable homes" for them.[67]

This second principle was the basis for the "suitable home" rules that were retained in many states throughout the operation of the Mothers' Pension program and its successors. In her classic study, *Aid to Dependent Children,* Winifred Bell argues that this rule became a convenient means by which welfare officials could identify black mothers of "illegitimate" children as "unfit" and "undeserving" of aid.[68] The available statistics suggest that the operative definitions of "fit" and "deserving" implied white and widowed.[69] Moreover, Bell suggests that receipt of a Mothers' Pension grant was thought to bestow prestige upon these mothers and to "set them apart from the totality of mothers" as those who were expected to "achieve the ideal of devoted, selfless, and competent motherhood."[70]

In reality, the Mothers' Pension grants did not provide sufficient support to enable these chosen few to devote themselves solely to their child-rearing duties. The program requirements presented contradictory obligations, defining "worthy" women as those who did not leave their children yet still managed to earn as much as possible.[71] Some states limited the amount of time a "worthy" mother could leave the home to three days a week. Many women resolved this dilemma by taking in laundry, thus simultaneously earning money and the status of "worthiness."[72]

The stated rationale behind the Aid to Dependent Children (ADC) program, established under the 1935 Social Security Act, seemed to remove this contradiction, asserting that mothers should be relieved of the double burden of wage-earning and caring for children. The Committee on Economic Security published a report in 1935 stating that the ADC program was designed "to release from the wage-earning role the person whose natural function is to give her children the physical and affectionate guardianship necessary not [only] to keep them from falling into social misfortune, but more affirmatively to make them citizens capable of contributing to society."[73] Thus, with the inception of the ADC program, federal policy proposed that the first obligation of women with children should be to nurture children into productive citizens and that this maternal mission should not be hindered by work in the paid labor force.

Sylvia Law argues that from 1935 to 1968, federal policy embodied the principle that women with children were unemployable.[74] Under federal ADC and then-AFDC guidelines in effect from 1939 to 1969, "Considerations Regarding Employment of Mothers" advised that exerting pressure on mothers might lead them to neglect their maternal or homemaking duties:

> The time available for domestic responsibilities is limited for an employed mother. She must either neglect her home or make inroads on her physical resources. The resulting nerve strain may affect her contribution to industry as well as to the well-being of her family.... The role of the public assistance agencies is, by assistance and other services, to help the mother arrive at a decision that will best meet her own needs and those of her children.[75]

In most cases, however, the interests of local employers competed with the needs of mother and child. For certain groups of women, the ideal of state-supported, full-time mothering was sacrificed to the demands of capitalism. Officially, federal policy "discouraged" states from using public assistance to coerce mothers to work outside the home. For example, the *Handbook of Public Assistance Administration* advised: "The Bureau of Public Assistance recommends against any policy of denying or withdrawing aid to dependent children as a method of bringing pressure upon women with young children to accept employment."[76] Nevertheless, individual caseworkers and local state agencies exercised wide discretion over the administration of grants and used a variety of mechanisms to deny women of color this protection against compulsion to work outside the home.

In many states and localities, ADC and AFDC administrative rules contained explicit wage work requirements for mothers but applied them selectively to poor women of color while preserving the option of full-time mothering for others.[77] Often these rules functioned as a pretext for expelling or denying women of color access to welfare, thus forcing them to seek work in the marginal labor market. For example, Louisiana adopted the first "employable mother" rule in 1943, requiring all AFDC families with children seven years or older to be denied assistance if the mother was presumed "employable" in the fields. Undoubtedly, the rule was directed at nonwhite mothers since this seasonal labor was almost exclusively performed by nonwhites.[78]

The statements of caseworkers suggest that racist assumptions often influenced them to view black mothers as particularly well-suited for employment, and these views guided their eligibility determinations. These assumptions included the beliefs that black mothers had always worked in the past, that appropriate employment opportunities were more abundant for black women, and that child-care needs did not pose a problem for these mothers, ostensibly because the children were cared for by extended family members—or, perhaps more to the point, because caseworkers did not believe it necessary to maintain the same standards of proper home life and maternal care for black children. One Louisiana caseworker unabashedly expressed these assumptions about the unique employability of black mothers:

> [The] Negro mother has always worked in the past. The grandmother was there to look after the children. Now the mother has quit work. She stays at home and sits on the porch and rocks. Nobody wants to make the children suffer. What they want is for the mother to get out and work.[79]

A colleague of this caseworker replied:

> What the people who make these criticisms are chiefly interested

in is cheaper servants. It makes no difference to them one way or
the other what happens to Negro children. They are not interested in whether the mother has someone to leave the children
with or not. What they want is to get a cook at $5 a week as they
used to.[80]

One can only infer from such statements that caseworkers recognized (though perhaps did not accept uncritically) the function of
their agencies in accommodating local demands for cheap labor. As
the remarks of one observer indicate, the attitude that the "employable Negro mother" could and should be coerced to remain in agricultural or domestic work often translated into the practice of
denying black families public assistance:

> The number of Negro cases is few due to the unanimous feeling
> on the part of the staff and board that there are more work op-
> portunities for Negro women and to their intense desire not to in-
> terfere with local labor conditions.... There is hesitancy on the
> part of lay boards to advance too rapidly over the thinking of their
> own communities, which see no reason why the employable Ne-
> gro mother should not continue her usually sketchy seasonal la-
> bor or indefinite domestic service rather than receive a public
> assistance grant.[81]

Thus, both explicit administrative measures such as the suitable
home and employable mother rules, and the biases of some caseworkers making eligibility determinations, operated to bar or expel
women of color from the rolls, compel them from their homes, and
deliver them to local employers for domestic or agricultural work.
The widespread use of these rules and the prevalence of these attitudes from the 1940s through the 1960s need to be viewed in their
historical context. After World War II, vigorous efforts were made
to encourage white middle-class women to return to the home as
guardians of their children and of domesticity. Simultaneously, efforts were made to direct black women back to these same homes as
domestic workers.[82] The overall result was to create altogether separate standards and conditions under which women of color and
white women had to mother, relegating each group to particular

functions within the system of patriarchal capitalism and thus rein-forcing race- and class-based divisions between women.

In the late 1960s, a series of legal challenges to restrictive wel-fare regulations succeeded in overturning some of the mechanisms that had been used to perpetuate these differential standards. Among these was a challenge to the Georgia employable mother rule in a class action suit, *Anderson v. Burson* (1968), filed on behalf of a group of AFDC mothers. The Georgia rule, enacted in 1952, per-mitted welfare officials to deny aid to mothers with children over one year of age on the assumption that the women were employable if suitable work was available.[83] "Suitable" meant employment at any wage, and the rule prohibited county welfare departments from supplementing that wage, even if it was lower than the welfare grant levels. Moreover, the rule authorized county welfare officials to deny all new applications and to close all existing cases of mothers deemed employable during "periods of full employment"—that is, during cotton-picking season.[84]

The plaintiffs in *Anderson v. Burson* argued that the rule had been used much more frequently to keep black women off the rolls than white women, thus violating the equal protection provisions under the 14th Amendment of the US Constitution. On April 5, 1968, a three-judge federal court in Atlanta struck down certain portions of the Georgia "employable mother" rule, validating the charge that it violated equal protection standards.[85] The court argued that the practice of denying supplementary benefits to mothers who were employed for less money than they would receive on welfare contra-dicted the purpose of the AFDC program. The plaintiffs also re-quested the right to refute the assumption that they could obtain work merely because a welfare official claimed that they were em-ployable.[86] The court struck down a provision requiring the appli-cant to demonstrate that suitable employment was not available.[87]

In many ways, the INS regulations challenged in the *Zambrano* case were implemented to produce much the same results as the "employable mother" rules. First, the improper INS regulations were used more frequently to discourage Latina mothers from using AFDC or other public benefits and to discourage these women from receiving benefits in the future, even after they were legalized. Second, as has already been argued, the INS practices contradicted the purpose of the "special rule" under IRCA: to expand access to legalization and its benefits to the undocumented working poor. Finally, it seems that INS officials assumed that these mothers had adequate means of supporting their children through employment while at the same time ensuring that, without legalization and the accompanying work authorization, these women could not acquire jobs providing a decent wage. Yet if they attempted to supplement their inadequate wages with AFDC, they eliminated their chances of gaining legal status themselves and the possibility of better providing for their families in the future.

The regulation of undocumented Latina mothers under IRCA closely resembles the regulation of black mothers under the "employable mother" rules. In each case the notion of nonwhite mothers as employable exists alongside prevailing dominant culture's view that a mother's employment outside the home harms her children's development. For each group of women, their construction as those who can and should work outside the home rationalizes the practice of denying support to them as mothers. This denial of aid forces these women to forego full-time mothering and to seek or remain in marginal work, for which they are seen as better suited. The parallel suggests that the notion of nonwhite mothers as uniquely employable has never been eradicated but, rather, has been enforced through a variety of government policies and practices.

Some feminists have proposed that subsidies to women with children should be expanded in the recognition that full-time mothering is work and should be properly rewarded. Wendy Sarvasy, for one, has called for us to recapture some of the original principles behind the Mothers' Pension program—for example, that mothers be seen as civil servants and provided with pensions as compensation for their services in nurturing future citizens.[88] Such proposals repeat the original flaw of the Mothers' Pension program. They limit support to an elite group of women by defining "deserving" mothers as full-time mothers, while few women actually find full-time mothering viable. Under the current racial division of reproductive labor, some women cannot stay at home with their own children while they mother other people's children and keep other people's homes. Moreover, many women of color, as well as working-class white women, have the same aspirations for "meaningful work" outside the home as do privileged white women, although they may not have the means to pursue such career ambitions. Ironically, it is the assumption of reproductive labor by women of color and immigrant women for privileged white women that allows the latter group to forego full-time mothering, opting for careers and other pursuits they desire. Thus, proposals to reward full-time mothering offer nothing to most women of color, for whom this occupation may not be an option or the ideal.

Historically, women of color have had to work, even while raising small children, either to supplement inadequate wages garnered by men in their families, or to provide for families in the absence of male providers. In response, communities of color have often constructed alternatives to dominant society's model of the family in which men are providers, women are dependents, and biological mothers exclusively are assumed to be the natural and proper caretakers of children. For example, Patricia Hill-Collins traces the strong tradition of shared mothering responsibilities among blood mothers, community mothers, and church mothers in African-American communities.[89]

Carol Stack and Linda Burton report that male and female, old and young members of low-income African-American families negotiate cycled or intergenerational caretaking responsibilities. Such arrangements enable young women to earn wages during childbearing years while their elders (mothers, fathers, aunts, uncles) are still young enough to care for children.[90] Similarly, the Mexicana mothers in Denise Segura's study viewed employment as compatible with mothering, as it enabled them to contribute toward the collective good of the family.[91]

Proposals to reform the welfare system through revaluing the work of full-time mothers fail to address the needs of women of color and further marginalize them in their struggles to provide for their families. A more radical proposition—and one that might begin to address the plight of women of color who are poor working mothers—would be to recognize and reward women for the services that they provide through both their productive and reproductive labors. Beyond income supports, these women should be offered adequate wages, access to better employment options, and the same services for "working mothers" (for example, child care) available to many of their employers. Initiatives on this order will certainly meet great resistance from those employers who rely on the "affordability" of immigrant women and women-of-color workers.[92]

During the Zoë Baird controversy, it was anticipated that a coalition of immigrant advocacy, child-care advocacy, and women's groups might form around the "shared interests" of women's work in housekeeping and child care. This was seen as an opportunity to champion the cause of "working" mothers from all social locations and to make the case for proper compensation for "housework"—whether performed by "housewives" or service workers. Yet no such coalition emerged.[93] It is telling that the major women's groups were conspicuously silent during Baird's confirmation hearings.[94] The few individuals from the National Organization for Women who attended the Immigration Reform Commission hearings on home-care worker programs were not acting as NOW representatives.[95] Perhaps this is not so surprising, as white professional women have historically relied on the "affordability" of immigrant women workers.[96]

Fear of being discovered with an undocumented employee might have compelled some to be silent, or some might have wished to avoid formalizing or regulating this industry. Whatever the cause of the paralysis around this issue, prospects for a "feminist" stance on home-care workers or immigrant women's rights have seemed grim. Efforts to improve conditions and wages for domestic workers and child-care providers have historically drawn a poor response from mainstream women's groups. Sociologist Diana Pearce reports that one women's rights organization declined to take a stand on the question of whether their city's minimum wage for household and child-care workers should be raised because the women on staff disagreed on this issue. Many argued that they could not afford to pay higher wages to their housekeepers and child-care providers.[97]

Pearce says it would be a mistake to interpret this as a "situation in which middle-class lawyers' and other professionals' interests conflicted with lower-class clients' interests." Pearce instead suggests that "[t]he real issue is one of inadequate pay for all women workers."[98] While I agree that the latter issue is one concern here, the former is precisely the central issue at stake. Pearce's interpretation neglects the fact that these women employers were protecting class and racial privileges they enjoyed.[99]

When the Malibu Democratic Club was presented with the proposals for a minimum-wage campaign in Los Angeles, the female membership, predominantly comprising wealthy "West LA" feminists, immediately inquired, "Does this mean that we will have to pay our baby-sitters and maids more?"[100] This incident offers a perfect example of how the interests of privileged "working" women and working-class women will always clash if the former insist on maintaining these privileges over the latter.

Debating Motherhood

On May 7, 1998, a full ten years after the *Zambrano* class-action suit was filed against the INS, the Ninth Circuit Court of Appeals dismissed the case from Superior Court.[101] This transpired after the INS had tried repeatedly to appeal to both the Ninth Circuit Court of Appeals and to the Supreme Court with no success, then ultimately resorted to trying to achieve its goals through the legislative process. Congress enacted, as part of the Illegal Immigration Reform and Immigrant Responsibility Act (IIRIRA) of 1996, section 377, which stipulated that the courts' jurisdiction over legalization matters would be limited to cases in which people had filed their applications or had attempted to file but were rejected by the INS. The stipulation was also made retroactive such that it applied to the *Zambrano* case. Subsequently, the INS filed another motion and succeeded in having the prior orders vacated and the case dismissed based on the new law's retroactivity.[102]

As Pauline Gee of California Rural Legal Assistance, co-counsel for the plaintiffs in *Zambrano*, said: "INS went to Congress because it couldn't win in the courts and had Senator Simpson, as his last act before retiring, pass this statute." Vibiana Andrade of the Mexican American Legal Defense and Education Fund, also co-counsel for the plaintiffs, commented: "Congress can do all kinds of things. In immigration law, it has unfettered discretion to do so. It has been a really frustrating ten-year fight." Andrade said it was particularly maddening that throughout the court battle the INS never contested the rulings against the agency, that it had implemented the law improperly, and that it had violated IRCA in applying its own public-charge standards. Instead, the INS reduced the case to a jurisdiction issue and ultimately won on the grounds that these matters should not be within the courts' discretionary powers.[103]

The *Zambrano* litigation brought important results for tens of thousands of immigrant families seeking to legalize their status. Under the early *Zambrano* rulings and injunctions, many people who had been denied or prevented from obtaining legal status because of the INS's improper public-charge standard implementation were able to have their legalization applications reconsidered or to file late applications for amnesty or work authorization.[104] However, the ultimate dismissal and the lengthy wait for this disappointing final outcome brought extreme hardship for many immigrant women and their children. Ten years represents a long period in many innocent children's lives—for some perhaps the bulk of their childhoods—during which time their mothers' lack of work authorization or legal immigration status meant that the entire family lived in poverty, in "the shadows," and at the service of dominant society.

Moreover, after the *Zambrano* case was dismissed, applications were considered only from those who could prove that they were "front desked"—that is, that they had tried to apply for amnesty but were turned away from even submitting an application at an agency office on the basis of the incorrect INS regulations.[105] Andrade argues that this is extremely unfair as it fails to address those who had not attempted to file applications because they had heard they would not be eligible if they had received public benefits or services. Andrade and co-counsel had argued that these people formed the largest group of plaintiffs in *Zambrano*, and that the INS contributed to these people's declining to apply by publicizing misinformation on the radio and television.

A year after the *Zambrano* case dismissal, the federal government made a long-overdue clarification of the public-charge provisions. This new guidance, issued May 25, 1999, defines "public charge" as a person who cannot support herself or himself without depending on cash assistance such as Temporary Aid to Needy Families, SSI, or General Assistance for income, or who needs long-term institutional care. The guidance emphasizes that the INS should look at many factors to determine if an applicant is likely to become a public charge in the future, and it cannot make its decision based solely on receipt of cash assistance in the past. Instead, it must consider all of the following factors: age, health, income, family size, education, and skills. The California Immigrant Welfare Collaborative, a coalition of immigrant rights organizations providing outreach and education around the issue, recommends that applicants who have received welfare in the past highlight information such as current employment or the availability of support from family members in the country during their INS interviews.[106]

The new INS guidance also clarifies that the use of Medi-Cal, Healthy Families (a new health-insurance program in California for children ages one to nineteen with family incomes at or below 200 percent of the federal poverty level), or other health services by an applicant or family members will not affect her or his immigration status unless it is for long-term care. Nor will the use of food stamps, WIC (Women, Infants, and Children aid), public housing, or other noncash programs by an applicant or family members. Finally, the use of cash assistance by an applicant's children or other family members is not grounds to refuse entry (or re-entry) to the United States or to deny permanent residency or citizenship unless it is the applicant's family's only income.

It is important to understand that the 1999 INS guidance issued on the public-charge standard was not a change but a clarification of the existing law as it should have been implemented originally. Ironically, the INS guidance cites the *Zambrano* case in the clarification.[107] Throughout the *Zambrano* litigation, the INS never disputed that its regulations and practices contradicted IRCA, nor did it rush to issue corrections to its improper regulations even once they were enjoined. This lends credibility to the argument that the public-charge provisions were not only misinterpreted or improperly implemented by the INS but perhaps deliberately obscured. These INS practices rendered immigrants, particularly those with dependents, more exploitable in the labor market. Moreover, they facilitated US employers' abilities to extract cheap labor from these women and at the same time allow the state to evade responsibility for the welfare of resident and citizen children.

The case of the Latina mothers in *Zambrano* highlights the need for a demystification of immigrant women as welfare dependent and a recognition that they are working mothers, often single heads of households, who benefit US capital and society at large through grossly under-compensated productive and reproductive labor, for other people's families as well as their own. At the very least, women should be offered a means to gain work authorization, permanent residence, or citizenship. The fact that in raising their own children, they, too, provide a service in nurturing future adult citizens should not be obscured by ideologies casting their children as somehow less worthy.

During the 1995 congressional hearings on welfare reform, Senator Lauch Faircloth made a statement capturing perfectly the ignorant sentiments and beliefs driving the immigration and welfare debates of the day. He proclaimed:

> [M]iddle-class American families who want to have children have to plan, prepare, and save money because they understand the serious responsibility involved in bringing children into the world. But welfare recipients do not have to prepare or save money before having children because they know they will get money from the federal government and that the taxpayers of the country will take care of their children.[108]

In my experience as a middle-class "American" mother, I have found that, quite to the contrary, my socio-economic peers rarely demonstrate greater financial or other planning but have children in the haphazard ways and for the full spectrum of reasons that people do. In fact, the only difference I have observed is that some middle-class families are able to rest assured that, when the time comes, they can rely on finding a poor woman (most likely an immigrant woman) to hire as an in-home nanny for their babies.[109] Saving money is not necessarily seen as an issue of great anxiety until the baby is preschool age, because an immigrant woman can always be found who is desperate enough to take the wages being offered for in-home care instead of costly day care. Thus, middle-class "American" families do not have to prepare before having children because they know that they will get an immigrant woman, often courtesy of the federal government, and that she (indeed a taxpayer) will take care of their children. The question is whether this woman will be able to take care of her own family on the wages she earns, and the crime is that most likely she will not.

1   The *San Francisco Chronicle* reported that, although no precise figures exist, "experts believe a large percentage of the estimated 3 million undocumented workers now residing in the United States are employed in child-care and domestic work." See "Hiring of Aliens Is a Widespread Practice," *San Francisco Chronicle,* January 15, 1993, p. A-6.

2   Deborah Sontag, "Increasingly, Two-Career Family Means Illegal Immigrant Help," *New York Times,* January 24, 1993, p. A-1.

3   Sontag, "Increasingly, Two-Career Family Means Illegal Immigrant Help," p. A-13.

4   Sontag, "Increasingly, Two-Career Family Means Illegal Immigrant Help," p. A-13.

5   Felicity Barringer, "What Many Say About Baird: What She Did Wasn't Right," *New York Times,* January 22, 1993, p. A-1.

6   Barringer, "What Many Say About Baird," p. A-10.

7   Carla Marinucci, "Immigrant Abuse: 'Slavery, Pure and Simple,'" *San Francisco Examiner,* January 10, 1993, pp. A-1, A-8.

8   Marinucci, "Immigrant Abuse."

9   Chris Hogeland and Karen Rosen, "Dreams Lost, Dreams Found: Undocumented Women in the Land of Opportunity" (San Francisco: Coalition for Immigrant and Refugee Rights and Services, Immigrant Women's Task Force, 1991), pp. 10–11.

10 Carla Marinucci, "Silence Shields Abuse of Immigrant Women," *San Francisco Examiner,* January 11, 1993, pp. A-1, A-10.

11 Interview with Patricia Tejada (pseudonym), Los Angeles, California, February 16, 1998.

12 Interview with Amalia Hernandez (pseudonym), Los Angeles, California, February 15, 1998.

13 The CIRRS report suggested that the availability of "underground" service jobs for women in housecleaning, child care, and the garment industry encourages women to migrate alone or without families. As one respondent, Rosa, explained: "I am very worried because we left the children with my parents, who are very old. We have not been able to send money home as planned because everything costs so much here." See Hogeland and Rosen, "Dreams Lost, Dreams Found," p. 5.

14 Interview with Warren Leiden, executive director of AILA, Washington, DC, March 22, 1993; interview with Lina Avidan, program director of CIRRS, San Francisco, March 15, 1993. Several proposals for a visa for "home care workers" (i.e., domestic workers, child-care workers, and home-health aides) emerged in response to the Zoë Baird affair.

15 The arguments in this chapter build on socialist feminist theory proposing that the welfare state mediates the conflicting demands for female home and market labor by subsidizing some women to remain home in order to

reproduce and maintain the labor force while channeling others into low-wage work.

16   Undocumented workers who worked for 90 days in agriculture between May 1985 and May 1986 could gain temporary legal resident status as special agricultural workers (SAWs). If the SAW pool dropped below sufficient numbers, additional workers could be admitted as replenishment agricultural workers (RAWs). Finally, the category of nonimmigrant, temporary agricultural workers (H-2As) was maintained so that growers could obtain laborers if they were unable to find legal resident or citizen workers. Those entering under this type of visa are presumed to be here temporarily without the intention to remain. Immigration Reform Task Force, "Report from the States on the State Legalization Impact Assistance Grant Program" (Washington, DC: American Public Welfare Association, May 1989), pp. 1, 28–30. See also Leonard Dinnerstein and David M. Reimers, *Ethnic Americans* (New York: Harper & Row Publishers, 1988), pp. 103–106, for an overview of IRCA and its origins.

17   In a report of the House Judiciary Committee, the plight of the undocumented was aptly described: "These people live in fear, afraid to seek help when their rights are violated, when they are victimized by criminals, employers or landlords, or when they become ill." House of Representatives Report No. 682 (I), 99th Congress, 2nd Session (1986), cited in *California Rural Legal Assistance (CRLA) v. Legal Services Corporation (LSC)*, No. 89-16734., DC No. CV-89-1850-SAW, Opinion, October 26, 1990, p. 13299.

18   Congressional Record H10596-7 (daily edition, October 15, 1986), cited in *CRLA v. LSC*, p. 13299.

19   A Senate Judiciary Committee report states: "The Committee notes the concern expressed by state and local governments regarding the potential fiscal impact arising from participation in public assistance programs by the legalized population. This concern is related to the experience … with refugee populations, whose dependence on special Federal entitlement programs has reached 70 percent in the past year, thereby thwarting the primary intent of the … program, which is to encourage economic self-sufficiency among refugees." Report of the Committee on the Judiciary on S. 2222, Senate Report No. 485, 97th Congress, 2nd Session, (Washington, DC: Government Printing Office, June 1982), p. 49.

20   Charles Wheeler, "Alien Eligibility for Public Benefits," *Immigrants' Rights Manual of the National Immigration Law Center* (September 1990), pp. 11–45.

21   Charles Wheeler and Beth Zacovic, "The Public Charge Ground of Exclusion for Legalization Applicants," *Interpreter Releases* 64: 35 (September 14, 1987), p. 1046.

22   Wheeler, "Alien Eligibility for Public Benefits," pp. 11–48.

23   Wheeler and Zacovic, "The Public Charge Ground of Exclusion," p. 1047.

24   8 USC section 1255a (d) (B)(iii). "Public cash assistance" includes only those programs that provide monetary assistance, not in-kind benefits such as food stamps or medical services. See Wheeler, "Alien Eligibility," pp. 11–49.

25 Wheeler, "Alien Eligibility," pp. 11–49.

26 Wheeler and Zacovic, "The Public Charge Ground," p. 1047.

27 Wheeler and Zacovic, "The Public Charge Ground," p. 1047. Also see L. Chavez and R. Rumbaut et al., *The Politics of Migrant Health Care* (San Diego: University of California, August 1985). This study estimated that 30 to 40 percent of undocumented persons had incomes below the federal poverty level guidelines, although more than 90 percent of these men and 64 percent of these women were employed. Thus, a large proportion of legalization applicants might be viewed as potential public charges, solely on the basis of their low incomes. With the "special rule," Congress tried to prevent the use of income as the sole criterion for determining the excludability or admissibility of applicants such as these.

28 Wheeler and Zacovic, "The Public Charge Ground," p. 1047.

29 The Ninth Circuit includes Alaska, Arizona, California, Guam, Hawaii, Idaho, the Mariana Islands, Montana, Nevada, Oregon, and Washington.

30 Second Amended Complaint, *Zambrano v. INS*, Civ. No. S-88-455 EJG/EM (E.D. Cal. August 26, 1988), pp. 18–19.

31 The only named male plaintiff was himself temporarily disabled by kidney failure and received county General Assistance while undergoing treatment and therapy.

32 Second Amended Complaint, pp. 3–5.

33 Second Amended Complaint, pp. 3–5.

34 Second Amended Complaint, pp. 3–5.

35 Second Amended Complaint, pp. 10–11.

36 Second Amended Complaint, pp. 10–11.

37 Second Amended Complaint, pp. 3–11.

38 Second Amended Complaint, p. 2.

39 Second Amended Complaint, p. 2.

40 Second Amended Complaint, p. 18.

41 Second Amended Complaint, p. 19.

42 Order Granting Plaintiffs' Motions for Partial Summary Judgment, Permanent Injunction and Redefinition of Class, *Zambrano v. INS*, Civ. No. S-88-455 EJG/EM (E.D. Cal. July 31, 1989), pp. 8–19.

43 Order Granting Plaintiffs' Motions, p. 19.

44 First, INS challenged the order to review the cases of those class-two members who applied for amnesty under the extended deadline. Second, INS contended that the courts do not have jurisdiction over this matter, arguing that the plaintiffs should be required to exhaust the administrative remedies before gaining judicial review. This jurisdictional issue was raised by INS in the *Zambrano* case as well as in a number of other cases involving the legalization program (e.g., *Ayuda v. Thornburgh, Catholic Social Services v. Barr,*

LULAC v. INS, and *Perales v. Thornburgh*). Third, INS has contended that plaintiffs' counsel should not have access to the names of the class-one members. (This information was conveyed to me in interviews with Susan Drake, lawyer, National Immigration Law Center, October 1990, and Stephen Rosenbaum, lawyer, California Rural Legal Assistance, November 25, 1991.)

45 *Zambrano v. INS* (972 F2d 1122), 9th Cir., 1992.

46 Petition for certiorari pending, *INS v. Zambrano* 92-849, 61 USLW 3404 (1992).

47 Second Amended Complaint, p. 19.

48 Second Amended Complaint, p. 19.

49 Declaration of Beth Zacovic, Legal Aid attorney, at *Zambrano v. INS*. Civ. No. S-88-455 EJG-EM (E.D. Cal. May 17, 1988). Zacovic obtained these statistics in an interview with a legislative analyst for Los Angeles County in April 1988; cited in Diane Bessette, "Getting Left Behind: The Impact of the 1986 Immigration Reform and Control Act Amnesty Program on Single Women With Children," *Hastings International and Comparative Law Review* 13: 2 (Winter 1990), p. 301.

50 Bessette, "Getting Left Behind," p. 300.

51 Bessette, "Getting Left Behind," p. 303.

52 Declaration of Mavis Anderson, cited in Bessette, "Getting Left Behind," p. 304.

53 Bessette, "Getting Left Behind," 302.

54 I use the term *underclass* here as I would the term *underdeveloped nation* to indicate a group of people that has been marginalized or deliberately deprived of the means to achieve economic autonomy and political power.

55 Belkin, 1990.

56 California Health and Welfare Agency, "A Survey of Newly Legalized Persons in California" (San Diego: Comprehensive Adult Student Assessment System, 1989), sections 7–3 through 7–12. See also Immigration Reform Task Force, "Report from the States," pp. 10–11, and Hogeland and Rosen, "Dreams Lost and Dreams Found," p. 19.

57 Order, pp. 5–6.

58 Second Amended Complaint, p. 19.

59 Bessette, "Getting Left Behind," p. 300.

60 Interview with Stephen Rosenbaum, lawyer, California Rural Legal Assistance, November 25, 1991.

61 In this chapter, I draw on socialist feminist theory, which proposes that the state regulates the labor of women through welfare policy. Internal colonialist theory proposes that the state regulates the labor of immigrants through immigration policy. This is achieved through immigration policies that allow for the importation or "recruitment" of foreign labor and through policies that deny these laborers the rights of citizens, thus rendering them more easily exploitable. For a more extensive discussion of this topic, see note 15 above and Mario Barrera, *Race and Class in the Southwest: A Theory of Racial Inequality* (Notre Dame, IN: University of Notre Dame Press, 1979), especially pp. 116–22.

62 Frances Fox Piven and Richard Cloward, *Regulating the Poor: The Functions of Public Welfare* (New York: Random House, 1971), pp. 123–31.

63 Mimi Abramovitz, *Regulating the Lives of Women: Social Welfare Policy from Colonial Times to the Present* (Boston: South End Press, rev. ed. 1996), pp. 313–18.

64 Evelyn Nakano Glenn defines reproductive labor to include "activities such as purchasing household goods, preparing and serving food, laundering and repairing clothing, maintaining furnishings and appliances, socializing children, providing care and emotional support for adults, and maintaining kin and community ties." See Evelyn Nakano Glenn, "From Servitude to Service Work: Historical Continuities in the Racial Division of Paid Reproductive Labor," *Signs* 18: 1 (Autumn 1992).

65 Glenn, "From Servitude to Service Work."

66 "Home life is the highest and finest product of civilization. It is the great molding force of mind and or character.... Children of parents of worthy character, suffering from temporary misfortune, and children of reasonably efficient and deserving mothers who are without the support of the normal breadwinner should, as a rule, be kept with their parents, such aid being given as may be necessary to maintain suitable homes for the rearing of the children." Proceedings of the conference on the Care of Dependent Children (Washington, DC, January 25–26, 1909), cited in Roy Lubove, *The Struggle for Social Security 1900–1935* (Cambridge, MA: Harvard University Press, 1968), p. 98.

67 Winifred Bell, *Aid to Dependent Children* (New York: Columbia University Press, 1965), p. 5.

68 Bell, *Aid to Dependent Children,* pp. 93–110, 111–23.

69 Bell, *Aid to Dependent Children,* p. 9.

70 Bell, *Aid to Dependent Children,* p. 13.

71 Sylvia A. Law, "Women, Work, Welfare and the Preservation of Patriarchy," *University of Pennsylvania Law Review* 131: 6 (1983), p. 1258.

72 Bell, *Aid to Dependent Children,* pp. 3–19, cited in Law, "Women, Work, Welfare," p. 1257.

73 Abramovitz, *Regulating the Lives of Women,* p. 314.

74 Law, "Women, Work, Welfare," p. 1254.

75 Law, "Women, Work, Welfare," p. 1257.

76 US Department of Health, Education and Welfare's *Handbook of Public Assistance Administration* (1943), cited in Law, "Women, Work, Welfare," p. 1257.

77 As discussed previously, the "suitable home" rules, instituted ostensibly to monitor the moral fitness of mothers, enabled welfare officials to rationalize limiting the coverage of black and "illegitimate" children (Bell, *Aid to Dependent Children,* p. 181). Thus they had much the same effect as the "employable mother" rules, necessitating that women denied assistance for their children seek low-wage work. Abramovitz argues that these rules were used specifically to pressure black women back into domestic work if they tried to avoid returning to it after holding other jobs during World War II (Abramovitz, *Regulating the Lives of Women,* p. 326).

78   Piven and Cloward, *Regulating the Poor,* p. 134.
79   Bell, *Aid to Dependent Children,* p. 64.
80   Bell, *Aid to Dependent Children,* p. 64.
81   Bell, *Aid to Dependent Children,* pp. 34–35, quoting a review of a Southern field supervisor's report; citing Mary S. Larabee, "Unmarried Parenthood Under the Social Security Act," *Proceedings of the National Conference of Social Work, 1939* (New York: Columbia University Press, 1939), p. 449.
82   Abramovitz, *Regulating the Lives of Women,* p. 326.
83   Piven and Cloward, *Regulating the Poor,* pp. 134–35.
84   Piven and Cloward, *Regulating the Poor,* pp. 134–35.
85   The judgment stated that the provisions prohibiting supplementation of wages "violated equal protection as imposing discrimination bearing no reasonable relation to financial needs or discriminating on [the] basis of source of income" (*Anderson v. Burson,* 300 F. Supp. 401 [1968], p. 401). Thus, the decision did not address the charge that the discrimination was racially based, as the plaintiffs suggested.
86   Piven and Cloward, *Regulating the Poor,* p. 308.
87   *Anderson v. Burson,* 300 F. Supp. 401 (1968), p. 403.
88   Wendy Sarvasy, "Reagan and Low-Income Mothers: A Feminist Recasting of the Debate," in *Remaking the Welfare State: Retrenchment and Social Policy in America and Europe,* ed. M.K. Brown (Philadelphia: Temple University Press, 1988), pp. 253–276, especially p. 269. See also Lubove, *The Struggle for Social Security 1900–1935,* p. 102, and Susan Tiffin, *In Whose Best Interest? Child Welfare Reform in the Progressive Era* (Westport, CT: Greenwood Press, 1982), p. 125.
89   See Patricia Hill-Collins, *Black Feminist Thought: Knowledge, Consciousness, and the Politics of Empowerment* (New York: Routledge, 1991), especially chapter 6.
90   Carol Stack and Linda Burton, "Conscripting Kin: Reflections on Family, Generation, and Culture," in *Mothering: Ideology, Experience, and Agency,* eds. Evelyn Nakano Glenn, Grace Chang, and Linda Rennie Forcey (New York: Routledge, 1994).
91   Denise Segura, "Working at Motherhood: Chicana and Mexican Immigrant Mothers and Employment," in *Mothering: Ideology, Experience, and Agency,* eds. E. Nakano Glenn, Grace Chang, and Linda Rennie Forcey (New York: Routledge, 1994).
92   See Evelyn Nakano Glenn, "From Servitude to Service Work"; Mary

Romero, *Maid in the U.S.A.* (New York: Routledge, 1992); and Bonnie Thornton Dill, "Race, Class, and Gender: Prospects for an All-Inclusive Sisterhood," *Feminist Studies* 9: 1 (Spring 1983), pp. 131–48. All cite evidence of middle-class employers' deliberate attempts to seek out immigrant women, particularly undocumented women, for low-wage household work.

93 Interview with Warren Leiden, AILA, Washington, DC, November 29, 1993.

94 "And while voices can be heard in her defense, questioning the law or the country's preoccupation with moral purity, the major women's groups have been largely silent, leaving unanswered the angry chorus that now threatens to kill the nomination of the first woman ever chosen to be attorney general," from Barringer, "What Many Say About Baird."

95 Interview with Warren Leiden, November 29, 1993.

96 For discussions of middle-class employers seeking immigrant women, particularly undocumented women, as low-wage household workers, see Glenn, "From Servitude to Service Work"; Romero, *Maid in the U.S.A.*; Debbie Nathan, *Women and Other Aliens: Essays from the U.S.–Mexico Border* (El Paso, Texas: Cinco Punto Press, 1991); Rosanna Hertz, *More Equal Than Others: Women and Men in Dual-Career Marriages* (Berkeley, CA: University of California Press, 1986); Judith Rollins, *Between Women: Domestics and Their Employers* (Philadelphia: Temple University Press, 1985); and Dill, "Race, Class, and Gender," pp. 131–48.

97 Diana Pearce, "Welfare Is Not for Women: Why the War on Poverty Cannot Conquer the Feminization of Poverty," in *Women, the State, and Welfare,* ed. Linda Gordon (Madison: University of Wisconsin Press, 1990).

98 Diana Pearce, "Welfare Is Not for Women."

99 For similar analyses, see Glenn, "From Servitude to Service Work"; Romero, *Maid in the U.S.A.*; and Dill, "Race, Class, and Gender." See also Cynthia Enloe, *Bananas, Beaches and Bases: Making Feminist Sense of International Politics* (Berkeley: University of California Press, 1990), pp. 193–94, for an account of women organizers' struggles to put the issues of migrant women workers on the agenda at the 1985 UN "Decade for Women" conference in Nairobi.

100 Interview with David Rolf, then–deputy general manager of Local 434B of SEIU, July 27, 1997.

101 The National Immigration Law Center in Los Angeles is providing a service to advise those previously eligible to apply for work authorization under *Zambrano* to investigate other possibilities for legalization.

102 Interviews with Pauline Gee and Vibiana Andrade, November 1999; "Memorandum of Points and Authorities in Support of Plaintiffs' Motion for Award of Reasonable Attorneys' Fees Under Equal Access to Justice Act," *Zambrano v. INS,* US District Court, Eastern District of California, August 10, 1998, pp. 7–11.

103 Moreover, Andrade explained that the broader impact of IIRIRA has been devastating for immigrant rights, as it drastically limits the Court's jurisdiction in immigration and deportation matters. See also Anthony Lewis, "The Mills of Cruelty," *New York Times,* December 14, 1999, p. A-31, on efforts to modify IIRIRA in order to restore immigration judges' discretion or some process by which a deportation can be stayed in cases of extreme hardship or cruelty.

104 Approximately 25,000 members of Class 1 benefited from the preliminary and permanent injunctions by having their legalization applications reopened and considered under the correct, more favorable standards. Most Class 1 members were able to legalize their immigration status because of the *Zambrano* lawsuit. At least 11,000 Class 2 members received the right to file late applications because INS had failed to publicize the "clarification memos" with the correct public-charge standards. See "Memorandum of Points and Authorities," pp. 10–12.

105 Interview with Sheila Neville, lawyer, National Immigration Law Center, Los Angeles, November 1999.

106 California Immigrant Welfare Collaborative, "New INS Guidance on Public Charge: When Is It Safe to Use Public Benefits?," May 25, 1999. Available through National Immigration Law Center at 213-639-3900.

107 Interview with Vibiana Andrade, November 18, 1999.

108 Dorothy Roberts, *Killing the Black Body: Race, Reproduction, and the Meaning of Liberty* (New York: Vintage Books, 1999), p. 218.

109 In fact, I have even met an upper-class German couple who moved from their home in Germany to Los Angeles in order to take advantage of the great supply of nannies available there. The couple bemoaned the fact that in Germany there are too many laws regulating the hours and even the age of those employed as caregivers.

The Nanny Visa
The Bracero Program Revisited

The notion that immigrants can be treated as expendable commodities, to be used then expelled from the country or simply from any public concern, has guided immigration law and labor practice throughout US history. This view can be traced back to at least 1911, when the Dillingham Immigration Commission reported on the particular advantages of using Mexican laborers: "While they are not easily assimilated, this is of no very great importance as long as most of them return to their native land. In the case of the Mexican, he is less desirable as a citizen than as a laborer."[1] One will find this attitude to be thriving today in any work site where there are immigrant women, although it may be couched in more covert rhetoric. The tale of Filipina/o workers at Casa San Miguel, a nursing home in suburban Concord, California, illustrates this all too well.

Most of the workers identify the unfair termination of sixty-five-year-old Natie Llever as the beginning of the struggle. Llever had been working at Casa San Miguel as a Certified Nursing Assistant (CNA) when she injured her back while trying to move a patient in December 1991. When she reported to work three months later, she was told by the director of nursing, Esther Van Buren, to quit her job. In other words, she had been terminated. According to Llever, Van Buren said: "You can no longer do this job because of your age. You are a sickly woman, and we want a young and strong worker for this job."[2] Ben Medina, a coworker, said that the Filipina/o workers' "hearts began to burn" when Llever was fired, and they knew they had to find a way to challenge this unfair treatment. They began organizing to unionize the staff, 87 percent of whom were Filipina/o.[3]

Demonstrating outside the facility before the union election in September 1992, workers marched and shouted *"Makibaka"* ("Let's fight" in Tagalog) and *"Huwag Matakot"* ("Don't get scared"), flying in the face of one of their employers' most egregious practices, an English-only policy.[4] Workers active in the union reported that, once they realized their intention to form a union, their employers stepped up selective enforcement of the English-only policy against Filipina/os, along with "extreme verbal and mental abuse."[5]

Reports of these worker abuses prompted Filipina/o community and religious leaders in the Bay Area to form the Citizens' Commission for Justice at Casa San Miguel. In public hearings before the Commission in December 1992, several workers, including those charging unfair termination, testified about workplace abuses they endured at the hands of their employers, Lenore and Moshe Shenker. Ben Medina reported that the Shenkers had wrongfully fired or suspended all of the strongest union leaders and had openly made racial slurs and threats. For example, in a meeting in July 1992, Moshe Shenker screamed at the Filipina/o workers, "If you don't understand English, just bow your heads and go back to your country. I'll call the police and send you back to the Philippines. You Filipinos are dumb-headed." Medina pointed out that all of the Filipina/o workers were citizens or permanent residents, with only one exception.[6]

Another former employee, Carol Bagley, a registered nurse (RN) who had been hired as the evening/night shift supervisor, testified that she had been told explicitly that she was hired to take care of the "Filipino problem." She was instructed by Assistant Director of Nursing Karen Meagher:

> They've been in control too long and it's time to clean house, getting rid of all of them if necessary. I want everything and everyone written up. Write up anyone speaking Tagalog outside their lunch room, using our telephone for private calls, leaving the facility for food, sitting at stations eating or reading, and so forth. The Filipinos are terrible, and this whole place stinks like fish because of them.[7]

Bagley explained that she was criticized for not removing the Filipina/os quickly enough, so the nursing directors began firing Filipina/o workers themselves, then demanding that she produce the write-up for their firings after the fact. Four weeks after she was hired, Bagley herself was fired. As Bagley said, her termination came as no surprise, since management had fired almost every Filipina/o union leader by then.[8]

Another worker, Remedios Hall, testified to an exchange with Meagher during this "purge" period that haunted her afterward. During that time, Hall recalls, the workers were very nervous because they did not know who would be fired next. Meagher patted her on the shoulder one day and said she dreamed "that Casa San Miguel turned into a big boat and all the Filipinos fell off one after the other into the water. They were struggling to get back onto the boat." Hall said she was plagued by worries afterward that this had been a premonition that "we were going to drown, or maybe it was a big plan that I don't know about."[9]

The workers testified that they were terminated ostensibly for violating the English-only policy, although they understood clearly that these were trumped-up charges to cover the real intent, to intimidate and harass leadership in the union movement. One CNA, Caridad Gusman, said she was reprimanded for addressing an older CNA in Tagalog using a title of respect, "Auntie Love."[10] On another occasion, she was reprimanded by her superviser, Thelma Smith, when a nurse asked her name one day and she responded, "Caridad."

In an eloquent statement, Luisa Yuson defended herself and coworkers who had been terminated or reprimanded for speaking Tagalog, and presented their position on the language issue:

> We are aware that the residents deserve that we be sensitive to them by avoiding speaking in a language foreign to them. And it is understandable that the families of the residents expect this…. We are in basic agreement with this position…. We love and respect the residents of Casa San Miguel. Their welfare, happiness, and security are of great concern to us. So, it is because of our sensitivity to the residents that we choose not to speak Tagalog

when we are giving direct care or when we are working in the presence of any resident. It is simply a matter of respect.

Yuson went on to express her shock that the Shenkers routinely spoke Hebrew in the presence of residents and workers.[11] Others testified that other workers spoke other languages as well, including Hindi and Spanish, with impunity. Clearly the English-only policy was applied selectively to Filipina/os, and was effectively a "No Tagalog" policy.[12]

Some of the workers at Casa San Miguel were attending school to advance in the nursing profession and had secured management's approval for arriving 10 to 15 minutes late for work on school days. Jennifer Hitosis reported that six women, including herself, were cited for late arrival despite their prior permission to do so for educational purposes. Hitosis also pointed out that the Shenkers and management applied a number of policies regarding sick leave, job-related injuries, and physical exams for employees only to Filipina/o workers, thus creating spurious reasons for termination. She described an environment of constant harassment and threats that she "would be the next" to be terminated, and recounted one of the worst follies by the Shenkers:

> The day before Thanksgiving we were advised at a meeting that there would not be a Thanksgiving dinner for us. Ladies and gentlemen, we don't want turkey dinners! We just want to do jobs and do them well. We just want all this discrimination, mental harassment, and retaliation to stop.[13]

Remarkably, the last worker to testify, Levi Elegado, expressed workers' concerns for their patients in the midst of the turmoil they were suffering themselves. He listed a number of remedial measures the workers suggested to prevent accidents and injuries to patients and staff. Indeed, the Shenkers were cited by state licensing officials a year later for the death of an 87-year-old patient, who had choked to death on a hot dog at a July 4 picnic in 1994. According to Maria Griffith-Cañas, an organizer for Service Employees International Union (SEIU) Local 250, the CNA assigned to the patient noticed that he was supposed to be on a diet of chopped and pureed foods, but when she alerted the superviser who had served the food, he scolded her, "Don't tell me what to do."[14] The Shenkers disputed the state's findings, but a watchdog group, California Advocates for Nursing Home Reform, supported them, having listed Casa San Miguel as one of the 50 worst facilities they reviewed in a 1993 report. Between October 1993 and January 1994, licensing officials twice recommended that Casa San Miguel's certification for Medicare and Medi-Cal payments be rescinded because of the frequency and severity of violations there.[15]

Although the workers voted to join SEIU Local 250 as early as September 25, 1992, the Shenkers refused to negotiate with the union. The Shenkers carried their resistance to great lengths, appealing the election and thus delaying negotiations for years. The National Labor Relations Board rejected the Shenkers' objections and certified the union on April 8, 1994. Meanwhile, Local 250 filed charges against Casa San Miguel with the Equal Employment Opportunity Commission (EEOC) on January 31, 1994, claiming that the employers "deliberately and intentionally discriminated against individuals … because of their national origin of the Philippines or because of their Filipino ancestry."[16] The union also filed charges of age discrimination on behalf of Natie Llever, 62, and Bienvenido Mercado, 65. Finally, the complainants charged that Casa San Miguel's English-only rule violated their rights under California Code Section 12940 by creating a hostile environment for some workers because of their national origin.[17]

According to EEOC guidelines, a rule requiring employees to speak only English on the job violates the 1964 Civil Rights Act unless the employer can show that this is "necessary for conducting business." If the employer believes that an English-only rule is "critical for business purposes," then the employer is responsible for informing employees when they must speak English and the consequences for not doing so. Otherwise, any "negative employment decision" based on breaking an English-only policy will be considered evidence of discrimination.[18] The guidelines state that prohibiting workers from speaking their main language can create "an atmosphere of inferiority, isolation, and intimidation based on national origin."[19]

This principle was challenged in a 1991 case, *Garcia v. Spun Steak Co.,* which has since been the "controlling" case regarding the English-only issue in the Ninth District.[20] The case involved a meatpacking company in South San Francisco, where two Spanish-speaking workers had allegedly made derogatory and racist remarks in Spanish against an African-American and a Chinese-American worker. The employer imposed an English-only rule that did not extend to workers' lunch hours, breaks, or free time. The employer asserted that the rule would

> promote racial harmony in the workplace, ... would enhance
> worker safety because some employees who did not understand
> Spanish claimed that the use of Spanish distracted them while op-
> erating machinery, and would enhance product quality because
> the United States Department of Agriculture inspector in the
> plant spoke only English.[21]

The court rejected the claim that the English-only rule created an atmosphere of inferiority, isolation, and intimidation for the workers, and argued that the bilingual employees, who spoke English and Spanish, could comply with the rule and "still enjoy the privilege of speaking on the job."[22] Prior to this decision, many employers had been eliminating English-only policies.[23] Language rights advocates hope to see another case involving nonbilingual workers or a language policy outside the Ninth District that may provide an opportunity to challenge the unfavorable decision in the *Spun Steak* case.[24]

Whether or not this principle is challenged in a future case, perhaps the more important dimension raised in the Casa San Miguel struggle that needs to be addressed is the use of English-only rules as an antilabor practice. In many cases, like Casa San Miguel, the point of English-only policies is not exclusively social control but also— and in some cases, primarily—labor control. The goal is not actually to encourage or even force people to assimilate, learn English, or become "American," but to make the assertion that immigrants or people of color are unassimilable, incapable, or unwilling to learn

English or become "American," and thereby to exclude them from workplaces or society once they have served their purpose. As in the case of Casa San Miguel, English-only rules serve as a covert tool for ejecting immigrant speakers of a particular language out of a work site, rather than infusing "American" culture into the site or the workers.

In the *Spun Steak* case, the productivity of the workers was the primary focus, although lip service was paid to striving for "racial harmony" in the plant. In fact, it can be argued that better interracial relations was only a goal of the employers to the extent that it would contribute to higher productivity. In the case of the Casa San Miguel workers, it is even more obvious that the employers had no genuine interest in workers educating themselves, given that they failed to honor the prior commitments allowing for workers' nursing training. Instead, the English-only policy served only as another means to label Filipina/o workers "unassimilable," as backup if age could not be used as pretense for discarding them.

This view of immigrants as unassimilable seems to diverge from the rationale behind the "Americanization" programs of the 1910s and 1920s, which operated on the assumptions that immigrants could and should be assimilated and that immigrant women could play key roles in either the cultural maintenance or transformation of their communities.[25] While these ideologies appear to contradict each other, they can be seen as two sides of the same coin. The early 20th-century programs and contemporary practices share much the same goals: capturing immigrant women's labor separate from their human needs or cultural attributes. Indeed, in the case of the Americanization programs, immigrant women were targeted as potential agents to aid in the destruction of their traditional immigrant cultures. Through working in the homes of their American employers, immigrant women were to shed their own "backward" cultures and learn the values and habits of good American homemakers and "worker-machines." Furthermore, they were deputized with the task of guiding their children to adopt these new ways in preparation for their service roles in the new industrial order.

In "Go after the Women: Americanization and the Mexican Immigrant Woman, 1915–1929," George Sanchez documents these government efforts to target immigrant women, steering them into domestic work through so-called Americanization programs. These were intended to provide the dual benefits of supplying immigrant women as household servants and as reproducers of the immigrant labor force. Immigrant women served in the latter capacity through bearing children, but more importantly by inculcating in their sons and daughters the proper American values and work ethic. For example, Pearl Ellis, who "worked with" Mexican immigrant communities in southern California through the 1920s, wrote in *Americanization through Homemaking:*

> [The mother's] ideals and aspirations will be breathed into [the child's] spirit, molding its character for all time. The child, in turn, will pass these rarer characteristics on to its descendants, thus developing the intellectual, physical, and spiritual qualities of the individual, which ... are contributions to civilization.[26]

These women's "contributions to civilization," of course, were most often from the sweat of their brows in their employers' kitchens, while their children, now imbued with higher intellectual and spiritual qualities, were tracked into vocational training in weaving, domestic science, basketry, and "manual training" in segregated public schools.[27]

Moreover, the moral value of Mexican immigrant women apparently changed with the market, particularly in agricultural areas of New Mexico and Colorado, where domestic work was only an off-season or winter job for women who were otherwise farm laborers.[28] The surplus of women available for labor in agriculture or domestic work ensured that wages in both of these industries could be kept at a minimum, however great the women's contributions to American civilization. Whether through toiling in the fields or in their employers' households, Mexican immigrant women fulfilled the Americanists' dream, if not the American dream. While they were explicitly targeted to serve as agents in the transformation of their communities, many simply served Anglo-American society.

Alien-ated Labor

Identifying immigrant women either as unassimilable or as agents of assimilation into American society serves the same purpose: to capture their low-wage or unpaid labors as worker-machines without human needs or rights. Employers attempt to justify this extraction by constructing immigrant women as unable to absorb "American" culture and unable to contribute value to "American" society, beyond destroying their own cultures. The contemporary rhetoric, de-emphasizing or ignoring immigrant women's potential roles as cultural transformers, may reflect only the "modern" preference of employers for exploiting immigrant women's productive functions over their reproductive services. Or, as Maria Mies observes in *Patriarchy and Accumulation on a World Scale*, First World efforts to increase the productivity of Third World women through education, on the one hand, and their knowledge and willingness to practice contraception, on the other, are "part and parcel of the same strategy to integrate poor women's supposedly underutilized productivity into the global accumulation process."[29]

Similarly, June Nash explains that the practice of distributing birth-control pills to women workers at the checkout clock in *maquiladoras* reflects the multinational corporations' multiple goals of "intensifying the appropriation of surplus and accelerating the pace of capital accumulation—but in such a way as to destroy the reproduction of society."[30] In other words, global capital prefers to exploit women as producers, rather than reproducers, and can accomplish this through a variety of tactics, including outlawing or otherwise preventing women of color and immigrant women's cultural and biological reproduction. Increasing immigrant women's production while limiting their reproduction facilitates utilizing immigrant women as expendable workers by ensuring that they will not bear more unwanted consumers or expand a population that has needs.

Several scholars have analyzed the systematic use of people of color and immigrants as expendable workers or as a reserve labor army in the United States. Robert Blauner's theory of internal colonialism, developed in *Racial Oppression in America*, proposes that the state channels people of color into a colonized labor force within the United States by restricting their physical and social mobility and political participation. Elaborating on this model in *Race and Class in the Southwest,* Mario Barrera observes that immigration policies allowing for the "recruitment" or importation of foreign laborers are coupled with policies denying these laborers the rights of citizen workers, thus rendering them more easily exploitable.[31] In *Inside the State: The Bracero Program, Immigration and the INS,* Kitty Calavita proposes that the state formulates immigration policy not only to accommodate capital's demands for cheap labor, but to fulfill its own agenda. Calavita says that the state seeks to maximize the utility of immigrants as laborers while minimizing its own costs and responsibilities associated with maintaining a surplus labor army of immigrants.[32]

Clearly Proposition 187 and the Personal Responsibility Act suit well the agenda of limiting state costs and responsibilities for immigrant workers. These act in conjunction with immigration policy allowing for the "recruitment" or direct importation of immigrants as expendable commodities. A number of examples of migrant contract-labor programs in recent US history illustrate how the state fulfills this agenda, maintaining a reserve labor force of immigrants without having to provide citizen-worker rights or benefits. The Bracero program involved hundreds of thousands of Mexican, primarily male, migrant workers imported to labor in agriculture in the American Southwest in the 1940s through 1960s. While the conventional wisdom is that contract labor programs are a thing of the past, such programs are not merely a phenomenon of distant history, as many people may think. Furthermore, efforts to resurrect something closely resembling the Bracero program are underway in a number of industries. Recently, a proposal was made to bring in female migrants as domestic, child-care, or elderly-care workers under a special, temporary worker visa called the "nanny visa."

The Bracero Program: An Army of "Arm-Men"

Confining the analysis for the moment to the history of male, Mexican migrant workers in the United States, the Bracero program is one of the best examples of systematic, government-sanctioned exploitation of migrant laborers. The program was instituted in response to wartime demands for labor by Southwestern agricultural employers.[33] Although it was originally conceived of as a temporary measure, it allowed for the importation of hundreds of thousands of Mexican men each year from 1942 to 1964.[34] "Bracero" translates roughly as "farm hand" (from "brazo," Spanish for arm) and literally as "arm-man." Calavita suggests that this term reflects "the function these braceros were to play in the American economy, supplying a pair of arms and imposing few obligations on the host society as human beings."[35]

While certain guidelines were established in an agreement with the Mexican government to give braceros basic protections, these were rarely enforced. Braceros tried in vain to report poor conditions to Mexican consuls in the United States. Among the most common complaints were substandard food and housing, inadequate wages, harsh working conditions, and insufficient work during the contract period. It was a common practice of growers to over-contract or apply for more braceros than they anticipated needing, or to keep braceros unemployed for portions of a day or even for weeks at a time because of bad weather or a late harvest. Some employers maneuvered a system much like debt bondage, charging braceros for room and board during these off-periods and deducting these expenses from future wages.[36] Testifying to the subhuman treatment of these men, one Border Patrol memo from Arizona reported that braceros were "fumigated prior to their departure to the United States ... by spraying them [with] airplanes, much in the same manner as agricultural fields are sprayed."[37] Once they arrived in the United States and were contracted to certain growers, braceros were obligated to stay on these farms, rather than migrating to the cities for work, until they were to be returned to Mexico at the end of their contract periods.[38] A number of sources confirm that this was strictly enforced, confining braceros to a given crop and employer by law. One immigration official told the President's Commission: "The contract worker is tied down to one employer [and] is not a free agent to leave whenever he desires and seek more lucrative employment elsewhere."[39]

The wage-setting process was also maneuvered to the advantage of growers. Theoretically, the Bureau of Employment Security (BES), under the Department of Labor, was responsible for certifying that domestic labor had been sought at "prevailing wages," but the BES merely took the growers' lead. Growers offered employment to domestic laborers at a certain wage and, when they had no takers, could then contract braceros at the wage found unacceptable by domestic workers.[40] Although technically growers were eligible for braceros only if there was a labor shortage, they could set wages low enough so that domestic workers would not apply and thus create the necessary preconditions.[41]

In a 1944 report for the head of the Office of Labor and Social Information for the lobby group *Unión Panamericana,* Ernesto Galarza documented the work and living conditions suffered by braceros, based on interviews with approximately 200 braceros housed in 20 camps in California, Colorado, Illinois, Michigan, and New Mexico. Some of the complaints voiced by the men interviewed reveal the employers' clear intentions not to allow braceros to "escape" into other employment sectors and to send braceros back to Mexico once they were utilized:

17. Some local shopkeepers will not sell to Mexicans.
18. The dance halls, pool halls, and beer halls will not serve nationals.
19. There is no opportunity to learn anything about the United States.
20. There are no means to better the vocational abilities of men who have certain knowledge or types of work to which they will be returning in Mexico.
21. There are no materials or classrooms for those who wish to learn English.[42]

Despite its origins as a "temporary" measure, the Bracero program operated officially or otherwise for more than two decades to import an uninterrupted supply of close to 5 million workers in total. Many scholars agree that the Bracero program had two enduring consequences after its termination in 1964. First, it was a major stimulus for illegal migration from Mexico to the United States during and subsequent to the program.[43] Second, as Barrera says, it "established a type of worker who was clearly set off as a Mexican national only temporarily in the United States."[44] More broadly, it set the precedent for the temporary or "guestworker" programs used extensively by US employers to secure cheap contract labor.

The nonimmigrant, temporary visa is understood by scholars to be a legacy of the Bracero era. Now a staple of US immigration practice, it can be issued once the Department of Labor certifies that there is a shortage of domestic (that is, citizen or resident) workers in any given industry. Those entering under this type of visa are conferred nonimmigrant status and are presumed to be residing temporarily in the United States to work, not intending to remain. Much like braceros, guestworkers are seen as offering the advantages of being tied to one employer or sector of the economy and imposing few costs to the "host" society.

Guestworkers have probably been used most often in the agricultural sector, where the concept originated. For example, three provisions were included in the Immigration Reform and Control Act (IRCA) of 1986 as concessions to agribusiness, which protested that they would suffer a shortage of workers. First, undocumented workers who had worked for 90 days in agriculture between May 1985 and May 1986 could be given temporary legal-resident status as special agricultural workers (SAWs). If the SAW pool dropped below sufficient numbers, additional workers could be admitted as replenishment agricultural workers (RAWs). Finally, if growers were unable to find legal resident or citizen workers, they could apply for temporary workers under H-2A visas.[45]

In 1986, Pete Wilson, then a US senator, was instrumental in pushing for these provisions to be included in IRCA, over objections by some House Democrats that temporary workers would most likely be subject to exploitation. Many critics have since observed that these programs, like the Bracero program, stimulate or exacerbate "illegal" immigration.[46] Yet growers continue to lobby vigorously with their friends in Washington for such programs. Only six months after the passage of Proposition 187, California growers clamored in Congress for a guestworker program that would bring people from Mexico and elsewhere to work in the United States temporarily as field hands. Ironically, then-Governor Pete Wilson, the self-proclaimed champion of eradicating the "illegal immigration problem," endorsed the proposals.

Some critics pointed to the history of the Bracero program. Others pointed out that growers already could avail themselves of H-2A visas for temporary workers. But most growers rely on the ready supply of undocumented workers and cannot be bothered with the red tape of the H-2A program or its requirements to provide workers with free housing, transportation, and higher wages. Growers seek an ultimately convenient, super-exploitable labor pool. As Don Villarejo, director of the California Institute for Rural Studies in Davis, said, "What growers are interested in is a 1-800-SEND-A-WORKER program."[47] With great regularity, proposals are raised in Congress to make guestworker programs even more favorable to growers. Recent proposals would provide for guestworkers to be imported during peak harvest seasons on two- or three-month visas, tied to particular employers, with no option to apply for legal immigrant status. Wages would be set at the "prevailing wage," rather than the "adverse effect wage," the rate required under current provisions to prevent wage depression caused by guestworker importation. The employers will be able to set wages according to results of their own prevailing wage studies. Moreover, 25 percent of the guestworkers' wages would be withheld in a trust fund until the workers leave the country.

A number of protective measures for guestworkers and employer obligations would be wiped out under such proposals. While current provisions require the Department of Labor to certify that there is a shortage of domestic workers in the region, this would not be required under the proposed programs. Employers would not be required to provide housing or transportation from the workers' country of origin. Nor would they be required to provide at least 75 percent of seasonal work or pay its equivalent, as is now guaranteed under H-2A provisions. As Mark Schacht, deputy director of California Rural Legal Assistance (CRLA) Foundation, said: "If the employer fires you for any reason, you're out of status on your visa and you're subject to deportation. Every guestworker that comes into this country knows the employer has that power over them."[48]

Many farmworker advocates have observed that enforcement of existing agricultural-worker protections has been weak, and the proposed guestworker-program changes would only exacerbate poor conditions and abuses in the industry. A Farmworker Justice Fund (FJF) alert points out that the number of undocumented workers certainly would not be reduced by the program, while the labor surplus would increase, depressing wages and working conditions even further. Moreover, chances for other low-skilled workers to enter and stay "legally" would be drastically reduced by the proposed programs. According to one estimate, every two new guestworkers brought in would eliminate the possibility for someone to gain permanent residency under the Diversity Visa Program and the Permanent Labor Certification Program. Bruce Goldstein of FJF suggests, "If we need more farm laborers in this country, they should be invited as immigrants who have the right to switch jobs if the employer mistreats them or if another employer offers a better deal, who have the opportunity to become citizens with the right to vote, and who could raise a family here."[49] While US employers and elites might like to have someone raise *their* families for them here, they show little interest in offering any other "opportunities" or rights to immigrant workers.[50]

The "Nanny Visa"

In 1953, a group of women in El Paso, Texas, organized the Association for Legalized Domestics. Contrary to what its name suggested, this group of Anglo women were housewives calling for a program to facilitate hiring Mexican women to work for them as maids. The association proposed that potential workers could be screened for age, health problems, and criminal records. Employees were to earn a minimum wage of $15 a week and were to be given room, board, and one and a half days off on weekends. A group of Chicana women working as maids in El Paso organized to try to block these efforts. They protested that the housewives merely wanted to import Mexicana women to work for lower wages, while local workers were readily available but demanded higher wages. Ultimately, the association's efforts to enlist government support in obtaining cheap "household help" were frustrated when the Department of Justice rejected the proposal.[51]

Forty years later, proposals with much the same goals as those of the El Paso housewives' association emerged in the wake of the Zoë Baird controversy. When Baird lost the nomination for US attorney general because she had employed two "illegal aliens" as a baby-sitter and a driver, she attempted to defend herself, claiming: "I was forced into this dilemma to care for my child.... In my hope to find appropriate child care for my son, I gave too little emphasis to what was described to me as a technical violation of the law."[52]

Apparently, this did garner the sympathies of many people. While some condemned Baird for what was seen as a flagrant violation of the law and a white-collar crime, others flocked to her defense. Many argued that what she did should not be considered a crime, that the law should be changed to make it easier (and legal) for working women or two-career couples to do what she had done. Writing for the *New York Times,* Deborah Sontag reported: "Many say, at the least, that household employers should be exempt, or that household workers should get a special visa."[53] Sontag quoted sociologist Philip Kasnitz: "A law that forces thousands of illegal immigrants and middle-class families to engage in criminal activity desperately needs to be reformed."[54] Soon after the Baird controversy began to quiet down, proposals began to be circulated to allow private household employers to legally hire those who might otherwise be "illegal" immigrant workers.

The federal Commission on Immigration Reform held meetings in February 1993 to hear testimony on the need for some type of immigration program for domestic workers, child-care workers, and home-health aides (all encompassed under the rubric of "home-care workers"). Plans following two different models emerged. One plan proposed to create a new classification for home-care workers within the existing unskilled labor visas. This initiative would work in a similar but expedited manner to temporary agricultural-worker visas. Under this plan, a household employer (for example, a parent or a disabled adult) would identify a position, swear by affidavit that he or she could not find a qualified US citizen or resident to fill the position, and petition to hire a foreign-born person.[55] This proposal was modeled after the Canadian "Live-in Caregiver Program."[56]

A second plan proposed to require the Department of Labor to determine when there was a shortage of domestic (that is, citizen or resident) workers and then to allow potential or current employees to apply for visas themselves. An applicant would qualify by demonstrating that he or she had worked in the home-care industry for a certain period of time and by stating an intention to continue in this work for some time. This proposal was modeled after the SAW and RAW programs under IRCA.[57]

These proposals obviously have very different implications for household workers' rights and protections. The first proposal favors the employers and allows for potential employer abuses, such as threatening a current employee with termination unless she accepts the wages and conditions offered. Proponents of the second proposal point out that it favors those who have already worked here and focuses on worker rights, rather than on creating opportunities for employers to bring in new workers.[58] Members of the domestic workers' group *Mujeres Unidas y Activas* (MUA) also favored the second proposal, since it would enable undocumented workers to apply for visas themselves, instead of having to rely on their employers.[59]

Responses to the Baird controversy indicate that neither heightened "awareness" nor fear of the law have influenced household employers to change their practices or attitudes about the use of immigrant workers, undocumented or otherwise. One woman explained that she would continue to flout the law, employing an undocumented Peruvian as a housekeeper: "After Zoë Baird, my husband and I discussed whether it was now an issue for us, and decided that neither of us will ever run for office."[60] Another woman, seeking specifically to hire an "illegal" immigrant, said: "I want someone who cannot leave the country, who doesn't know anyone in New York, who basically does not have a life. I want someone who is completely dependent on me and loyal to my family."[61] These comments should give us pause before considering home-care worker visa proposals relying on the good graces or ethics of household employers to uphold their employees' rights.

The experience to date with nonimmigrant, temporary worker visas in sectors besides agriculture has been just as bad as in the agricultural sector. For example, in response to the claim that trained nurses were in short supply, hospitals were allowed to bring in skilled nurses through H-1 visas under the Nursing Relief Act of 1989.[62] Many Filipinas entered the United States under the H-1 visa classification in the late 1980s and early 1990s. Cathleen Yasuda of the Asian Pacific American Labor Alliance says that during this period, many schools were set up in the Philippines designed just for the export of women to be H-1 nurses in the United States. She adds that H-1 nurses typically work six or seven days a week, 12 hours a day, often for two employers.[63] Maria Griffith-Cañas, lead organizer in Local 250's campaign at Casa San Miguel, reports that in 1995 she found 18 H-1 nurses from the Philippines living in the basement of Golden Cross nursing home in Santa Cruz. They were woken up at any time to go on duty and were paid what amounted to $1 an hour after various "fees" were deducted. The union succeeded in having the operation shut down, and Griffith-Cañas pleaded with Philippines President Ramos to take measures to ensure that Filipina migrants would be informed of their rights as H-1 workers.[64]

Duty-Free Employers

When US employers lobby for access to cheap immigrant laborers yet at the same time call for an end to the "illegal" immigration problem, it poses quite a contradiction. Illegality lies not with the immigrants who do the most scorned work for a pittance; the true crimes are perpetrated by exploitative employers of undocumented workers and by the government, which facilitates these abuses.

Several immigration scholars have proposed that illegal immigration is not merely tolerated but actively encouraged by the US government.[65] Much historical evidence suggests that the INS and Border Patrol function to regulate the flow of immigration to ensure a reserve army of labor.[66] For example, immigration officials reported in 1950 that farmers would complain to the Commissioner of Immigration during cotton-picking time to create some pretense for an investigation to disrupt border patrol work.[67] During harvest season, Border Patrol officials and growers traditionally had an implicit agreement that efforts to round up or deport illegal immigrants would be eased.[68] Kitty Calavita documents that lax border enforcement during harvests "seems to have been the official policy through much of the 1940s and early 1950s."[69]

Calavita suggests that the rise in illegal immigration following the Bracero program "was not simply a by-product of the ... [p]rogram, but was encouraged by INS enforcement policies."[70] She emphasizes, however, that the government preferred braceros over undocumented immigrants and exerted considerable effort to persuade growers to adopt this preference, as well. The preference stemmed from the fact that, although either type of worker could just as easily be drawn in or expelled from the labor force, only braceros could be expelled from the country on demand. As one critic of the program said, "Like the sprinkling systems of mechanized irrigation, braceros could be turned on and off."[71]

Finally, Calavita points to an unofficial policy after 1954 that braceros would not be regarded as prospective immigrants, or that immigrant visas were not to be granted to Mexican farmworkers. This potentially controversial policy was adopted in a secret meeting between top State Department and INS officials. Calavita says that the policy was designed to preserve the vulnerability of Mexican agricultural workers inherent in their bracero status.[72] This policy provides another good example of how the state acts to render immigrant workers more easily exploitable and simultaneously limits its own ethical and financial responsibility to these workers.

In the contemporary period, this pattern of state complicity continues. The federal government persists in creating a militarized border by pouring money into increasing Border Patrol efforts, using high-technology equipment and building high-security fences and steel walls at border cities.[73] Moreover, while employer sanctions were instituted ostensibly to reduce the employment and abuses of undocumented workers, they have actually functioned to facilitate these abuses by making all immigrant workers more vulnerable to retaliation for organizing.[74] Many other provisions in current immigration law enabling employers to avoid prosecution or penalties for employing undocumented workers suggest that this may be the real goal of such laws—to enable immigration agencies to secure the cooperation of employers, without imposing penalties, just as in the Bracero era.[75]

The 1992 Federal Commission on Agricultural Workers found a number of provisions exempting farmers from providing their workers with overtime pay, housing with toilets, unemployment insurance, workers' compensation, or the right to organize. The commission recommended that this system of "agricultural protectionism" would have to be tackled to control "illegal" immigration.[76] Expanding on this observation, one might say that the illegal and abusive practices of employers of undocumented and other vulnerable immigrant workers will not be remedied until "employer protectionism" is ended.

In March 1995, New York State Senator Frank Padavan introduced a five-bill package prohibiting the use of state funds for health, education, and welfare for undocumented immigrants. Padavan said that the legislation was drafted "in the spirit of California's Proposition 187."[77] Clearly, US lawmakers will continue to attempt to "have it both ways"—that is, to have an endless supply of immigrants as cheap laborers without having to provide basic rights and protections for them as workers and human beings. As Calavita notes:

> Confronted on the one hand by the economic utility of immigrants as cheap labor and on the other by the political and fiscal costs of nurturing a surplus labor supply, lawmakers have historically attempted to resolve the ensuing conflicts ... [by] tampering with restrictive measures ... to reduce the costs associated with a destitute immigrant population.[78]

This is precisely the aim of Proposition 187 and legislation modeled after it on every governmental level. None of these measures suggest that we punish exploitative employers or require them to share the "costs" of the immigrant labor they rely on by providing decent wages or benefits. Instead, they propose that we punish immigrant women and children by denying them critical nutrition, medical care, and schooling.

"Caring Till It Hurts"

Immigrant women workers may battle internalized forces, as well. Dominant US ideology identifies women as caretakers and women of color/Third World women especially as servants to nurture and clean up after First World elites. This may reinforce roles often defined for immigrant women in their home countries as dutiful daughters, mothers, and wives, raised in cultures emphasizing respect for elders and the protection of children. Explains Maria Griffith-Cañas, who emigrated from El Salvador and worked in convalescent homes for many years before she began organizing home- and health-care workers in SEIU Local 250: "You see minorities as the ones tending because our cultures say that we care for elders."[79]

The workers she organizes now in nursing homes around the East Bay tell of grueling work conditions at the same time that they express great emotional attachment to and concern for their patients. A typical day shift begins at 7:30 a.m. and ends at 3:30 p.m., with a half-hour lunch break, and usually entails tending to six or seven patients each for two to three hours, including waking, bathing, toileting or "diapering," dressing, and seating them in wheelchairs for lunch by 11 a.m., then returning them to bed. Many have done this work as CNAs for years, earning from $5.39 per hour as a starting wage to a maximum of $7 per hour, earned by one woman who had worked in the industry for nine years.

Many of the workers are somewhat elderly themselves, and are tested by the physically demanding nature of the work. A report by SEIU, "Caring Till It Hurts," documents that nursing-home workers are also at great risk of assaults by patients suffering some form of dementia and of injuries from lifting and moving patients, particularly when there is understaffing and outmoded equipment.[80] In response to these high injury rates, employers have introduced an insidious invention in nursing homes around the country called "safety bingo." Whenever a week passes without staff reporting an injury, they draw a bingo number. If an injury is reported, everyone has to throw their bingo card out and start over. The grand prize is a color televison.[81] A poster announcing "safety bingo" was posted prominently in the lunchroom of a Santa Cruz facility I visited in 1998. I witnessed one associate administrator congratulating the shop steward there: "You're tough, Reina. What has it been, eight or nine years since you [have] called in sick?"[82]

When asked to name the most difficult part of their job, workers responded that they worried about the quality of care that was possible to give within such short time periods; there were too many patients assigned to staff. One woman responded that the hardest thing for her is when a patient she has cared for and grown close to over a long period of time is moved or dies. This woman added, "But I have learned a lot here about nursing, and more English; and I think old people need us a lot."[83]

Even amidst their employers' assaults on them, many of the workers at Casa San Miguel could not bring themselves to leave their patients. Ireneo Llever recalled that worker morale was so low after Shenker's "dumb-headed" remark that "We wanted to resign but ... we just couldn't leave the residents." Ultimately, of course, they were fired.[84] The statement of Ben Medina, one of the Casa San Miguel workers, captures well the beliefs that may motivate many immigrants—men and women—who work as care-takers. Medina represented the group of aggrieved workers in introducing the testimony before the Citizens' Commission for Justice at Casa San Miguel:

> Our main duty as health-care workers is to give our utmost and sincere service to the residents. We are to love and respect them because we know the residents are not there by choice, and they need our care, love, and attention. For this, the residents pay our wages, which we, in turn, use to feed our families. This career we have chosen—to take care of the elderly—comes naturally to us, as we Filipinos believe and practice respect and dignity to our elders. This is part of our culture that we will always practice and are proud of.[85]

Cathleen Yasuda, a longtime union leader in the health-care industry, encountered similar beliefs, citing them as one obstacle in organizing RNs and CNAs. Yasuda noted that health-care professionals are often "caregivers" (in the popular usage of the term) and "codependent." Standing up for themselves is "something they won't do if it's at the possible risk of the patients." Only recently have people begun to see that hospitals are corporations concerned with profit and not with care, she explained. Thus, her new organizing tactic is to market their campaigns as an issue of quality of patient care. Nurses "will go out on the streets for that, then they begin to see that better wages and conditions will attract better nurses."[86]

My aim here is not to suggest that immigrant women are in need of feminist consciousness-raising or politicization, but to suggest that immigrant women's culturally inscribed values and identities may play into the hands of employers eager to capture these women's "labors of love" for themselves, their dependents, and clients. Thus, employers are able to exploit immigrant women's beliefs and roles that may be deeply engrained. When these ideologies are formalized in government policy and employer practice, immigrant women are doomed to become disposable workers.

In stark contrast to care workers' attachments to and concern for their clients, employers often refuse to acknowledge or take responsibility for the human and workers' rights of the undocumented people who live and work in their midst. If policy makers and employers of immigrant workers—who are often one and the same—are going to insist that we solve the "illegal immigration" problem, then they must take responsibility for their own complicity in this system. Further, they are going to have to be prepared to relinquish their own benefits from it. Few California employers were willing to take a stand publicly on Proposition 187, though they feared they had much to lose if it passed. In a rare exception, Russ Williams of Agricultural Producers, one of the largest trade associations representing growers and processors in California and Arizona, said baldly: "Who benefits by having [undocumented workers in California]? You benefit, I benefit, we all benefit."[87]

Recently, a long line of statespeople—from Zoë Baird to Pete Wilson, the newest member of the cast—have been exposed as having enjoyed the services of undocumented workers.[88] Wilson's employment of an undocumented woman from Mexico as a maid is particularly scandalous, given that his recent political career has focused on attacking "illegal" immigrants. His insistence that he had no knowledge of this employee's existence, and his ex-wife's transparent statements assuming responsibility for this little embarrassment, make the entire affair only more sordid.

Wilson probably would have liked to have disposed of his undocumented employee, Josefina Delgado Klag, after he was finished with her.[89] Indeed, he might have liked to have seen her deported right out of the country, his conscience, and the American public's memory. Apparently, Wilson's memory is just so short, as he endorsed the remake of the Bracero program for his grower friends and filed suit appealing the 1998 ruling that struck down Proposition 187 before he left office. The American public cannot remain so isolated from the constant reminders in our view of some people's comfort and careers being built on the precarious lives and toil of others.

While the proposals for a home-care worker visa ultimately did not gain momentum, similar policy proposals will undoubtedly arise again. When they do, it will be crucial that provisions are made to ensure fair wages and conditions for household workers and some means of holding employers accountable to these standards. Without these, immigrant women are in danger of becoming the new "braceras"— a pair of arms to rock the cradle or scrub the floors for their employers, then go home tired and empty-handed to their own children.

1   "Senate Immigration Commission Report," Senate Document No. 747, 61st Congress, 3rd Session, 1911, pp. 690–91; cited in Kitty Calavita, *Inside the State: The Bracero Program, Immigration, and the INS* (New York: Routledge, Chapman and Hall, 1992), p. 180.

2   H. Lupa, "Filipinos Accuse Convalescent Owners of Age and Race Discrimination," *Maharlika,* January 1993, pp. 1, 20.

3   Astrid Manuel-Barros, "Leaders Air Support for Care Home Workers [sic]," *Philippine News,* March 2–8, 1994.

4   Joyce Rouston, "Workers to Vote on Union," *Contra Costa Times,* September 25, 1992, pp. 2A, 2E.

5   Tracie Reynolds, "Filipino Employees Say Hospital Is Racist," *Oakland Tribune,* December 4, 1992.

6   Statement of Ben Medina, Citizens' Commission for Justice at Casa San Miguel (Walnut Creek, CA), December 3, 1992.

7   Statement of the Citizens' Commission for Justice at Casa San Miguel to the Contra Costa County Human Rights Commission, January 1993, p. 3.

8   "Testimonies of Employees of Casa San Miguel Presented to Citizens' Commission for Justice at Casa San Miguel" (Walnut Creek, CA), December 3, 1992.

9   See "Testimonies of Employees of Casa San Miguel."

10 Anna Viray, "Testimonies on Alleged Abuses vs. Filipinos Heard," *Philippine News,* December 16–22, 1992.

11 See "Testimonies of Employees of Casa San Miguel."

12 Abraham F. Ignacio Jr. and H.C. Toribio, "The House of Pain," *Filipinas,* September 1994, p. 19.

13 See "Testimonies of Employees of Casa San Miguel."

14 Interview with Maria Griffith-Cañas, March 2, 1998.

15 Sharon Ezekiel, "Nursing Home to Sue over Citation," *Contra Costa Times,* August 26, 1994.

16 "Discrimination Suit Filed Against Health Care Home," *Filipino Monitor* 3: 4, February 17–March 2, 1994.

17 See "Discrimination Suit Filed Against Health Care Home."

18 George Avalos, "Concord Hospital Workers Vote for Union," *Contra Costa Times,* September 26, 1992.

19 "Campaign at Casa San Miguel Takes on Added Meaning," *Unity,* May/June 1994.

20 The Ninth District includes Alaska, Arizona, California, Guam, Hawaii, Idaho, the Mariana Islands, Montana, Nevada, Oregon, and Washington.

21 William R. Tamayo, regional attorney for US Equal Employment Opportunity Commission, "National Origin Discrimination in Violation of Title VII of the Civil Rights Act of 1964: English Only, Accent Discrimination and Language Fluency," paper presented at training on workers' rights issues, San Francisco, April 17, 1998, p. 4.

22   Tamayo, "National Origin Discrimination in Violation of Title VII of the Civil Rights Act of 1964," p. 4.

23   See "Campaign at Casa San Miguel Takes on Added Meaning."

24   Interview with Donya Fernandez, Language Rights Project of the Employment Law Center, Legal Aid Society of San Francisco, May 25, 1999.

25   Deutsch, "Women and Intercultural Relations," p. 735.

26   Sanchez, p. 256, citing Pearl Ellis, *Americanization through Homemaking* (Los Angeles: Wetzel Publishing Co., 1929), p. 65.

27   Deutsch, p. 98, and Garcia, "Americanization and the Mexican Immigrant," pp. 74–75.

28   Deutsch, "Women and Intercultural Relations," p. 734.

29   Maria Mies, *Patriarchy and Accumulation on a World Scale: Women in the International Division of Labor* (London: Zed Books, 1986), p. 122.

30   June Nash, "Cultural Parameters of Sexism and Racism in the International Division of Labor," *Racism, Sexism and the World-System,* eds. Joan Smith et al. (New York: Greenwood Press, 1988), p. 27.

31   Robert Blauner, *Racial Oppression in America* (New York: Harper and Row, 1972); Mario Barrera, *Race and Class in the Southwest: A Theory of Racial Inequality* (Notre Dame, IN: University of Notre Dame Press, 1979).

32   Kitty Calavita, *Inside the State.*

33   Dubbed the "productive rearguard" by some observers, the braceros were most commonly called the "nationals," meaning Mexicans, by Americans. John Mraz and Jaime Vélez Storey, *Uprooted: Braceros in the Harmanos Mayo Lens* (Houston: Arte Publico Press, 1996), pp. 46–47.

34   Barrera, *Race and Class in the Southwest,* pp. 116–17, and Calavita, *Inside the State,* p. 1.

35   Calavita, *Inside the State,* p. 1.

36   Mraz and Storey, *Uprooted,* pp. 46–52.

37   US INS, Border Patrol. "Monthly Sector Activity Report," Yuma, Arizona, October 1958. Accession 63A1359, Box 3; cited in Calavita, *Inside the State,* p. 63.

38   Barrera, *Race and Class in the Southwest,* p. 118.

39   The chief of the Farm Placement Service of the Department of Labor and a grower testifying in Congress corroborated this statement; cited in Calavita, *Inside the State,* p. 56.

40   Calavita, *Inside the State,* p. 63.

41   Richard B. Craig, *The Bracero Program: Interest Groups and Foreign Policy* (Austin: University of Texas Press, 1971), p. 67.

42   Mraz and Storey, *Uprooted,* pp. 48–49.

43   Barrera, *Race and Class in the Southwest,* p. 122; Arthur Corwin, "Causes of Mexican Emigration to the United States," in *Perspectives in American History* (1973), p. 627.

44   Barrera, *Race and Class in the Southwest,* p. 121; Calavita, *Inside the State,* p. 198.

45 Immigration Reform Task Force, "Report from the States on the State Legalization Impact Assistance Grant Program" (Washington, DC: American Public Welfare Association, May 1989), pp. 1, 28–30.

46 "Haunted by Past Immigration Policies," *New York Times*, October 15, 1994, p. A-1.

47 Louis Freedberg, "Growers Push for 'Guest' Field Hands," *San Francisco Chronicle*, June 30, 1995, p. 1.

48 Camille Taiara, "Many Hands Make Less: Legislation Would Import Cheap Farm Labor," *San Francisco Bay Guardian*, June 12, 1998, p. 14; California Institute for Rural Studies, "Proposed Agricultural Guest Worker Program Key Talking Points."

49 Farmworker Justice Fund, *FJF Alert*, May 3, 1999. Contact number: 202-776-1757.

50 In the most recent proposals, under Senate bills S. 1814 and S. 1815, the cosponsors Senator Gordon Smith (Republican–Oregon) and Senator Bob Graham (Democrat–Florida) attempt to frame the proposals as "amnesty" programs for farmworkers. The fine print reveals, however, that a farmworker must work 180 days each year exclusively in agriculture for five years to be eligible to apply for legal permanent-resident status through the proposed program. In reality, a farmworker can only find an average of 130 days of work each year, so most people participating in the program will ultimately be disqualified and deported if they can't find enough work. Interview with Jonathan Brier of CAUSA, January 6, 2000. A number of groups are organizing to defeat these new Bracero bills. They include CAUSA in Oregon (contact number: 503-363-1895) and PCUN in Oregon (contact number: 503-982-0243).

51 Mary Romero, *Maid in the USA* (New York: Routledge, 1992), p. 91; citing *El Paso Times*, September 25, 1953, and *El Paso Herald Post*, October 12, 15, and 30, and November 9 and 18, 1953.

52 "Baird Apologizes for Illegal Hiring," *New York Times*, January 20, 1993, pp. A-1, A-12.

53 Deborah Sontag, "Increasingly, Two-Career Family Means Illegal Immigrant Help," *New York Times*, January 24, 1993, p. A-13.

54 Sontag, "Illegal Immigrant Help."

55 Interview with Warren Leiden, executive director of AILA, Washington, DC, March 22, 1993. Leiden emphasized that the applicant would gain temporary legal status on the first day of the job, and would retain this status even if s(he) changed employers. Also, s(he) would be encouraged to apply for permanent-resident status after three years.

56 Interview with Ms. Greenhill of the Canadian Consulate in Los Angeles, December 1993; see Cynthia Enloe, *Bananas, Beaches and Bases: Making Feminist Sense of International Politics* (Berkeley: University of California Press,

1990), for a discussion of government programs exporting women from the Third World to work as nurses, nannies, and maids in the First World.

57 Interview with Lina Avidan, program director of CIRRS, San Francisco, March 15, 1993. Avidan stated that many proposals are still in preliminary stages and that advocacy groups such as hers have not formally endorsed particular proposals yet.

58 Interview with Lina Avidan.

59 Statements of Nohemy Ortiz and Maria Olea, representing Mujeres Unidas y Activas, at meeting of CIRRS, March 4, 1993.

60 Sontag, "Illegal Immigrant Help."

61 Sontag, "Illegal Immigrant Help."

62 Interview with Andy Prazuch, AILA, March 18, 1993.

63 Interview with Cathleen Yasuda, July 29, 1997.

64 Interview with Maria Griffith-Cañas, August 16, 1996, and March 2, 1998.

65 See Robert Bach, "Mexican Immigration and US Reforms in the 1960s," *Kapitalistate* 7 (1978), pp. 73–80; Michael Burawoy, "The Functions and Reproduction of Migrant Labor," *American Journal of Sociology* 81: 5 (1976), pp. 1050–87; Jorge Bustamante, "Commodity-Migrants: Structural Analysis of Mexican Immigration to the US," in *Views Across the Border,* ed. Stanley Ross (Albuquerque, NM: University of New Mexico Press, 1978); Gerald Lopez, "Undocumented Mexican Migration: In Search of a Just Immigration Law and Policy," *UCLA Law Review* 28 (April 1981), pp. 615–714.

66 Barrera, *Race and Class in the Southwest,* p. 126.

67 George Coalson, *The Development of the Migratory Farm Labor System in Texas, 1900–1954* (San Francisco: R & E Research Associates, 1977), p. 81.

68 Lyle Saunders and Olen Leonard, *The Wetback in the Lower Rio Grande Valley of Texas* (Austin: University of Texas Press, 1951), and Ellwyn Stoddard, "A Conceptual Analysis of the 'Alien Invasion': Institutionalized Support of Illegal Mexican Aliens in the US," *International Migration Review* (Summer 1976), pp. 157–89; cited in Barrera, *Race and Class in the Southwest,* pp. 126–27.

69 Calavita, *Inside the State,* p. 33.

70 Calavita, *Inside the State,* p. 32.

71 Calavita, *Inside the State,* p. 58.

72 Calavita, *Inside the State,* pp. 80–82.

73 For more information on human-rights abuses at the border by Border Patrol officials, contact Rubén Solís, chair, Border Justice Campaign, Southwest Network for Economic and Environmental Justice, 226 Wicks, San Antonio, TX 78210. See also José Palafox and Matthew Jardine, "Hardening the Line: The Growing American War on 'Illegals,'" *Colorlines* 1: 3 (Winter 1999), pp. 20–21; and José Palafox, "Militarizing the Border," *CovertAction Quarterly* 56 (Spring 1996), p. 14.

74 For an excellent dicussion of the origins and consequences of employer sanctions, see David Bacon, "An Immigration Policy Based on Human

Rights," in *Immigration—A Civil Rights Issue for the Americas,* eds. Susanne Jones and Suzie Thomas (Wilmington, DE: Scholarly Resource Books, 1999), p. 157.

75　Calavita, *Inside the State,* p. 169.

76　Peter T. Kilborn, "Law Fails to Stem Abuse of Migrants, US Panel Reports," *New York Times,* October 22, 1992, pp. A-1, A-10.

77　"The Spirit of Prop. 187 Comes to New York," *Torch* (newsletter for the New York Association for New Americans, Inc.), April 8, 1995, pp. 1–3.

78　Calavita, *Inside the State,* p. 179.

79　Interview with Maria Griffith-Cañas, March 16, 1996.

80　"Caring Till It Hurts: How Nursing Home Work Is Becoming the Most Dangerous Job in America," special report by SEIU, second edition, 1997.

81　"Caring Till It Hurts," p. 15.

82　Meeting at the facility in Santa Cruz, California, March 12, 1998.

83　Interviews with workers in Santa Cruz facility, March 1998.

84　*Philippine News,* February 1994.

85　Statement of Ben Medina, Citizens' Commission for Justice at Casa San Miguel (Walnut Creek, California), December 3, 1992.

86　Interview with Cathleen Yasuda, Asian-Pacific American Labor Alliance (APALA), July 29, 1997.

87　Marcos Breton, "State Economy Lures Immigrants, Some Say," *Sacramento Bee,* October 23, 1994, p. A-30.

88　Robert Gunnison, "Wilson Maid Was Illegal Immigrant," *San Francisco Chronicle,* May 4, 1995, p. A-1; Marc Sandalow, "Question Is, How Much of Wilson's Time Will It Take to Explain?" *San Francisco Chronicle,* May 5, 1995, p. A-3; Robert Gunnison and Kenneth Garcia, "Wilson Says He Doesn't Recall Maid," *San Francisco Chronicle,* May 5, 1995, pp. A-1, A-15.

89　On December 4, 1997, immigration judge Rico Bartolomei ruled that Klag did not have to return to her native Mexico. After the ruling, Klag said that Wilson knew she was in the country "illegally" when he hired her and that there were other undocumented domestics on staff at the Wilsons' home when she was there. "Judge Rules for Ex-Wilson Maid at Deportation Hearing," *Oakland Tribune,* December 5, 1997, p. A-15.

Global Exchange

The World Bank, "Welfare Reform," and the Trade in Migrant Women

> We in the Third World are being told by the IMF [International Monetary Fund] and World Bank, "Here are the models in the West," and [we are] having conditions put on us that take away what little we have achieved in our own countries.
>
> —woman trade unionist, India[1]

> We are told to tighten our belts—but in this belt-tightening, others are loosening.
>
> —Winnie Byanyima, Uganda[2]

> We see migration as the result of structural adjustment programs—we give up our lands, our products, and finally our people.
>
> —Eileen Fernandez, Malaysia[3]

Each of these testimonies, given in China in 1995 at the Non-Governmental Organizations (NGO) Forum on Women, speaks to the real impacts of structural adjustment programs (SAPs) felt by poor women of the Third World. They reflect these women's clear recognition that their land, products, labor, and lives are extracted for other people's profit through these programs. Since the 1980s, the World Bank, the International Monetary Fund (IMF), and other international financial institutions (IFIs) based in the First World have routinely prescribed structural adjustment policies to the governments of indebted countries as preconditions for loans. These prescriptions have included cutting government expenditures on social programs, slashing wages, liberalizing imports, opening markets to foreign investment, expanding exports, devaluing local currency, and privatizing state enterprises. While SAPs are ostensibly intended to promote efficiency and sustained economic growth in the "adjusting" country, in reality they function to open up developing nations' economies and peoples to imperialist exploitation.

SAPs strike women in these nations the hardest, and render them most vulnerable to exploitation, both at home and in the global labor market. At the Fourth World Conference on Women and the NGO forum in China in 1995, poor women of color from Africa, Asia, Latin America, and the Middle East spoke of increasing poverty and rapidly deteriorating nutrition, health, and work conditions that have emerged for women in their countries as a result of SAPs. When wages and food subsidies are cut, women as wives and mothers adjust household budgets often at the expense of their own and their children's nutrition. As public health care and education vanish, women suffer from lack of prenatal care and become nurses to ill family members at home, while girls are the first to be kept from school to help at home or join the labor force. When export-oriented agriculture is encouraged, indeed coerced, peasant families are evicted from their lands to make room for corporate farms. Many women are forced to become seasonal workers in the fields or in processing areas, or to find work in the service industry, in manufacturing, or in home work producing garments for export.[4]

When women take on these extra burdens and are still unable to sustain their families, many have no other viable option but to leave their families and migrate in search of work. At the NGO forum, Asian women organizers in particular pointed to the massive migration from their countries as a result of SAP-driven poverty. Asian women migrate by the millions each year to work as servants, service workers, and sex workers in Canada, Europe, Japan, the Middle East, and the United States. Not coincidentally, the demand for service workers and especially for private household caregivers and domestic workers is exploding in wealthy nations of the First World undergoing their own versions of adjustment.

For example, in the United States, domestic forms of structural adjustment, including cutbacks in health care and the continued lack of subsidized child care, contribute to an expanded demand among dual-career, middle-class households for workers in child care, elderly care, and housekeeping. The slashing of benefits and social services under "welfare reform" helps to guarantee that this demand is met by eager migrant women workers. The dismantling of public supports in the United States in general, and the denial of benefits and services to immigrants in particular, act in tandem with structural adjustment abroad to force migrant women into low-wage labor in the United States. Migrant women workers from indebted nations are kept pliable not only by the dependence of their home countries and families on remittances, but also by stringent restrictions on immigrant access to almost all forms of assistance in the United States. Their vulnerability is further reinforced by US immigration policies, designed to recruit migrant women as contract laborers or temporary workers ineligible for the protections and rights afforded to citizens.[5]

Both in their indebted home countries and abroad, women suffer the most from the dismantling of social programs under structural adjustment. In the Third World, women absorb the costs of cuts in food subsidies and health care by going hungry and foregoing proper medical care. Ironically, these same women continue to pick up the slack for vanishing social supports in the First World by nursing the elderly parents and young children of their employers for extremely low wages. Thus, there is a transferral of costs from the governments of both sending and receiving countries to migrant women workers from indebted nations. In both their home and "host" countries, and for both their own and their employers' families, these women pay most dearly for "adjustment."

Women are keenly aware that they bear the brunt of these hardships under structural adjustment, while their nations' governments and elites reap fat rewards in the form of women's cheap or unpaid labor and remittances from migrant women workers abroad. SAPs are founded upon the tacit assumption that poor women of color can make do with less and work more. It is assumed that women will manage, out of sheer resourcefulness, to keep their families afloat in the face of "austerity measures" in the Third World and "welfare reform" in the First World. Further, they will continue to do low-wage service work, servicing their home countries' debts while providing greater comfort for the elite around the world. As Pamela Sparr puts it, structural adjustment policies "bank on women: they reinforce women's oppression and rely on it in order to work."[6] Expanding on Sparr, we could say that the elite of the First World and Third World quite literally bank on women, profiting immeasurably from women's paid and unpaid labor under structural adjustment.

Recently, there has been a growing challenge to the assumption that poor women of color can continue to "adjust" without limits, that women will always be able to pick up the slack for vanishing social supports, or that they will be willing to do so at their own expense and for the gain of others. At the Beijing NGO forum, women from around the world shared stories of struggling to secure basic needs for their families and bitter accounts of exploitation as migrant workers. At the same time, they called for accountability from the IMF and World Bank and their own governments, and connected with other women organizing for migrant worker rights around the world. During the November 1999 protests in Seattle against the World Trade Organization (WTO), the Workers' Voices Coalition, representing communities of color, immigrant rights groups, and women's organizations, mobilized to protest what it sees as a "profound deterioration in the conditions of immigrant and women workers worldwide as a direct result of Free Trade policies, globalization, and privatization."[7]

Testimonies of Women Living Under SAPs: Living Without Basic Needs

At the NGO forum of 1995, women from the Third World gave first-hand testimony on the impacts of SAPs on their daily lives and struggles for survival. The phenomenon consistently reported is that overall standards of living, and conditions for women and girls in particular, have deteriorated dramatically since the onset of SAPs. Often this has occurred after periods of marked improvement in women's employment, health, education, and nutrition following national independence movements.

In a workshop on the impact of SAPs on women, an organizer from rural India spoke of the particular hardships women face as those most affected by cuts in social programs and as the first to be displaced from their farmlands. She reported that lands in India formerly used to produce rice have been rapidly converted to shrimp farms and orange orchards. While rice has always been a staple for local consumption, shrimp are purely cash crops for export to Japan, and oranges are exported to the United States for orange juice. In her community, peasant women ran in front of bulldozers to try to prevent these lands from being taken over, but to no avail.[8]

Women from many other Third World countries reported similar conditions. An organizer from Malaysia observed, "We are adjusting with no limits to capital mobilizing everywhere. Malaysia has used all of the SAP principles, including privatization of services and deregulation of land acquisition." This woman reported that land once held by small farmers in Malaysia has also been shifted to shrimp cultivation; and Sri Lankan peasants see their lands being taken up to cultivate strawberries for export to other countries.[9] Similarly, peasant women from the Philippines testified that under SAPs, they have been forced to relinquish all the profits of their labor to landlords; lands once used to grow rice, corn, and coffee have been converted to growing orchids and "other exotic flowers that you can't eat" for export.[10]

In each of these countries, women bear the brunt of SAP-induced poverty daily through lack of health care, housing, and food.[11] Filipina rural women have reported going without power for four to eight hours of every day and coping with little or no water.[12] Urban women from the Philippines reported working an average 18-hour day doing domestic work, laundry work outside their homes, and begging, while men face increasing unemployment. Their children are most often on the street rather than in school, and many families are becoming homeless due to the high price of housing and the demolition of houses under development. Families often eat only once or twice a day because they can't afford to eat more often. Most go without any health care, as the public hospitals demand payment up front and prescription medicines are prohibitively expensive.[13] Similarly, one rural organizer from India reported that prices for essential medicines have gone up 600 percent since the onset of SAPs, severely reducing Indian women's access to proper health care.[14]

One woman from Egypt, typically considered a "medium developing country," testified that IMF-dictated SAPs in her country have also resulted in food shortages and even the first occurrences of deaths from starvation in recent Egyptian history. Egyptian women report hardships from frozen wages and tax increases by the government to pay its debts (for example, sales taxes of 18 percent on food and clothes). The end of free education and health services has been most devastating to women and girls, with girls being kept home from school, sent to work, and married off earlier. While girls in Egypt once were educated at levels comparable to boys, now 66 percent are illiterate and only 50 percent of girls continue on to high school. Finally, there has been a growing trend of early pregnancy with no prenatal or postnatal care.[15]

The "official" figures corroborate these first-hand testimonies of women in countries under structural adjustment. Between 1969 and 1985, per capita food production declined in 51 out of 94 developing countries. Simultaneously, access to food has been severely limited by increased food prices with the devaluation of local currencies under SAPs. Expenditures on education in all poor developing countries except China and India declined from 21 percent of national budgets in 1972 to 9 percent in 1988. Health-care expenditures were also reduced from 5.5 percent to 2.8 percent of national budgets during this period.[16]

As women have been displaced from their lands and homes under structural adjustment, women who were once small farmers have been forced to do home work, to migrate to cities to work in manufacturing and the electronic industry, or to migrate overseas to do nursing, domestic work, sex work, and "entertainment."[17] Commentary of women organizing in countries impacted by SAPs reflects an acute awareness of the ways in which the governments and economic elites of their countries and First World countries profit at the expense of women's labor conditions, education, nutrition, health, and safety. As one labor organizer from India remarked:

> Our governments are surrendering to these multinational corpo-
> rations and Western agencies. These magnates and mafias, in the
> name of globalization, want to exploit our workers and resources.
> Our real concerns are food, water, clean, sanitary conditions,
> health, shelter, and no exploitation. These are the human rights
> we want. All these governments are telling us to talk about human
> rights. What are they doing?[18]

Exporting Women: The "New Heroes"

Each day, thousands of Filipinas leave their homes and families in
search of work abroad. The Philippine government estimates that
more than 4 percent of the country's total population is overseas
contract workers. About 700,000 Filipina/os were deployed through
a government agency, the Philippine Overseas Employment Administration (POEA), each year in 1993 and 1994.[19] In 1991, women
constituted a larger proportion of the country's overseas workforce
(41 percent) than its domestic workforce (36 percent). Of those
overseas, approximately 70 percent are women working as domestic
servants in middle- and upper-class homes in Europe, Japan, the
Middle East, the United Kingdom, and the United States. Many of
the others work as nurses, sex workers, and entertainers.[20] Such
massive migrations of women have led to public outcries that the
Philippine government is selling or trafficking women.

Indeed, this massive migration is no mere coincidence of individual women's choices to leave the Philippines. The Philippine government receives huge sums of remittances from its overseas workers
each year. "Host" country governments and private employers welcome the migrant women workers for the cheap labor that they perform. These governments and employers accrue savings not only by
paying extremely low wages, but by denying public benefits and social services to these temporary workers. Finally, recruiting agencies
and other entrepreneurs on each end of the trade route reap tremendous profits from providing employers in "host" countries with ready
and willing service workers and caregivers of all kinds.

In 1994, the Central Bank of the Philippines recorded the receipt of $2.9 billion in remittances by overseas workers. Remittances through informal channels have been estimated at $6 to 7 billion annually. These remittances are the country's largest source of foreign exchange—surpassing income from either sugar or minerals—and provide currency for payments toward the country's $46 billion debt. In 1993, overseas contract workers' remittances were estimated at 3.4 percent of the Gross Domestic Product, which is the equivalent of 30 percent of the trade deficit or the entire interest payments on the country's foreign debt. These estimates are based on official figures alone and do not include money that entered through informal channels. As the Freedom from Debt Coalition has put it, "Indeed, what the country cannot achieve through export of goods, it compensates for through the export of human resources."[21]

Of less importance to the Philippine government, but certainly significant in explaining the continued massive migration flows, are estimates that approximately 30 to 50 percent of the entire Filipina/o population is dependent on migrant worker remittances.[22] Furthermore, it has been found that migrant women workers send home a larger proportion of their wages than their male counterparts do, even though they tend to earn less than men.[23] Such contributions led one ambassador from the Philippines to Canada to proclaim: "The migrant workers are our heroes because they sustain our economy."[24]

"Host" countries are eager to receive these female mercenaries, as they bolster their economies also. As many countries of the First World undergo downsizing and the dismantling of public supports, migrant women workers offer an ideal source of cheap, highly exploitable labor. These women are channeled directly into the service sector, where they do every form of care work for a pittance and no benefits. Ironically, immigrant domestic workers, nannies, in-home caregivers, and nurses pick up the slack for cuts in government services and supports that pervade the First World, as well as the Third World. Overseas, they provide care for the ill, the elderly, and children, while their own families forego this care because of the economic restructuring that drives them overseas.

Nurses and Home-Care Workers

Currently, there are 100,000 registered nurses in the Philippines, but almost none actually reside in the country. Similarly, 90 percent of all Filipina/o medical-school graduates do not live in their country. Since the 1970s, the United States has imported women from the Philippines to work as nurses, ostensibly in response to domestic shortages in trained nurses. This importation system became institutionalized in the H-1 nursing visa, which enables a hospital or nursing home to sponsor or bring a nurse with a professional license from abroad to work here for two years.

Under the H-1 program, applicants must take the US nurses' licensing exam. If she passes, she can gain permanent residency after two years. During those two years, she is nearly captive to her original sponsoring employer. If she fails the exam, she loses her sponsorship and technically must leave the country. More often, such women go underground until they can take the exam again. Sometimes, they work in nursing homes, where they are paid as little as $5 an hour; others arrange green-card marriages.

In 1988, the Filipina Nurses Organization fought for the Nursing Relief Act, which has provided some rights and stability to H-1 nurses in the last decade. The law grants nurses permanent residency after five years of living in the United States and working in the nursing profession. Prior to this act's passage, H-1 nurses had to go home after five years and could only return and apply to have their H-1 visas renewed after one year's residence in their home countries. This system served to keep nurses in low-wage, temporary positions, forcing them to begin again and again at entry level with no seniority or benefits. The Immigration and Naturalization Service routinely conducted raids at hospitals to ensure that this turnover of temporary workers occurred.

Mayee Crispin, a Filipina nurse, organizes H-1 nurses at St. Bernard's Hospital on the south side of Chicago. At St. Bernard's, 80 percent of the nurses are single Filipina women on H-1 visas. The starting wage is $14 an hour, in contrast to $16 an hour at other hospitals, and the ratio of patients to nurses is high. But many of the nurses are reluctant to organize, fearful of losing their jobs or their employers' immigration sponsorship if they are identified as being pro-union. Many are sending remittances to their families at home and struggling to pay off their debts from migration.

Crispin proposes that importing nurses from the Philippines is a moneymaking venture for hospitals and the nursing recruiters they contract. According to Crispin, a hospital typically gets workers from overseas by making an official certification that they cannot find US workers to fill its nursing positions. (This is usually because the hospital offers wages that few US workers are willing to accept.) The hospital is then free to contract a recruiter to go to the Philippines in search of nurses. A nurse must pay, on average, between $7,000 and $9,000 to the recruiter. Ostensibly, a portion of this fee goes to the recruiter's salary, and a portion goes to a lawyer to arrange the woman's visa. Since most women cannot afford this fee, they agree to have it deducted from their wages. After paying off such fees and sending roughly 25 to 30 percent of their wages to their families at home, their monthly wages disappear quickly. In essence, most of these women live in a situation much like indentured servitude or debt bondage for at least two years. Crispin says that hospitals, by hiring migrant nurses, not only get cheap labor, they also get a workforce that is extremely vulnerable, fearful, uninformed of its rights, and thus likely to resist unionization.

Ninotchka Rosca of Gabriela Network USA observes the ironic history of Filipina nurses in the United States. In the 1980s, the nursing profession in the United States was extremely low-paying, with salaries at about $20,000 a year. So the country experienced a drastic shortage of nurses. With few US citizens going into the field or willing to work for such low wages, many Jamaican and Filipina women migrated here to do this work. With the downsizing in health care, many of those same nurses who have been here for more than a decade are now finding themselves just as vulnerable as new migrants. Hospitals are attempting to reduce costs by firing their most experienced, and thus highest-paid, nurses. Rosca suggests that US hospitals and the health-care industry would collapse without Filipina nurses. She comments: "We take care of everybody else's weaker members of society, while we let our own society go to hell."[25]

Home health care is another industry in which immigrant women are highly concentrated and fall prey to both profit-seeking agencies and the cost-cutting US government. Many home-care workers are employees of the state, working under a state-funded program called "in-home support services" (IHSS). Some of these women are registered nurses, while others are not trained as nurses at all. The program provides no training, no regulations, and no monitoring of the work, which includes everything from performing medical procedures to preparing meals and cleaning to helping elderly, frail, or ill clients to get to the toilet, to bathe, and to move about. To keep costs down, the state pays workers a minimum wage of $4.50 an hour and provides no benefits, including no sick leave, family leave, overtime pay, compensation for injuries on the job, or reimbursement for bus fares or gasoline to run errands for patients or to take them to the doctor.[26] In California, there are 170,000 of these workers statewide, of whom approximately 80 percent are women, 60 to 70 percent are people of color, and 40 percent are immigrants.

Josie Camacho—at the time, an organizing leader for SEIU (Service Employees International Union) Local 250, a union of home-care workers in Alameda and San Francisco Counties in California—points out that, particularly with the restructuring of hospitals under the ongoing privatization of health care, patients are being sent home too early and thus home-care workers are having to provide what should be trained nursing care, often without any formal training. For example, routine duties can include giving enemas and insulin shots, changing bandages, and hooking up dialysis machines.[27] In addition to the grueling work and low pay, immigrant workers in particular frequently report sexual harassment and other forms of abuse from their clients, including threats of deportation and general treatment as slaves. One worker was ordered to clean the bathroom with a toothbrush.[28]

The union is demanding the workers' rights to dignity and respect, proper training in health and safety procedures, and better wages. Camacho explains that these demands are aimed not only at improving the standard of living and rights for the workers, but also at improving the quality of care provided to clients. Patients are typically Supplementary Security Income (SSI) recipients and must have assets under $2,000 to qualify for care under the state program. Thus, the government is relying on the weak positions of both impoverished patients, who have no control over the quality of care offered them, and low-wage workers, who have little recourse to fight these low wages and highly exploitative conditions.

Employing an IHSS worker saves taxpayers approximately $30,000 a year, the difference between the cost of keeping a patient in a nursing home and the typical salary of $7,000 a year earned by an IHSS worker who works 30 hours a week. This savings is reaped by state, county, and federal governments, which share the program's annual cost. Robert Barton, manager of the adult-services branch of the California Department of Social Services overseeing the program, commented: "It's a good deal for the government." The union's health-care organizing director in Washington, David Snapp, retorts: "It's a scam."[29] The IHSS program provides one of the best illustrations of the tremendous savings to governments through the low-wage labor of migrant care workers. Other savings to the state and employers have not been measured, such as those from not providing public benefits, services, and protections to these workers.

In the private sector, the situation is no better, with agencies and companies turning a profit from placing these workers instead of the state saving money by underpaying workers. Home-care agencies, just like hospitals, make huge profits from recruiting and placing home-care workers. For example, an agency will typically contract out a live-in caregiver to a client for $120 to $200 a day, while the worker herself receives only $80 of that daily rate.[30]

Domestic Workers and Nannies

The majority of migrant Filipina workers are domestic workers and nannies. Many of them work in Canada, which has had a "live-in caregiver program" since 1992 to facilitate the importation of these migrants. Through this program, a Canadian employer (either an individual or employment agency) may apply through the Canadian

Employment Office for a prospective employee. The employer must show that it first tried to find a Canadian to do the job. The prospective employee must have six months of formal training or 12 months of experience in caregiving work and be in good health. If approved, the employee can gain temporary employment authorization for one year, and this can be extended for an additional year. A nanny must undergo a personal interview with Canadian consular officials and must receive security clearance. Once matched with an employer, she must notify the Ministry of Citizenship and Immigration if she wishes to change employers. After two years of live-in work, a nanny can apply for landed-immigrant status. She can then sponsor her immediate family to join her if they can prove that they have a source of steady income. Three years after applying for landed-immigrant status, she can become a Canadian citizen.[31]

The film *Brown Women, Blonde Babies,* produced by Marie Boti, documents the conditions for Filipina migrant women working as domestics and nannies in Canada. The film shows women who typically work around the clock, from 7 a.m. to 10 p.m. and beyond. They earn an average of $130 a month (in US dollars) after taxes. Women who wish to leave their employers must persuade an immigration officer to let them. In response to one woman's pleas for release from an employer, an immigration officer said coldly, "You didn't come here to be happy."[32]

In stark contrast to the conditions revealed in this documentary, employers of domestic workers and nannies in Canada romanticize the work and the "opportunities" they offer to immigrant women. For example, a Toronto newspaper, *The Globe and Mail,* boasted that Canada is the first-choice destination for Filipina migrant workers:

> For the women themselves, improving their economic status helps them challenge the Philippines' traditional stereotype of women as submissive homemakers who need to rely on their husbands, fathers, or brothers to survive. The huge exodus of female contract workers from the country in the past decade has created a generation of women who are more confident and independent about their role in a society that has now been forced to ask some hard questions about many of its traditional paternalistic attitudes.[33]

Clearly, if Filipina women's roles in their society are subservient, as this statement implies, then those roles are not overturned but reinforced when migrant women are forced to serve as low-wage workers overseas instead of as homemakers. The only difference is that they provide domestic services to employers in the First World, instead of to their own families, while servicing their government's foreign debt at the same time. The Kanlungan Foundation Centre, an advocacy group for Filipina migrant workers, points out:

> We do not migrate as totally free and independent individuals. At times, we have no choice but to migrate, to brave the odds ... Even from the very start, we are already victims of illegal recruitment, victims of our government's active marketing of our cheap labor.... [S]uffering the backlash of states that fail to provide adequate support for child-care services, we enter First World countries that seek to preserve patriarchal ideology.[34]

This statement reflects migrant women workers' understanding that they are being used to maintain patriarchy in the First World, as governments in these wealthy nations cut social supports.

Just as employers try to justify exploiting servants by romanticizing the "opportunities" they provide these women, the Philippine government attempts to rationalize the trade in women by glorifying its migrant women exports. In 1988, on a state visit to Hong Kong, President Corazón Aquino declared migrant women the new heroes of the Philippine economy.[35] Since then, many officials have taken this up as the party line in justifying the trade in women. The Freedom from Debt Coalition (FDC), an organization working to counter SAPs, notes: "Because of their economic contributions, migrant workers are hailed by the administration as the new heroes and labor export is elevated into a national policy, the appalling social costs and the prevalence of abuses notwithstanding."[36]

Women's Resistance

In July 1994, Sarah Balabagan, a 15-year-old Filipina working as a maid in the United Arab Emirates (UAE), was raped at knifepoint by her employer. In self-defense, Balabagan stabbed and killed her rapist/employer and was sentenced to seven years of imprisonment. In response to protests, Balabagan was retried but was then sentenced to death. In outrage, many overseas Filipinas joined protests staged by Gabriela Network USA in front of the UAE mission and the Philippine government consulate in the United States. Again, Balabagan's sentence was revised. This time, she was sentenced to one year in prison and 100 lashes. She was also ordered to pay her deceased employer's family 150,000 dirhams, or the equivalent of $41,995. Gabriela's Ninotchka Rosca speculates that the main reason the UAE government rescinded the death sentence was fear of a walkout by the approximately 75,000 Filipina/os working in the United Arab Emirates, which would have paralyzed the country.

Protests continued after this last sentence, with activists pointing out that 100 lashes could actually kill Balabagan. Despite this, the Philippine government agreed to the sentence, reinforcing outrage at its willingness to sacrifice women's lives to maintain good relations with its chief trade partners. Many Filipinas working in the United Arab Emirates have collected a scholarship fund for Balabagan to complete her education once she finishes her prison sentence. She had quit school to work in the United Arab Emirates to support her parents and help pay for her brother's education. Balabagan has since become a symbol for Filipina overseas workers fighting for the recognition and protection of their human and worker's rights.[37]

Teresita Tristan is a widow who left two children behind in the Philippines for a job in Britain as a domestic worker. Before leaving, she had been promised a salary of $400 a month; when she arrived, her employers took her passport and informed her that she would be paid $108 a month. On her first day in the country, she was taken for a medical exam, given medicine to clean her stomach, and instructed to take a bath and not to touch the dishes with her bare hands until five days had passed. Her daily work consisted of cleaning the entire house, taking the children to school, and preparing the family's meals, of which she ate only leftovers. She was not allowed to eat from their plates or glasses or to use the toilet inside the house. When her male employer kept making sexual advances, asking her to go to the guest house with him, she asked to be released and return home. Instead, she was transferred to her employers' daughter's home, where she was treated just as badly. The children pulled her hair and kicked her, and when she complained, she was told, "They are just children."[38]

One day, Tristan went to the park and met a British woman who took her phone number and called the police for her. The Commission for Filipina Migrant Workers helped her to leave her employer's home and find shelter. For many weeks, she feared that her employer would come to find her. Now, Tristan belongs to an organization of unauthorized workers fighting for migrant workers' rights. Tristan's story is typical of that of migrant workers, according to Kalayaan, an organization working for justice for overseas domestic workers in Britain. Between January 1992 and December 1994, Kalayaan interviewed 755 workers who had left their employers. These interviews revealed widespread abuses of overseas domestic workers from Brazil, Colombia, Ghana, India, Nigeria, the Philippines, and Sri Lanka. Eighty-eight percent had experienced psychological abuse, including name-calling, threats, and insults; 38 percent had endured physical abuse of some form; 11 percent had experienced attempted, threatened, or actual sexual assault or rape. A full 60 percent had received no regular food; 42 percent had no bed, while 51 percent had no bedroom and were forced to sleep in a hallway, kitchen, bathroom, or storeroom; 34 percent reported being imprisoned or not being allowed to leave the house; 91 percent reported working for an average of 17 hours a day with no time off; 55 percent were not paid regularly; and 81 percent were paid less than what had been agreed upon in their contracts, with an average monthly wage of $105.

A spokeswoman from Kalayaan says that these widespread abuses are made possible by British immigration law. In 1979, the British government abolished work permits for overseas domestic workers but continued to allow overseas employers and returning British residents to bring domestic workers into the country. This was a concession granted to rich people returning from traveling abroad with their employees. As Maria Gonzalez of the Commission on Filipina Overseas Domestic Workers puts it: "In the United Kingdom, migrant women are brought into the country like the baggage of their employers."[39] Migrant women enter with their employers' names stamped on their passports and cannot change employers after entering. Even in the rare case that a woman negotiates a contract with her employer, she has no bargaining power or legal recourse if the employer violates it.

Migrant workers have mobilized worldwide to expose these abuses and to fight for protection of their rights. Women in countries including Britain, Canada, Japan, and the United States have organized grassroots groups to offer support and legal advocacy and to lobby for the protection of Filipina and other migrant workers abroad. Kalayaan lobbies to change British law to allow migrant workers to receive permits directly, to change employers freely, and to stay and work in the country while pursuing legal action against former employers.

INTERCEDE is a similar organization, based in Toronto, Ontario, undertaking research and advocating for Filipina and Caribbean migrant domestic-worker rights. It provides direct services, such as individual counseling on labor and immigration rights, educational meetings, and social activities to aid settlement. The organization also lobbies the Canadian government. In 1981, INTERCEDE succeeded in convincing the Canadian parliament to grant the same rights to foreign domestic workers on temporary visas that Canadian citizens have under labor laws.[40] Currently, INTERCEDE is pressuring the government to recognize domestic work as an occupation, to do away with the live-in requirement, and to allow immigrants to gain "landed-immigrant" status immediately upon entering Canada, instead of having to wait two years.

In the United States, the Campaign for Migrant Domestic Worker Rights, a project launched in September 1997 in Washington, DC, is a coalition of lawyers, social-service providers, unions, and human-rights, ethnic, and religious organizations working to monitor and end abuses of migrant domestic workers employed in the private homes of diplomats and officials of the World Bank, the IMF, the United Nations, and other international agencies. The majority of the workers served by the coalition are poor Third World women who have immigrated to the United States on special visas (A-3 and G-5) to work as cooks, drivers, nannies, housekeepers, gardeners, and other personal servants. Just prior to the coalition's formation, Aegypiidae Bolos, a Filipina housekeeper, sued her former employer, a retired employee of the World Bank, for sexual assault. Bolos had been attacked several times by Robert Mabouche, including one night after her husband, who had worked for the Mabouches, was fired and sent back to the Philippines. She said she did not report the attacks earlier because she was afraid of being deported. In an unprecedented case, Bolos was awarded $120,000 by a Montgomery County jury for suffering emotional distress, sexual assault and battery, and wrongful termination of employment. Bolos said, "I am so happy because I have found justice…. This is a big help, because the employers take advantage of housekeepers. They think we do not have the money to get justice."[41]

The coalition aims to hold employers and institutions such as the World Bank and the IMF (which alone have about 1,000 G-5–visa workers) accountable for their employees' abusive practices and to educate workers about their rights and available social services and legal assistance. The approach of this campaign seems to be well directed at the source of the problems on more than one level. The coalition addresses reported abuses of workers, including gross underpayment or nonpayment and physical, sexual, and psychological abuse. (In one case, a Filipina woman's employer forced her to wear a dog collar and sleep outside with the family's dogs.) On another level, the project targets the institutions and actors that are responsible for the imposition of SAPs and "austerity measures," which wreak havoc on these women's lives in their home countries and force them to migrate.[42]

Health-care workers, many of whom are migrant women, are employed in the fastest-growing service industry in the United States and are also a prime target for labor organizers as some of the most exploited and, until recently, least organized workers.[43] A recent victory by SEIU against the state of California represents the fruits of a five-year struggle by the union on behalf of more than

50,000 home-care workers. In the summer of 1990, the California legislature and Governor Pete Wilson failed to reach an agreement on a budget, and the state stopped issuing paychecks. IHSS home-care workers were the first to feel the impact of the budget crisis. Some workers' paychecks were delayed up to two months. During the budget impasse of 1992, workers suffered the same series of events.

The union brought a class-action suit against the state (*Caldman v. California*) on behalf of more than 10,000 IHSS workers. It argued that the workers suffered extreme hardship because of the delayed payments, including having electricity turned off in their homes and not having enough money for food. Judge Levi of the US District Court for the Eastern District of California ruled on March 17, 1994, that the delayed payments violated the Fair Labor Standards Act. A settlement reached in May 1995 awarded damages of $4 million to be divided among approximately 50,000 workers who joined the action. It has taken as long as six years for the workers to receive individual settlements of between $126 and $340, or $680 if their payments were delayed in both 1990 and 1992.[44] This SEIU struggle represents a victory over a government that all too easily evades responsibility for the well-being and basic rights of both its impoverished and ill citizens and the migrant workers it actively recruits to care for them.

Josie Camacho, then-organizer for SEIU Local 250, points to the ongoing challenges of organizing home-care workers. First, there is no central workplace, with workers scattered among as many as 6,000 different work sites in a county. Second, some immigrant workers feel indebted to their employers and are not only reluctant to join the union but have reported other workers who do. Third, the union has had to identify an "employer" on which to make their demands, as the state is unwilling to identify as much. The union has had to create an employer, called the "public authority," made up of disability advocates, clients currently receiving IHSS, and senior citizens.

This need to create an employer illustrates a central challenge in organizing for migrant worker rights. No party is willing to admit responsibility for, or to be held accountable for, the rights and protection of these workers. All parties, including both the sending and receiving countries' governments, employers, and employment agencies, evade or completely disclaim responsibility. Yet all benefit immensely from these workers' labor, extracting foreign currency, profits, savings, and care services.

Groups such as the Campaign for Migrant Domestic Workers' Rights, INTERCEDE, Kalayaan, and SEIU Local 250 focus on organizing immigrant workers and providing direct services to them in "host" home countries while lobbying these sending-country governments to change oppressive immigration and labor policies. Other organizations have a different emphasis, putting pressure on the Philippine government and IFIs to recognize the impact of SAPs on poor women of the Third World at home and abroad. They work to demonstrate that migration is not a matter of an individual woman's free choice, but a response to poverty created by First World imperialism and perpetuated by SAPs. They aim to expose how the Philippine government facilitates the export of women migrant workers, sacrificing women in the futile effort to keep up with debt payments. Finally, they pressure the Philippine government to redirect expenditures away from debt servicing, to institute protections for migrant workers abroad, and to stop the export of women from the Philippines and other impoverished countries.

As Merceditas Cruz of the FDC has commented, "While many analysts would root the cause of the problem of migration in poverty, I would like to be more pointed in the analysis of just what constitutes this poverty and what structural forces bring it about." Cruz described the rice crisis that forced the Philippines, once the leading rice producer in Asia, to import rice from Thailand and other Asian neighbors. Cruz cautioned that while many people mistakenly blamed the rice cartels for this crisis, she held the Philippine government and IFIs responsible. Under SAPs, farmers lost critical subsidies, and those in the hinterlands could not bring their produce to the market for lack of roads resulting from cuts in infrastructure spending.[45]

Compare Cruz's analysis with the following simplistic account put forth in the Toronto *Globe and Mail,* in the same article celebrating the fabulous employment opportunities in Canada for nannies:

Armed with little more than enormous optimism and pluck, more than 1,300 migrants a day leave the Philippines to escape crushing poverty and carve out a better future for their families. With few opportunities for them in the dysfunctional economy of the Philippines, a country plagued by corruption and political instability, they travel halfway around the world to work as nannies and housekeepers for middle-class working couples in New York, Hong Kong, Vancouver, or Toronto.[46]

This account reflects the prevailing mind-set in many "host" countries, highlighting the tremendous challenge the FDC and other organizations face in demystifying the causes and consequences of Filipina migration. Certainly many would agree that corruption has plagued the Philippine government and economy, but advocates for immigrants' rights propose that corrupt officials and imperialist systems supporting them should be held accountable. Gabriela demands that the Philippine government negotiate reduced payments and repudiate fraudulent loans; it also insists that the IMF collect any remaining debts from the Marcos family.[47]

At the 1995 NGO forum, the FDC demanded a commitment to freeing public resources currently devoted to debt service, redirecting them to rural infrastructure and social services such as primary health care, education, and housing:

> In order to prevent the hemorrhagic flow of migrant Filipinas to all corners of the globe, the FDC has always maintained that freeing the money that goes to debt payments will contribute significantly to the creation of jobs and a genuine and balanced industrialization, and ultimately to the development of the Philippine economy. Then and only then can we prevent the disintegration of the Filipino family, and the Filipino nation as a whole due to the debt, the SAPs, and migration.[48]

While many organizations focus on fighting for protections for migrant workers overseas, others propose that ultimately the global trafficking in women must stop. Gabriela has led the fight against the trade in Filipina and other migrant women. Gabriela accused the Philippine government of feeding young Filipinas into the sex industry in Japan after 35 violations were discovered within a four-month period when a Department of Labor and Employment policy prohibited women under age 23 from migrating to Japan to work as entertainers. Gabriela found that the department made exceptions for four "favored" recruitment agencies. The department's former secretary confessor admitted that it granted exemptions to the minimum age requirement, but denied that Filipina migrants were falling victim to prostitution in Japan.[49] In response, Gabriela asked who benefits from these exemptions and called the Philippine government the biggest pimp in the country. Gabriela has called for the government to begin weaning the economy away from—and ultimately stop—the export of labor. The Philippine government denies that it participates in such a trade.[50]

Mainstream US feminist responses to the issue of the trade in women have been lukewarm at best. When Gabriela called on women's organizations around the world to put the issue of the global trafficking of women on their agendas, the National Organization for Women declined to do so, stating that it does not deal with international issues.[51] Perhaps the real issue is that privileged women of the First World, even self-avowed feminists, may be some of the primary consumers and beneficiaries in this trade.

Even among grassroots organizations fighting for justice for migrant women workers, it may prove difficult to develop a unified position or strategy. The effectiveness and viability of one strategy, imposing a ban on recruitment of Filipinas for migrant work, has been debated since such a ban was imposed by the Aquino administration in 1988. A coalition of 22 migrant-worker groups in Hong Kong formed to press the Aquino government to repeal the ban, arguing that it hindered Filipinas' ability to secure employment, actually debilitating rather than protecting them.[52]

Almost ten years later, debate over the tactic of a ban continues. Felicita Villasin, executive director of INTERCEDE and executive board member of the National Action Committee on the Status of Women (NAC) in Canada, says that she does not embrace the strategy of calling for a reduction of or stop to labor migration. She sees this as an impractical measure that will only drive women to face greater danger and abuses as illegal migrants. Instead, she calls for structural changes in the Philippine economy that will make migration a choice, not a necessity. At least on this last point, Villasin asserts, there seems to be consensus among the women's groups involved in Filipina migrant-worker struggles.

Since before the NGO forum, INTERCEDE has undertaken popular education among its members and the public about the connections between labor migration and SAPs imposed on indebted countries of Asia and the Caribbean, exposing the structural reasons that many of its members have had to leave their families to migrate for work. INTERCEDE is a member organization of NAC, a coalition of 600 women's groups that, according to Villasin, "seek our counterparts in the South to work not just towards solidarity or sympathy but towards strategy on an international level."[53]

Asian/Pacific Islander and other feminists of color in the First World would do well to take the lead from groups like INTERCEDE and many of our Third World sisters who have been mobilizing around the issues of SAPs and the trafficking of women. At the NGO forum, many First World women remarked that they were the least well-informed or organized on global economic issues. Many First World feminists of color came home from the forum resolved to undertake or redouble efforts to understand and expose the links between economic restructuring in the First World, SAPs in the Third World, and the global trade in women.

In Canada, NAC and the Canadian Labour Congress cosponsored a monthlong, nationwide Women's March Against Poverty in May and June 1996. The march culminated in a rally at the nation's capital to demand that Parliament redress women's poverty in Canada and globally. Its call to action included the need to strengthen employment conditions and opportunities for women, to reinforce social services, and to adopt the elimination of women's poverty "as a foreign policy objective."[54]

In the United States, Miriam Ching Louie and Linda Burnham of the Women of Color Resource Center returned from the NGO forum committed to designing a popular education project, Women's Education in the Global Economy (WEdGE). The project includes a curriculum and set of trainings focused on a broad range of global economic issues and trends impacting women: the global assembly line; SAPs; women's unpaid, contingent, and informal work; welfare; environmental justice; women's human rights; sex trafficking and migration; and organizing around these issues.[55]

The goal in each of these efforts is to educate women broadly about global restructuring as a complex of interconnected systems that bolster patriarchy, racism, capitalism, and imperialism in oppressing poor women of color worldwide. In the United States, for example, more needs to be done to expose how "welfare reform," attacks on social spending, and SAPs in the Third World all contribute to the channeling and entrapment of migrant women and women of color in exploitative, low-wage service work.

SAPs and other economic restructuring policies affect Third World women in similar ways the world over, making survival more precarious, and women's unpaid labor burdens heavier, and exacerbating women's exploitation as low-wage workers both at home and abroad. Yet the struggles and triumphs of women like Balabagan and Tristan—and the efforts of groups such as INTERCEDE, Gabriela, Kalayaan, and SEIU Local 250—stand as testament to the ability of women to resist this global assault on Third World women workers.

Conclusion

In *Losing Control? Sovereignty in an Age of Globalization*, Saskia Sassen describes what she calls the trends of "denationalization" of economics and "renationalization" of politics in the new global economy. She argues that "the existence of two different regimes for the circulation of capital and the circulation of immigrants, as well as two different regimes for the protection of human rights and the protection of state sovereignty, poses problems that cannot be solved by the old rules of the game."[56] Sassen suggests that the rise of global capitalism has transformed the institution of citizenship into one of "economic citizenship" such that corporations and markets may now act in the accountability functions that states were once presumed to do. In such a system of a "global, cross-border economic electorate ... the right to vote is predicated on the possibility of registering capital."[57]

Sassen proposes that these transformations offer expanded potential for immigrant-rights movements to claim rights based on international human-rights codes and institutions, such as the 1990 International Convention on the Protection of the Rights of All Migrant Workers and Members of their Families adopted by the UN General Assembly.[58] That is, displaced communities of immigrants do not derive rights exclusively from citizenship in their nation-state but from a broader base with the denationalization of economics.

I believe that this is an optimistic view of the political transformations accompanying globalization. In reality, displaced migrant workers now have an even more limited base from which to claim rights as they look to their countries of origin for the protection of their political, economic, or social rights. Moreover, the extent to which an immigrant worker can derive such protections from her or his country of origin depends on the economic stature of that country within the global economy. This is amply illustrated in the stories of two young women who worked in live-in housekeeping and child care in the United States: the widely publicized case of Louise Woodward, the British "au pair," and the little-known case of Maria "Cuca" del Refugio Gonzalez Vasquez, a Mexican "maid."[59] Both of these young women were charged with and tried for the murder of infants in their care. I am less interested in the guilt or innocence of each of these women than in the gross differences in how each was treated at the hands of the US legal system, the public here, and the governments and public in their home countries.

Louise Woodward was a 19-year-old woman from Britain employed as an au pair by a married, professional couple in suburban Newton, Massachusetts, and charged with murder for shaking the eight-month-old infant under her care, Matthew Eappen, before his death. In Woodward's case, a jury found her guilty of murder prior to state judge Hiller Zobel's reduction of her conviction to involuntary manslaughter and of her sentence to time already served. The judge wrote, "I believe that the circumstances in which [Woodward] acted were characterized by confusion, inexperience, frustration, immaturity, and some anger, but not malice (in the legal sense) supporting a conviction for second-degree murder."[60]

Woodward had several factors in her favor, including her being a white citizen of a First World nation and having been recruited and sponsored by a high-priced agency that paid her lawyers' bills. Her attorneys brought in costly defense experts who showed that the fatal injury to the infant could have been an old one, inflicted prior to Woodward's admittedly "rough" handling. Woodward promised the judge that she would remain in Massachusetts and agreed to yield her passport while her lawyers appealed her conviction. She left the courthouse accompanied by her parents and a police motorcycle escort. Her team of lawyers, including Barry Scheck, who had been one of O.J. Simpson's lawyers, stated that they would shelter her from public attention in the meantime.

Woodward needed no shielding from the public response in her native Britain, though. As one observer wrote for the *New York Times,* "The ruling unleashed streams of champagne and tears in England, where thousands have rallied for Ms. Woodward's defense and nearly the entire country seemed obsessed by her case."[61] Woodward had gathered an extensive following of supporters in Britain who elevated her to heroine status, proclaimed her innocence, and celebrated her release in public news broadcasts to the tune of the theme song for England's soccer team, used in the 1996 European soccer championships. Woodward's supporters saw her as "the victim in the case, a young, naive girl who had traveled to Boston as a way to spend time between high school and college, and who had been treated with callousness and neglect by her employers."[62]

The similarities between Woodward's case and that of Vasquez, a young Mexican woman hired as a maid by a professional couple in El Paso, Texas, are uncanny. In both cases, the impetuous, momentary actions of teenage girls could have been seen as causing the deaths of the infants in their care, and each was subsequently charged with murder. But the parallels in the two cases stop there. Vasquez, who was 17 years old, had probably acted in "confusion, inexperience, frustration, immaturity, and some anger, but not malice," as the judge had characterized Woodward's actions, when she shook Michelle Duran, the two-month-old infant in her care, who died a few days later. The jury found Vasquez guilty of "reckless endangerment" and gave her a suspended sentence with ten years' probation to be administered by Mexican authorities in Juarez.

Vasquez did not have the benefit of an au pair agency hiring a team of lawyers for her defense. In fact, she had not been sponsored or recruited at all to be an au pair after high school and presumably before going on to university. Instead, she had only completed about three years of elementary school, and had been caring for the household and her four younger siblings from the age of 13 until she left her home in southern Mexico to look for work as a maid in Juarez. After working in Juarez for two months for a wealthy Mexican family, she crossed the border "illegally" to El Paso to begin working as a live-in maid for friends of her former Mexican employers. She earned the typical salary of room, board, and about $50 a week to care for four young children and the enormous house of a Mexican-American attorney and his wife.

The very definition of Woodward's employment situation was a world apart from Vasquez's. According to one au pair employer, an au pair is a young woman who comes to this country "as part of an educational cultural exchange program ... straight out of high school ... seeking international adventure in exchange for work."[63] Au pair candidates and their prospective host families go through an extensive application process requiring essays and interviews. Once a match is made, the host family pays a $400 placement fee, an $800 arrival fee, and a fee of $2,970 plus one-way domestic airfare to bring the au pair from New York to their home. Upon her arrival, the expenses paid by the family include a weekly stipend of $139 for the au pair, room and board, tuition (up to $500), and car insurance. This averages out to about $245 a week, not including airfares when the family vacations with the au pair, gas, phone, and temporary child care when the au pair is on vacation for two weeks each year.[64]

One woman, a veteran sponsor of au pairs, advised prospective "host" employers in a parenting magazine after the Woodward spectacle:

According to the guidelines in the program, an au pair's responsibilities may also include cooking, cleaning, and doing laundry for the children. Don't count on this. You'll be lucky if she cleans her own room, but if she's good with the children it may be worth it to not sweat the small stuff.[65]

Compare these expectations with the attitude of Vasquez's employer, Diana Duran, who in her testimony recalled scolding Vasquez because "she would carry around Michelle when she would be doing housework … [holding] her around the waist with one arm and [doing] work with the other hand." The most obvious difference in conceptions of European au pairs and Third World "maids" is reflected in the terms "sponsor" or "host family" for those employing the former, and "lady" or sometimes "padrona" for those employing the latter. Au pairs are expected to benefit from an educational and mutual cultural exchange with their host families, providing a minimum of child care, while maids are expected to serve their higher-class employers, earning a minimum of wages.

In an ironic twist, the jurors in Vasquez's case, many of whom were Latino, were sympathetic to Vasquez largely because of their resentment or animosity toward her employers, the Durans, who were upper-class Latinos. While the conviction and sentence were softer in Vasquez's case than in Woodward's, however, the long-term impact was far more damaging. Vasquez did not have a police escort from the courthouse nor a fan club celebrating her lighter sentence and anxiously awaiting her return to Mexico. Moreover, Vasquez cannot safely return to the United States ever again. Now, with a criminal conviction, she would certainly go to prison if she were to be caught by the INS, her attorney advised her.

The fate of Vasquez brings into sharp relief the treatment of Louise Woodward as a virtual saint, despite the almost identical criminal charges the two young women faced. Some observers speculated that the outcome for Woodward might have been different had her employers and the baby been white. In any case, we can see how the power relations between First and Third World nations are replicated in the treatment of one young woman from a debtor nation as defective goods to be removed and barred from the country, while under the same circumstances another young woman from a First World nation is treated as a heroine and celebrity to be protected and escorted safely home.

Walden Bello argues in his book, *Dark Victory: The United States, Structural Adjustment and Global Poverty,* that the original intentions of SAPs were to resubordinate the Third World—particularly those nations threatening to become developed—by crippling the authority of their governments, and to repress labor globally to free corporate capital from any hindrances to maximizing profits.[66] SAPs in the Philippines, austerity programs in Mexico, and other similar debt policies imposed by First World agencies to ensure favorable "trade" arrangements have been an uncontested success by these measures. Third World debtor-nation governments have been unable and unwilling to protect their female citizens abroad, often eager instead to protect relations with the First World. The trade in women from the Philippines and elsewhere has proven immensely profitable to sending countries' governments and entrepreneurs, and highly "economical" to the governments that recruit them and the elite who employ them. When debtor nations export their women as migrant workers in the futile effort to keep up with debt payments, these women live and work in conditions of debt bondage, mirroring the relationship between their home and "host" countries.

1   Testimonies, Non-Governmental Organizations Forum on Women, Huairou, China, September 1995.

2   Testimonies, Non-Governmental Organizations Forum on Women.

3   Testimonies, Non-Governmental Organizations Forum on Women.

4   Pamela Sparr, *Mortgaging Women's Lives: Feminist Critiques of Structural Adjustment* (London and New Jersey: Zed Books Ltd., 1994).

5   See Grace Chang, "Disposable Nannies: Women's Work and the Politics of Latina Immigration," *Radical America* 26: 2 (October 1996), pp. 5–20.

6   Sparr, *Mortgaging Women's Lives,* p. 184.

7   Kristyn Joy, "Gender, Immigration and the WTO," *Network News* (Winter 2000), p. 12.

8   Testimony of Fatima, workshop on the impact of SAPs, NGO forum, September 2, 1995.

9   Testimony of Eileen Fernandez, workshop on the impact of SAPs, NGO forum, September 2, 1995.

10 Gabriela workshop, NGO forum, September 3, 1995.

11 The "official" figures corroborate these firsthand testimonies of women in countries under structural adjustment: Between 1969 and 1985, per capita food production declined in 51 out of 94 developing countries. Simultaneously, access to food has been severely limited by increased food prices with the devaluation of local currencies under SAPs. Expenditures on education in all poor developing countries except China and India declined from 21 percent of national budgets in 1972 to 9 percent in 1988. Health-care expenditures were also reduced from 5.5 percent to 2.8 percent of national budgets during this period (UNICEF report cited in Peter Lurie, Percy Hintzen, and Robert A. Lowe, "Socioeconomic Obstacles to HIV Prevention and Treatment in Developing Countries: The Roles of the International Monetary Fund and the World Bank," *AIDS* 9: 6, pp. 542–43).

12 Testimony of Merceditas Cruz, Migration and the Globalizing Economy workshop, NGO forum, September 6, 1995.

13 Testimony of Carmen, Organization of Free & United Women under Gabriela, NGO forum, September 3, 1995.

14 Impacts of SAPs workshop, NGO forum, September 2, 1995.

15 Testimony of Marlene Kanwati of Egypt at workshop on the effects of the international economic system on women, NGO forum, September 4, 1995.

16 See UNICEF report cited in Lurie et al., "Socioeconomic Obstacles to HIV Prevention and Treatment in Developing Countries," pp. 542–43.

17 Testimony of representative from International Organization of Prostitutes, Gabriela workshop, NGO forum, September 3, 1995.

18 Plenary on Globalization, NGO forum, September 3, 1995.

19 This number does not include women who are trafficked, are illegally recruited, or migrate for marriage, or students or tourists who eventually become undocumented workers. Compiled by Kanlungan Foundation Centre

from Philippine Overseas Employment Administration (POEA) and Department of Labor and Employment (DOLE) statistics, 1995.

20   Isabel Vincent, "Canada Beckons Cream of Nannies: Much-Sought Filipinas Prefer Work Conditions," *Globe and Mail,* January 20, 1996, pp. A-1, A-6. Other authors address more extensively trafficking in women for the sex, entertainment, and mail-order-bride industries. See Ninotchka Rosca, "The Philippines' Shameful Export," *The Nation,* April 17, 1995, pp. 523–25; Elaine Kim, "Sex Tourism in Asia: A Reflection of Political and Economic Equality," *Critical Perspectives of Third World America* 2: 1 (Fall 1984), pp. 215–31; and *Sisters and Daughters Betrayed: The Trafficking of Women and Girls and the Fight to End It,* prod. Chela Blitt, Global Fund for Women, videocassette.

21   "Flor Contemplacion: Victim of Mismanaged Economy," editorial, *PAID! (People Against Immoral Debt),* newsletter of Freedom from Debt Coalition, April 1995, p. 7.

22   Kanlungan Foundation Centre fact sheet prepared for the 1995 UN Conference on Women.

23   Freedom from Debt Coalition (FDC), based on DOLE figures, 1995.

24   *Brown Women, Blonde Babies,* prod. Marie Boti, Montreal, Canada; videocassette available from Multi-monde Productions, 4067 Boul. St.-Laurent, Suite 201, Montreal, Canada H2W 1Y7, 514-842-4047.

25   Interview with Ninotchka Rosca, April 29, 1996.

26   Peter T. Kilborn, "Union Gets the Lowly to Sign Up: Home Care Aides Are Fresh Target," *New York Times,* November 21, 1995.

27   Kilborn, "Union Gets the Lowly to Sign Up," *New York Times.*

28   Interview with Josie Camacho, April 18, 1996.

29   Kilborn, "Union Gets the Lowly to Sign Up," *New York Times.*

30   Interview with Josie Camacho, April 18, 1996.

31   Interview with Ms. Greenhill of the Canadian Consulate in Los Angeles, California, December 1993; Vincent, "Canada Beckons Cream of Nannies," *Globe and Mail,* p. A-1.

32   *Brown Women, Blonde Babies.*

33   Vincent, "Canada Beckons Cream of Nannies," *Globe and Mail,* p. A-6.

34   Kanlungan Foundation Centre, *A Framework on Women and Migration,* prepared for NGO forum, 1995.

35   Interview with Ninotchka Rosca, April 29, 1996.

36   FDC statement prepared for NGO Forum, 1995.

37   *Kapihan Sa Kanlungan: A Quarterly Digest of Migration News,* newsletter produced by Kanlungan Foundation Centre, April–June 1995; interview with Ninotchka Rosca; Vincent, "Canada Beckons," p. A-6.

38   Testimony, workshop on violence and migration, NGO forum, 1995.

39   Testimony, workshop on violence and migration, NGO forum, 1995.

40   Cynthia Enloe, *Bananas, Beaches and Bases: Making Feminist Sense of International Politics* (Berkeley, CA: University of California Press, 1989), p. 190.

41 Pamela Constable, "Housekeeper Wins Suit Against Boss," *Washington Post*, June 10, 1997, p. E-5.

42 Stephen Fried, "Empowering the Powerless: The Campaign for Migrant Domestic Workers Rights," *The Progressive Response*, Institute for Policy Studies, August 1999.

43 Kilborn, "Union Gets the Lowly to Sign Up."

44 SEIU press release, "Delayed Payment Case for Home Care Workers Settled with State for $4 Million," May 30, 1995.

45 Migration and the Global Economy Workshop, NGO forum, September 6, 1995.

46 Vincent, "Canada Beckons Cream of Nannies."

47 Interview with Ninotchka Rosca, April 29, 1996.

48 Statement prepared by Merceditas Cruz of FDC for NGO forum, 1995.

49 Press conference, March 23, 1994, National Press Club, Manila; "Gabriela Accuses Philippine Government of Pimping," *Gabriela International Update*, August 1995.

50 Interview with Ninotchka Rosca.

51 Interview with Ninotchka Rosca.

52 Enloe, *Bananas, Beaches, and Bases,* p. 188. Slowly, the Aquino government exempted one government after another from its requirements, and by 1989, 22 countries enjoyed exemption from the ban.

53 Interview with Felicita Villasin, May 6, 1996.

54 National Action Committee on the Status of Women (NAC) bulletins on March Against Poverty (1996).

55 For information, contact Women of Color Resource Center, 2288 Fulton Street, Suite 103, Berkeley, CA 94704.

56 Saskia Sassen, *Losing Control? Sovereignty in an Age of Globalization* (New York: Columbia University Press, 1996), p. xvi.

57 Arnoldo Garcia, "'101 Damn Nations': A Critique for a Globalized Era," *Network News*, Fall 1996, p. 13.

58 Sassen, *Losing Control?,* p. 94.

59 Vasquez is a pseudonym.

60 Carey Goldberg, "In a Startling Turnabout, Judge Sets Au Pair Free," *New York Times*, November 11, 1997, late ed., p. A-1.

61 Goldberg, "Startling Turnabout," p. A-22.

62 Sarah Lyall, "Au Pair's Hometown Celebrates Release," *New York Times*, November 11, 1997, p. A-22.

63 Dona Nichols, "Mary Poppins vs. Louise Woodward: A Local Family's Au Pair Tale," *Valley Parent*, January 1998, pp. 20–25.

64 Nichols, "Mary Poppins," p. 24.

65 Nichols, "Mary Poppins," p. 25.

66 Walden Bello, with Shea Cunningham and Bill Rau, *Dark Victory: The United States, Structural Adjustment and Global Poverty* (London: Pluto Press, 1994).

Immigrants
and Workfare Workers
Employable but "Not Employed"

On April 3, 1997, in Virginia, just outside Washington, DC, about 60 law enforcement agents from the Virginia sheriff's office joined with federal agents from the Immigration and Naturalization Service (INS) to raid a construction site where workers were building a county jail. Agents gathered approximately 100 workers against a wall, searching for about a dozen undocumented workers. Barbara Bradley, reporting for National Public Radio, commented: "This looks like any raid of illegal immigrants, but, in fact, it's an experiment in welfare reform." She explained that the INS planned to coordinate with Virginia's social services to replace undocumented workers with welfare recipients.[1]

When asked for comment, INS spokesperson Russ Bergeron confirmed this, calling the operation a "win-win situation for everyone" and enumerating the benefits:

> Number one, the employers get the immediate cooperation of the state in filling the vacancies that have been created. Number two, people who are on entitlement programs get an opportunity to get jobs. Number three, the immigration service benefits because the positions being filled are being filled by legal workers in the United States, and so it's less likely that we're going to have to come back to this work site to remove illegal workers.[2]

Later that morning, Scott Osdyke, deputy secretary of Virginia Health and Human Resources Department, was notified that 14 people had been apprehended and removed. The department inquired into the skill levels required for the job "openings" so that they could be matched with applicants among welfare and unemployment recipients. Osdyke explained, "If the INS is going to go in ... and enforce the law, which they're going to do anyway ... we wanted immediate opportunity to have access to that labor market."[3]

"What this system allows," Bergeron added, "is a system where once the illegal workers are removed, they can get legal workers who are qualified workers and that lessens the chance that they're going to run afoul of immigration [the INS] in the future."[4] Bergeron's comment hinted at one great incentive for employers to cooperate with the INS plan, even if they would have no difficulty finding other workers to fill those jobs otherwise. The not-so-hidden message seems to be that if employers cooperate in relying on applicants provided by Health and Human Resources, they may not be subject to close surveillance by the INS in the future. In November 1996, the state of Virginia began a pilot program, adopting a formal policy to reserve job vacancies resulting from INS raids for welfare-to-work participants. An article in the journal of the Institute for Public Affairs entitled, "Are There No Workhouses?" announced, "If you're currently receiving welfare benefits in Virginia, the state's Department of Social Services has some good news for you: It may be able to set you up with a new job just as soon as the Immigration and Naturalization Service rounds up a few more undocumented immigrants."[5] Bill Strassberger, an INS spokesperson, added that while wages for these jobs average $7 to $8 an hour, a "lucky few" will be able to land higher-paying jobs in fields like asbestos removal. This is in keeping with INS Commissioner Doris Meissner's proclamation, "We expect that our enforcement actions will open job opportunities for people currently receiving public aid."[6] The INS hopes to expand the program to the states with heavy immigration flows, such as California, Florida, Illinois, New York, and Texas.[7]

While this proposal was not received with much support or interest at the 1998 National Conference of Governors, it actually has been bandied about in policy circles since at least 1985, when Harold Ezell, then commissioner for the INS Western Region, proposed a similar program. Ezell said that there had been discussions of a joint program with the Department of Labor, such that "when we raid a factory or [race] track or whatever, the Department of Labor would backfill with unemployed Americans." Ezell pointed to his agency's efforts in the horse-racing industry, where he claimed that pressure from the INS forced the industry to establish recruiting and training programs to "replace illegals with Americans."[8]

At the same time, Joe Nalven, a professor at San Diego State University, proposed to link INS activity with California's workfare program, Greater Avenues for Independence (GAIN), then in its incipient stages. Nalven had conducted a study for the New York firm Manpower Demonstration Research Corporation (MDRC), hired by California to study the workfare proposal in the early 1980s. Although MDRC was not receptive to the idea, California's director of GAIN at the time said that he thought it was a good idea, pointing out that the wages and transportation costs of workfare workers could be subsidized by GAIN to improve conditions for the replacement American workers.[9]

Perhaps this is precisely the goal of such proposals—to fill "vacancies" created by the removal of undocumented immigrant workers with workers who are equally exploitable and controllable, if not more so, but far more politically palatable because they are perceived as more "American." Replacing "illegal immigrant" workers with US-citizen welfare recipients in low-wage jobs holds great appeal for the American public because it is seen as solving two problems that have been hyped in the American public imagination: "illegal" immigration and "welfare dependency."

Putting welfare recipients to work in jobs vacated by "illegals" is touted as restoring jobs to Americans, even as "creating" jobs. This serves to distract attention from two realities. First, creating job vacancies is not the same as creating jobs. No new jobs are created by dislocating workers and replacing them with others. Second, workfare workers are possibly even more exploited than some immigrant workers. They don't get paid outside of work in exchange for public benefits, while employers receive subsidies for employing them. In addition, those on workfare can be replaced as easily as immigrant workers, particularly if they "make trouble" and complain about working conditions.

Raul Yzaguirre, president of the National Council of La Raza, expressed concerns about the implicit message that employers won't be watched or sanctioned for workplace violations if they hire welfare recipients. Yzaguirre criticized such programs as exacerbating racial conflicts in cities: "I think it increases racial tension. Undocumented immigrants tend to be Asian or Hispanic. Welfare recipients tend to be black and white. So I think it aggravates already explosive situations in many cities."[10]

Perhaps more importantly, this type of program serves to pit one group of exploited workers against another, creating two pools of cheap, super-exploitable labor from which employers can choose. Undocumented workers and welfare workers become two labor sources that employers can use as leverage against each other, just as undocumented workers and braceros were used by growers. Thus, these operations allow for divide-and-conquer tactics, reinforcing racial conflicts and their underlying racist images. This is evident in the remarks of Mac McCarthy, a welder at the Virginia construction site raided by the INS:

> What are you going to have to go through, 30 of them to find one? It's a waste of time. Who wants to … train somebody that—he's going to work a week and go, "I can collect welfare. I don't need to work." And after you spend all this time trying to train that individual, and then—the guy don't want to work—want to go back on welfare. I'd rather have Latinos.[11]

McCarthy's comment reflects pervasive public attitudes that Latinos (read: immigrants) are ideal workers, ultimately available and controllable, while welfare recipients (read: blacks) are undependable, untrainable, and lacking in work ethic or motivation to leave welfare.

The Multiracial Race to the Bottom

As welfare "deform" rapidly demolishes an already tattered safety net in the United States, the most vulnerable low-wage and poverty-wage contingent workers are falling to the same plight and often competing for the same exploitative and hazardous work. It is not surprising, then, that employers (including the federal and state governments) would pit these two groups against each other, utilizing coordinated welfare and immigration policy and administration. Employers also exploit racial conflicts and hierarchies, reinforcing racialized constructions of blacks as welfare cheats or dependents and immigrants as welfare cheats and "illegals" who are redeemable as good worker-machines. The welder from Virginia's "preference" for Latinos may represent a common attitude among resentful white workers, who perhaps are all too receptive to such myths. "Citizen" welfare or workfare workers and noncitizen immigrant workers are simultaneously disenfranchised through these parallel and interconnected practices and ideologies.

The work performed by these groups and their labor conditions are strikingly similar: invisible, unsafe, unsanitary, hazardous, low-paid service work. Their labor is not seen as contract labor, or a service that they provide to society for which they should be compensated. Instead, their labor is constructed as either charity, opportunity, privilege, community service, repayment of a debt to society, or as punishment for a crime. In the case of welfare recipients, the "crimes" are being poor, homeless, or "unemployed." In the case of immigrants, they are criminalized for entering the country (presumed "illegally," of course) and for consuming resources to which they allegedly have no rights. In both cases, employers invoke these constructions of immigrant and workfare workers as undeserving criminals indebted to society in order to coerce these workers into exploitative work, justify this exploitation, and counter organizing among these workers.

Emma Harris is one of almost 3,000 people doing workfare in San Francisco for $345 per month in county General Assistance (GA) benefits. She leaves home at 5 a.m. and catches a bus to report to work by 7 a.m., where she cleans city buses, inside and out, removing graffiti from the seats and walls for eight hours, until she goes home at 3 p.m. Other typical workfare assignments include sweeping streets, cleaning parks, doing laundry and collecting garbage at San Francisco General Hospital, and performing clerical duties and parking staff cars at the Department of Human Services, which administers the GA program. A street sweeper must be at the work site at 6:30 a.m. and is penalized with the loss of one month's benefits for being ten minutes late. Workfare workers have no holidays, sick days, or vacation days, and are subject to many health hazards, including exposure to blood, feces, and toxic wastes or detergents, without the proper safety trainings or protective gear.

Harris reports that many of her coworkers became ill or suffered burns from the chemical cleansers they used until People Organized to Win Employment Rights (POWER), a San Francisco–based workfare workers' union, fought to get protective masks and gloves. Although POWER won the California Occupational Safety and Health Administration's recognition of workfare workers' rights to coverage under health and safety regulations, the city has been slow to provide the required protective gear or trainings. A site captain for POWER, Harris says that workfare workers at her site were even prevented from using the bathrooms until POWER staged an action with ample media coverage.[12]

The city of San Francisco would like to treat workfare workers like indentured servants, Harris says. Workfare workers perform the same tasks as other unionized city employees, often alongside them, but for a fraction of the wages and without the same protections or benefits. While unionized city employees may sweep streets for as much as $15.04 an hour plus benefits, workfare workers receive monthly grants equivalent to about $5.31 an hour for the same work. "The city says we are not considered workers. They say we're volunteers, so we don't deserve to get paid more," Harris comments. "We know that's not right because they save millions of dollars each year from our work."

According to Steve Williams, founder and codirector of POWER, one of the union's main challenges has been to get officials to recognize these workers as employees who should earn prevailing wages and whose years on the job should count as experience. Williams says, "[San Francisco Mayor] Willie Brown has been portraying workfare workers as recipients of charity, doing nothing for these grants."[13] The primary tactic the city has used to deny prevailing wages is to argue that the tasks of workfare workers don't match the job descriptions of city workers, even though any workfare worker can tell you that they are doing the same tasks as city workers, often side by side with them. The only difference is that workfare workers wear the orange paper vests that have become symbolic of their servitude instead of the proper protective gear that should be provided to them.[14]

Official proclamations as to the nature of workfare are missionary in tone, adamantly denying that workfare is labor for which compensation is due. "We don't think of it as work, but as community service," Dorothy Enisman, director of San Francisco's GA program said. "It's not a job. They're participating in a program in exchange for a grant."[15] At a Civil Service Commission hearing to determine whether workfare workers' assignments qualified as experience comparable to city-worker classifications in order to apply for city jobs, Michael Josephers of the Department of Human Services (DHS) insisted: "The purpose of workfare has always been to give recipients the opportunity to repay society and re-enter the labor market by gaining skills, such as getting to work on time, wearing proper clothes, and using safety equipment properly."[16] Josephers's comment was an insult to the workfare workers present, who are often denied proper protective clothing and safety trainings, and who testified to being passed over for permanent positions doing work they had done as workfare for years, on the basis that they had "no experience."

Josephers went on to say that his agency had "discovered" that people were staying in workfare assignments for three, five, and seven years at a time, "so we decided to create new programs."[17] The new programs proposed include a rotation system that would force GA recipients to change workfare placements every three to four months. As Williams pointed out, the result would be that no one would have a chance of gaining adequate experience to be hired for permanent positions. Josephers also claimed that workfare is not intended to lead to permanent jobs but to provide experience for jobs in the private sector. Williams retorted that he had not seen any positions for street sweeping or bus cleaning in private industries the last time he looked.[18]

Moreover, Williams said, the reason DHS spokesmen always state that workfare is not meant to lead to permanent jobs is that "DHS has stolen these jobs, which used to be done by unionized city employees at prevailing wages."[19] Williams recounted the history of the workfare program in San Francisco, which has been used to erode the unionized city labor force slowly but surely. When workfare was first introduced in the city 15 years ago, unionized city workers numbered approximately 300. Now, they number just over 70, with most of them supervising the workfare workers who do the actual labor.[20]

Similarly, in New York, where the workfare program called the Work Experience Program (WEP) currently employs almost ten times as many workers as that in San Francisco, workfare workers have been used by the city to do critical services at low cost, replacing the ranks of higher-paid, unionized municipal workers. Williams points out that San Francisco went about replacing unionized city workers in a much more underhanded way than did New York and New Jersey. By refusing to refund civil-service positions upon attrition, the city managed to reduce the ranks steadily and quietly, thereby averting a public outcry or mass uprising. Williams also faults the unions for not having been on top of this issue for its constituency.

POWER members recognize that the workfare program has never been intended to move people into permanent jobs. At a Saturday morning meeting called by the San Francisco DHS for a "public dialogue" on four proposed county adult-assistance programs, one POWER member said:

> You are trying to remove me from my job to place me in a program to soak up federal money, only to return me to the same job at a lower wage.... Start calling people who work for their money "employees." You are calling people "trainees" and "volunteers" just to create a loophole for union-busting.[21]

At the same hearing, when one woman asked, "If workfare's not a job, then why is it that if you miss a day, you don't get paid?" DHS of-

ficial Newsome replied, "It's just the way the program is structured." Indeed, the program has been structured such that POWER
estimates that the city saved approximately $23 million in fiscal year
1994–95 by not paying workfare workers prevailing wages for their
labor. This figure does not include the city's profits from providing
no health benefits, Social Security, or unemployment insurance to
the workfare workers who provided the city with more than 73,000
hours per month of labor.[22] Moreover, Williams emphasizes that
this labor, although seen as tedious or menial, is absolutely vital to
the city.[23]

Suspicions High and Wages Low

Richard Schwartz, former senior adviser on welfare to New York
City Mayor Rudolph Giuliani, called New York's 36,000 workfare
workers a "windfall." He said, "If they were not out cleaning streets
or working in parks, the streets would simply be dirtier and the parks
more unkempt."[24] Exploiting welfare recipients through coerced labor has generated not only huge bonanzas of labor and profit for
many cities but has produced hostilities and fears, dividing workers
who might otherwise be allied. New York and Los Angeles each has
more than 30,000 workfare workers either partially or entirely replacing once full-time city employees. In San Francisco, the Bureau
of Street Maintenance and Environmental Services now has
workfare workers outnumbering city employees by two to one, at
anywhere from one-half to one-fourth the pay rate.[25] New York's
WEP workers and unionized city workers standing side by side doing
the same work are growing resentful and suspicious of each other.[26]

These tensions are surfacing at work sites all over the country,
as workfare and welfare-to-work workers are being assigned to public jobs, as well as private industries, and the threat of displacement
looms large. For example, at the Jersey City Medical Center, Jose-
phine Araujo and Sarah Thompson work together on the 17th floor,
sharing the duties of taking patients for X rays, rehabilitation, and
blood tests. Araujo began working at the hospital in the summer of
1996 as part of a welfare-to-work program—that is, for no wages.
Thompson was a full-time employee for 27 years until December

1996, when her hours were cut in half, slashing her salary from $22,000 to $11,000. Her managers claim that budget constraints forced this cut in her hours. Araujo, who took on some of Thompson's work, is not even listed as a trainee but as a volunteer. Jonathan Metsch, president of the Jersey City Medical Center, insisted, "There is no issue of displacement.... The workfare program is to get welfare people into the rhythm and habits of going to work and we folded it into our volunteer operation. This is work volunteers normally do in hospitals."[27]

In Baltimore, where the minimum wage was $4.75 an hour in 1997, public schools hired welfare recipients for $1.50 an hour instead of renewing contracts with agencies hiring out cleaning staff for $6 an hour. Baltimore's Citywide Bus Company also trained welfare recipients to be aides to assist disabled children on school buses for $1.50 an hour. The welfare recipients were the preferred workers because they continued to receive federal welfare benefits at no cost to the schools. The Industrial Areas Foundation, organizing low-wage workers in Baltimore, mobilized protests against worker displacement caused by welfare-to-work programs and attempts by the city to undermine a new living-wage ordinance by using welfare workers. The protests helped to pressure Maryland Governor Paris Glendening to sign an executive order banning the practice of hiring welfare recipients to replace workers.[28]

In the private sector, corporations are also capitalizing on welfare reform and congratulating themselves as models in welfare-to-work. Marriott International Hotels' Pathways to Independence program provides "training" to welfare recipients in housekeeping, reservations, kitchen work, and other jobs. Marriott captures the advantages of federal child-care and transportation subsidies that inflate the trainees' incomes, enabling Marriott to pay lower wages of $6 to $8 an hour. Marriott also receives tax credits given to employers hiring welfare recipients.[29]

Children Today, a publication of the US Department of Health and Human Services, featured an article on the Pathways to Independence program highlighting the program's emphasis on career planning, self-esteem enhancement, communications, cultural diversity, work ethics, and managing life issues. "In addition to these coping skills, instructors teach trainees how to become and remain productive employees by emphasizing the precise job skills necessary to the hospitality industry."[30] But one businessman's editorial in *Lodging Hospitality* trade journal warned his hotel-industry colleagues not to fall prey to trying to save the nation's poor or solve the nation's problems through welfare-to-work programs:

> The vast welfare population can be roughly divided into three unequal groups. At the bottom are hard-core drug addicts, lifelong criminals, and social misfits who will logically never be able to migrate to the workforce. At the top are those who probably have the desire, and even some skills, to work. They should be able to find jobs and, more importantly, keep jobs—particularly if they receive training, counseling, and encouragement from programs like Pathways to Independence.... In the broad middle lies the unknown—long-term welfare recipients who've either grown up in a culture of public dependence or who ... have lost the ethic and attitudes required for consistent, long-term employment.[31]

The author's antipoor bigotry even seems to outweigh his interest in what he calls the "attractive ... prospects of a large new pool of prospective workers," bringing with them tax credits to employers of up to $20,000.

All of these workers, the displaced and the replacements, have suffered the impacts of the 1996 welfare-reform legislation signed into law by Bill Clinton, which mandated that welfare recipients find work within strict time limits, without any dedicated effort on the state's part to create new jobs. Displacement, wage depression, and a deterioration of labor conditions and rights are inevitable results of these federal welfare-to-work requirements. These workers are also all victims of oppressive ideology casting welfare recipients as those who deserve, indeed should be grateful for, lives of servitude in whatever work they can get.

Be Our Guest (Worker)

This ideology has strong parallels with historical beliefs about immigrant workers and their particular "suitability" for the service work they have most often been forced to undertake. For both welfare workers and immigrant workers, the rhetoric espoused by government officials, corporate spokesmen, and private household employers emphasizes the benefits to those seen as "recipients" instead of workers. Immigrants and welfare workers are portrayed as the beneficiaries of opportunities, training, preparation, and assimilation to become productive members of society under the benevolent sponsorship of the state or private employers.

In Los Angeles County, where the official term for employers of workfare workers is "sponsors," Sandra Semtner, a division chief in the Department of Public Social Services (DPSS) said, "Theoretically, GR [General Relief] workers are working off their debt to the county. The other purpose is to provide working-world experience. It's very important for unemployed people to keep in the flow of work, to keep them exposed to productive activity."[32] Tony Coles, senior welfare adviser to Mayor Giuliani in New York, says that workfare imparts skills—such as turning up on time, taking orders, and completing a job—that workers need in the private sector. "This program is good for the recipients and good for the city. It instills basic values and structure that one would want to have," Coles says, "and the city gets done jobs that would not otherwise be done."[33]

Semtner's and Coles's visions bear remarkable resemblance to the rationale behind so-called Americanization programs aimed at steering Mexican immigrant women into domestic service in the American Southwest during the 1910s and 1920s. These programs targeted mothers in particular, in keeping with the belief that these women would be central to accomplishing cultural assimilation in their communities. One such program, through the California Commission of Immigration and Housing, involved an array of instructional services intended to foster skills and "habits" that were believed to facilitate the incorporation of Mexican women and children into US industrial society.[34] For example, an English primer was fashioned to drill the values of industry through this verse:

We are working every day,
So our boys and girls can play.

We are working for our homes and country, too.
We like to wash, to sew to cook,
We like to write, or read a book,
We are working, working, working every day.[35]

In addition, Americanization teachers tried to change Mexican diets—seen as too heavily laden with fried foods that were thought to make Mexicans lazy and prone to stealing—and hygiene practices, since "sloppy appearances" in women were thought to prevent them from acquiring waitress positions. Also, information about birth control was introduced whenever possible to persuade Mexican women of the value of fertility control in "freeing" them to engage in wage work.[36]

These Americanization programs were seen as yielding multiple benefits. First, the women could be "prepared" to fulfill the immediate and great demand for service workers. Second, by instilling these women with proper American values and habits, they could in turn nurture a future generation of workers well trained for their prescribed roles in the new industrial order. While these programs were intended to facilitate the destruction of Mexican culture and more efficient exploitation of immigrant communities, they were nevertheless touted as beneficial to the "trainees." For example, some mistresses who employed Mexican women as household servants actually rationalized paying low wages on the basis that the experience would ease the immigrant women's assimilation and, therefore, their upward social mobility.[37] Apparently, still other mistresses in El Paso hoped to find better service for their generous employment and pleaded with the city council in 1919 for help in replacing their Mexican servants, whom they said proved to be "inadequate despite higher wages."[38]

These attitudes continue to be pervasive today among employers of immigrant workers in private households. Work done by immigrant workers is defined as an opportunity or privilege bestowed on the worker by the employer. Asian-American studies and literature professor Sau-ling C. Wong observes that when people of color are represented as caregivers to white people, providing services ranging from spiritual guidance to elder care, as in popular films such as *Driving Miss Daisy, Ghost,* and *The Hand That Rocks the Cradle,* this is "depicted in a benign light … with emphasis placed on the benefits accruing to the care-receiver, the volitional participation of the caregiver, and the general mutuality of the exchange."[39] In reality, the benefits reaped by employers are not confined to free labor and profits but include emotional gratification derived from the employers' beliefs that they are providing "charity" or "assistance" to the "recipients." Employers of immigrants in private households live out their fantasies of nobility, seeing themselves as beneficent "padronas" or "padrones" in middle- and upper-class homes across the nation.

The story of Yuni Mulyono illustrates well the plight of many immigrant women who have lived through nightmares at the hands of employers fancying themselves magnanimous sponsors to their household servants. Mulyono (not her real name) was given a new name by a "consultant" who also arranged her passport and visa for the employers, Lina Nilam and Reginald Hall. Immediately upon arriving in Los Angeles on December 5, 1992, Mulyono began working as a live-in nanny for the wealthy couple in Los Angeles. She worked every day, 65 hours a week, in return for $100 a month, which she had been told was the minimum wage in California, and represented four times her monthly salary in Jakarta. Mulyono never saw this money, as it was sent directly to her family in Indonesia, who used it to support her brothers and sisters through high school and her young daughter, Zustin, who was one and a half years old when Mulyono left Indonesia.[40]

Mulyono's duties began at 5:30 a.m. on weekdays, waking and readying the couple's daughter for school; preparing lunch "to go" for the whole family; serving breakfast; cleaning the kitchen; feeding and cleaning up after the family's two dogs; and cleaning the entire house, including scrubbing the toilets, every day. She also washed the windows and gardened once or twice a week. After the child returned from school, Mulyono bathed and cared for her until 7 p.m., when Nilam came home and Mulyono served the family dinner. Her work ended around 9 p.m., after she cleaned up the kitchen. "I never thought they would treat me the way they treated me," Mulyono said, since in Jakarta she had her freedom "as long as the work was done." Yet, she said, when she came to the United States, she did not speak English and didn't know anyone, so she was resigned to the fact that she never left the house or had any real time off.

It was not until January 1994 that she began to leave the house for two hours each Saturday to attend English classes. In school, she met a friend, Marco Rodriguez, who asked her to go out. When she asked her employers if she could go, Nilam replied angrily, "You came to the United States to work for me, not to have fun," and Hall threatened that they had a responsibility to send her back to Indonesia unless she fulfilled her obligation to work for them for five years. Finally, her employers agreed to let her go out on Sundays, but they were furious when she was late coming home once. Mulyono was afraid that they would act on their threats to send her back to Indonesia, so she packed her bags. Mulyono reported that Nilam chased her out with only her purse in hand and Hall threatened to kill her when she tried to return for her things.[41]

After Mulyono finally escaped her employers' household on September 19, 1995, she went to the Coalition for Humane Immigrant Rights of Los Angeles (CHIRLA), which helped her find an attorney. The late Christina Riegos of CHIRLA predicted that the employers would insist that her pay had been "charity [we] gave her."[42] Indeed, when Mulyono filed suit for back wages, her employers claimed that she had been an ungrateful "guest" in their home who was treated "like family" and spent her time "lounging around" or in "vacation and leisure time activities." Mulyono's attorney, Michelle Yu, argued that under both California Code and the Fair Labor Standards Act (FLSA), "employ" is defined as "to suffer or permit to work," and under this definition, the defendants had an employment relationship with Mulyono, rather than one of friendship or sponsorship, as they claimed.

Yu referred to a ruling in *Brennan v. Partida* (1974), in which the court determined that two laundromat attendants were employees, rather than independent contractors, under the FLSA: "The employer's good faith does not excuse his obligation to pay what is due under the act. Nor does it matter that the parties had no intention of creating an employment relationship, for application of the FLSA does not turn on subjective intent."[43] Yu argued that Mulyono understood herself to be an employee of the defendants, regardless of what relationship the defendants now claimed was their intention to create with her.[44] Finally, Yu brought in an expert witness on Indonesian society's rigid ethnic and class divisions to testify that it would be highly implausible for the employer, a wealthy Chinese-Indonesian, to keep Mulyono, a poor Javanese-Indonesian, as a houseguest.[45]

Judge Jack W. Morgan, a Republican appointee of Governor Pete Wilson, rejected the employers' claims that Mulyono had been a guest and entered an unprecedented judgment awarding Mulyono $47,827 for back pay and overtime. Furthermore, he found that the charge raised by the employers of Mulyono's illegal entry into the country was a "nonissue," stating, "Whether or not a person is in the United States legally does not impact upon their ability to seek minimum wage for services performed."[46] Nevertheless, the judge did not award any damages to Mulyono, asserting that the employers "acted in good faith and in the honest but incorrect belief that whatever benefits they conferred on the plaintiff was adequate compensation for the services."[47] Thus, in principle, the decision in the Mulyono case was ambivalent at best. For Mulyono, it was a moral victory but amounted to little in practical terms. After the judge's ruling, the employers filed for bankruptcy and successfully avoided having to compensate Mulyono with any more than $5,000 to settle. Still, Mulyono felt vindicated, and she, along with many immigrants' rights advocates, believes that this will set a positive precedent: "Because of my case … there are lots of housekeepers like me, and it opened their eyes that there is hope and help."[48]

Mulyono's winning of a back-pay judgment was a rare victory, but her story is otherwise not exceptional. Sociologist Mary Romero reports that when she presented her study of the exploitation of Chicana domestic workers, many colleagues responded defensively, explaining that they treated their immigrant household employees "just like family" and felt that they were providing them with "bridging" opportunities.[49] Rosanna Hertz, in her study *More Equal Than Others: Women and Men in Dual-Career Marriages,* found that some employers rationalized paying low wages to their household employees on the basis of these claims as well.[50]

"Not Employment, But Assistance"

California state and county governments are employing strikingly similar rhetoric in their implementation of welfare-to-work policy. A debate between the federal Department of Labor and California's Department of Social Services (CDSS) illustrates well how easily this ideology is translated into antilabor practice. Defying labor department recommendations, California blocked the institution of basic protections for workfare workers, contending that welfare-to-work activities are "assistance" programs, providing "recipients" with training and preparation for entry into the workforce and productive society. CDSS circulated a memo instructing counties not to apply the FLSA, including the minimum-wage standard, to CalWORKs (California Work Opportunity and Responsibility to Kids Act) participants engaged in "work experience" and "community service" programs. This directly contradicted a US Department of Labor guidance, issued in May 1997, stating that welfare recipients would probably be considered employees in many, if not most, work activities under the new welfare law. The guidance specifically stated that "welfare recipients in 'workfare' arrangements which require recipients to work in return for their welfare benefits must be compensated at the minimum wage if they are classified as 'employees' under the FLSA's broad definition"—that is, persons "suffered or permitted to work." Furthermore, it stated that determining whether or not someone is an employee under the FLSA should turn on an assessment of what the worker is actually doing at the placement site and the economic realities of her or his relationship to her or his employer.[51]

Despite these clear directives from the labor department, CDSS issued a letter in May 1998 stating its position that no employment relationship exists for "work experience" and "community service," and that no individualized determination regarding the application of the FLSA is necessary for these nonemployment welfare-to-work activities. The CDSS letter asserts:

> The nature of the relationship with aid recipients is not employment, but assistance…. These activities are not provided by statute for the benefit of the state, CDSS, counties, or any entity providing an activity. Rather, the activities are provided for the training and rehabilitation of unemployed and unemployable recipients. Among other things, these activities contribute to recipients' sense of self-worth and accomplishment and their ability to overcome barriers to employment.[52]

The practical result of this CDSS position in Los Angeles County and elsewhere has been that with the reduction of benefits but maintenance or increase of number of "work activity" hours required, many workfare and welfare workers are receiving less than minimum wage.[53]

This deliberate depression of wages by the state of California should be viewed in the broader context of wage depression nationwide. An analysis by the Economic Policy Institute estimates that the influx of millions of welfare recipients pushed into the job market by welfare-to-work policies will cause the wages of low-wage workers to fall by an average of 12 percent, with wages in states with relatively large welfare-recipient populations dropping even more—17.8 percent in California and 17.1 percent in New York. As the study's authors point out, "Thus, the working poor, praised by welfare reformers as an example to be followed by current welfare recipients, will foot the bill for 'fixing' the system."[54] Workers already struggling in low-wage jobs now face increased competition with welfare recipients entering an insufficient job market. Also, each welfare recipient entering or returning to work under the reform plan will lose wages totaling an average of $38,800 per year.[55]

These analyses are corroborated by the statements of corporate employers who welcome the influx of people being pushed off welfare. Richard Reinhold, chair of a Salt Lake City–based temporary employment agency, SOS Staffing Services, said: "Without the welfare people, we cannot fill all our orders for temps. To get enough people without them, we would have had to raise the wage—not by a lot, maybe 5 percent—but we would have had to pay more." Reinhold's company pays assembly-line workers, office clerks, and telemarketers $6 to $8 an hour, and roughly 7 percent of its staff is "coming off welfare."[56] Similarly, Keith Wine, manager at Norell Services, another temporary agency, in Richmond, California, says that the influx of former welfare recipients will "stabilize" pay scales in the city, which previously suffered from labor shortages with a low unemployment rate of 3 percent. Wine said: "Everyone has been raising wages to get people, and this will make it possible to hold pay steady."[57]

Ilana Berger, former lead organizer for POWER, noted that although the official unemployment rate is often cited as 6 percent nationally, this does not account for those workers who worked only a few hours per week or who pursued a futile job search in a market that has no jobs for them, nor adequate services such as child care or transportation that would make permanent full-time work viable. If we account for these alternative workers, the unemployment rate is at least double the official number, and it is 23 percent for people of color, Berger said.[58]

The INS, "At Your Service"

Given the similar covert functions of the INS and state human-services departments to regulate labor, it is not surprising that collaborations between these agencies are becoming more common around the nation in the era of "welfare reform." That immigration policy used to regulate labor is not a new phenomenon; nor is the use of welfare policy to control labor. But the collaboration between immigration and welfare agencies is a relatively new and destructive phenomenon for all low-wage workers. "Welfare reform" has become inextricably intertwined with "immigration reform," and the development of these alarming new alliances have appeared both in formal policy and in administrative practice.

In a press release issued in March 1998, the INS's San Francisco district office proudly announced the arrest of seven undocumented workers at a Pizzeria Uno restaurant. The workers were from Mexico and Guatemala, ranging in age from 18 to 30, and had worked in the pizzeria as busboys and cooks and in food preparation for between two weeks and two years. The press release highlighted that this "operation climaxed a six-month investigation."[59]

At first glance, the report of a six-month investigation resulting in the apprehension of seven undocumented workers hardly seems newsworthy, much less an item that a federal agency would boast about as a good use of tax dollars. A statement by Acting District Director Charles H. Demore sheds light on the public-relations value of the announcement: "The men arrested today were only earning between $12,000 and $14,000 a year. These aren't high wages, but in a time when many people face the end of welfare benefits, there's a positive community impact in making entry-level jobs requiring limited skills available to people who have a legal right to work in the United States."[60]

In a similar press release, the INS's San Francisco office claimed that its removal of ten undocumented workers potentially made $300,000 in wages available to legal workers, particularly welfare recipients slated to lose their benefits through welfare reform. District Director Thomas Schiltgen pronounced, "We're in a unique position to open up jobs they can do, work that can help them hold their families together."[61] The bitter irony in Schiltgen's statement, of course, is that INS raids have devastating effects on immigrant families, as the National Network for Immigrant and Refugee Rights (NNIRR) documented in a recent report.[62]

The symbolic value of these INS notices in the face of welfare reform cannot be missed. Indeed, only weeks after the announcement, on April 1, 1998, thousands of welfare recipients in California faced the beginning of the time limits on their receipt of public assistance.[63] These proclamations don't just represent good public relations; they reveal a more accurate picture of one unacknowledged, but increasingly public, function of the INS. While ostensibly the INS's role is "gatekeeping"—that is, controlling the entries and departures of migrants to and from the United States—its true function is more specifically to regulate the movement, availability, and independence of migrant labor. Increasingly, this INS "service" is being utilized by corporations to obtain low-wage immigrant workers with complete impunity and by welfare agencies to secure "job openings" without the creation of jobs.

This compounds an existing challenge of organizing among immigrant workers: fear in the face of employers' threats of calling the INS on "troublesome" workers. Beyond this, there has been a growing trend of employers calling the INS on *themselves* in retaliation against immigrant workers known to be sympathetic to unions. A new report by the National INS Raids Task Force of the NNIRR, *Portrait of Injustice: The Impact of Immigration Raids on Families, Workers, and Communities,* documents numerous incidences in which INS raids have been staged just as workers are engaged in a union drive. For example, 50 INS agents entered Mediacopy, a video reproduction plant outside San Francisco, on January 7, 1997, gathered workers, and began calling out the names of people thought to be undocumented. Ninety-nine people were detained, some for two days in a women's jail, and then shipped by bus to a detention facility in Las Vegas. This raid, one of the largest enforcement operations in northern California in recent history, preceded a union drive that was to culminate in a March 24 vote on joining the International Longshoremen's and Warehousemen's Union (ILWU).

Mediacopy had long profited by classifying a large portion of its 500 employees, a majority of whom were immigrant women from Mexico, as temporary workers, providing them no benefits, sick leave, vacation, or health insurance. Some employees had worked there for five years, struggling to feed their families on meager wages and unable to refuse overtime work for fear of being fired. One woman reported, "If we refused to work Saturday and Sunday, they'd threaten to take a week's work from us."[64]

Several accounts suggest that Mediacopy collaborated with the INS to use the raids to intimidate workers. In the fall of 1996, workers began discussions about forming a union, and that December, INS agents reviewed employee records on site. With Mediacopy's cooperation, the INS attempted to identify unauthorized workers. After the raid, the National Network for Immigrant and Refugee Rights (NNIRR) worked with the ILWU to protest this collaboration.

The company admitted that it knew the INS was going to raid. As David Bacon, chair of the Northern California Coalition for Immigrant Rights (NCCIR) Board, points out, the fact that the timing of the raid occurred so close to the organizing drive at the plant suggests collusion.[65] Union leaders noted that those workers who were detained during the raid had been in support of joining the union.[66]

Mediacopy's anti-union efforts were relentless after a majority of workers signed union cards the day after the raid. The company's elaborate union-busting campaign included forcing workers to view a video about violent strikes and firing 200 employees who had to reapply for their jobs through temporary agencies. Perhaps even more telling was the company's response when the INS sent Mediacopy a notice demanding the "reverification" of documents of another 140 workers. The company did not post this notice to its workers until a month before the March vote. The INS provided no explanation as to why the company was allowed to delay response to the order for so long.[67] Moreover, Mediacopy utilized these tactics in spite of INS regulations warning against reliance on information "provided to the Service to retaliate against employees for exercising their employment rights."[68]

The case of Gloria Esperanza Montero and other garment workers at a sweatshop in Long Island City, New York, presents even clearer evidence of employer collusion with the INS against immigrant worker organizing. Montero, a citizen of Ecuador working at STC Knitting factories and active in union organizing, was arrested and ordered to be deported after her employers maneuvered a raid of their own facilities. As Muzaffar Chishti, co-counsel for Montero, reports, Local 155 of the International Ladies' Garment Workers' Union, now the Union of Needletrades, Industrial, and Textile Employees (UNITE!), had begun to organize workers at this sweatshop in 1992.[69] In the effort to quash union activity, STC threatened to report certain employees as undocumented to the INS. The union then responded by filing five charges of unfair labor practice against STC with the National Labor Relations Board (NLRB). In September 1992, the NLRB conducted an election, resulting in the union's certification. On October 19, 1992, just as the union was to begin collective bargaining, the STC factory was raided.

A number of facts implicate the INS as a partner of STC in questionable labor practice. In September 1992, Henry Dogin, STC's attorney, who had been the former district director of the New York office of the INS, sent a fax to the INS saying that some STC employees might be undocumented. While Dogin's association with STC was not known to the INS when the fax was received, the INS later learned that Dogin was STC's attorney. Later that month, the INS received two "anonymous" complaints about STC employing undocumented workers.[70] Also, during the union drive, Latino and Korean workers had been quite divided, with the groups even housed on different floors of the factory. While there was overwhelming support for the union among the Latino workers, few of the Korean workers were pro-union. When the INS raided, agents arrived with a list of "suspected" employees. All ten of those arrested were Latino. The union suspects that the owner, who was Korean, had tipped off the Korean workers not to show up on that day.[71]

Montero's attorneys appealed the Board of Immigration Appeals decision to deport Montero, arguing that the evidence of her alien status was obtained through a raid initiated by the employer's unfair labor practices and attempts to suppress union activity. The Second Circuit US Court of Appeals denied Montero's petition, arguing that while immigration law, particularly the employer sanctions, were not intended to "limit in any way the scope of the term 'employee' in … the National Labor Relations Act (NLRA), or the rights and protections of that Act," on the other hand, "no court has interpreted immigration law to constrain the Attorney General's ability to deport undocumented aliens." The court argued further that to exclude evidence of an alien's illegal presence in the United States because the evidence was obtained in connection with the unfair labor practices of an employer is "wholly inconsistent with enforcement of the [Immigration and Nationality Act]." The majority opinion stated, "Whether or not an undocumented alien has been the victim of unfair labor practices, such an alien has no entitlement to be in the United States."[72]

Finally, the judges responded to the concern raised by Montero's counsel and in the many amicus curiae briefs filed by lawyers, scholars, and labor and immigrant rights groups, which argued that allowing deportation based on evidence obtained "in connection with a labor dispute" would undermine labor law protections:

> This concern is misplaced. Under current law, an employer is subject to sanctions under both the NLRA and the INS if it identifies its undocumented employees to the INS in the course of a labor dispute. To the extent that these sanctions are insufficiently severe to deter such conduct that concern must be addressed to the Congress and not the courts.[73]

In the same breath, in other words, the court recognized that an employer might resort to reporting itself to the INS in the midst of a labor conflict and that the ostensible deterrence against such a tactic was weak; yet it ruled that this problem would have to be taken up by Congress. Based on an administrative fluke, rather than a principled decision, one of the seven defendants avoided deportation because the arresting INS agent also interrogated him, violating INS procedure and due process.[74]

Mike Wishnie, co-counsel for Montero, who was working with the American Civil Liberties Union's Immigrant Rights Project at the time, commented on another phenomenon threatening immigrant worker rights: collaboration between the INS and the Department of Labor. The labor department relies on worker complaints to initiate any investigations of employers. This leaves grim prospects of prosecuting abusive employers of immigrant workers, particularly since 1992, when the two agencies entered into an agreement known as the Memorandum of Understanding (MOU) that the labor department will refer claimants to the INSURANCE[75] As a result, Wishnie says that his organization advises clients not to go to the labor department. In addition, a new task force of the civil rights division of the Department of Justice trying to bring criminal prosecutions for cases of slavery is attempting to use the Department of Labor for "intake." Wishnie's group is trying to instruct the civil rights division that it will not get many cases this way because of the MOU. Finally, Wishnie says that new INS regulations stipulating that it has to inform employers before they raid will enable employers to do as STC did, bringing only union-active workers in and telling company loyalists to stay home on the day of a raid.[76]

Collaboration between the INS and employers to undermine labor organizing is becoming more common and more explicit across the country. Corporations are agreeing to cooperate with INS raids in direct exchange for, or with the implicit understanding that they will be subject to, less surveillance. For example, Charles "Chick" Allen III, president of Allen Family Foods poultry producers, approached the local INS office in Baltimore about a plan to "cooperatively control" undocumented workers after two of his plants had been raided in August 1996. Allen and the INS reached an agreement that the company would no longer suffer "disruptive" INS raids and in return would allow the INS access to payroll lists, random interviews with employees, and unannounced spot checks.[77]

Allen said that the "deal amounts to textbook cooperation between government and industry."[78] Baltimore district INS director Benedict Ferro boasted that the agreement was the first of its kind between the INS and a company in an industry where "illegal employment of unauthorized workers ... has been one of our greatest enforcement challenges." Indeed, Allen Family Foods has been fined $42,000 for knowingly employing undocumented workers. The poultry industry employs a large percentage of immigrant workers because other workers refuse these arduous and low-paying jobs.[79]

Arrangements such as the INS/Allen agreement and the INS/Department of Labor MOU do not bode well for immigrant labor rights. Maria Jimenez of American Friends Service Committee has observed, "With the help of the INS, employers can police their workforce at will using the only armed force in the country specifically designed to regulate labor." Alfredo Flotte, organizer for ILWU in the Mediacopy dispute, commented, "Immigrant workers should not have to face an unholy alliance of anti-union companies and the INS every time they try to organize a union to end low pay and nasty conditions on the job."[80] Moreover, as Sasha Kokha of the NNIRR suggests, "The strategy of conducting explicit raids may be giving way to more subtle forms of collusion between employers and the INS," which may be more difficult to counter.[81]

In October 1998, the National INS Raids Task Force of the NNIRR sponsored a national week of action against immigration raids, protesting the devastating impacts on families, workers, and communities in 27 cities. The NCCIR protested outside the San Francisco INS office and carried out popular education on how INS raids shatter families, undermine worker organizing, and violate human rights. In a supreme irony, then, the myth of immigrants as terrorists who steal jobs and depress wages masks the reality that jobs are being stolen from immigrants through terrorizing INS raids and given to, indeed forced upon, other impoverished people for no wages. Low-wage workers are building awareness of how their plights are connected and how they are under attack by the same rhetoric and practices, whether they are directed against welfare workers or immigrant workers.

Amy Schur of Los Angeles's ACORN, a nationwide union of workfare workers, makes this connection explicit: "We're saying, if you're in workfare and you have no benefits, no guarantees, then you're working like illegal immigrants," says Schur. "It's a legalized system of peonage."[82] ACORN of Los Angeles has a multiracial and multilingual membership and organizing staff. It works closely with other Los Angeles–based groups, such as the Asian Pacific-American Law Alliance and AGENDA (Action for Grassroots Empowerment and Neighborhood Development Alternatives), in countering welfare "deform," fighting against workfare abuses, and ultimately working for the abolition of workfare and the creation of real, living-wage jobs.

The similar plight of immigrant workers and workfare workers in this hostile labor market and society are unmistakable. While immigrants are forced to do "3D—dirty, dangerous, and degrading" work for sub-minimum wages in large part because they are excluded from public assistance and services that they need and deserve, workfare workers are forced to do this work for free or what amounts to poverty wages because they are threatened with losing their benefits otherwise. The parallels are both ideological and practical. Both groups of workers are criminalized and pathologized as lazy and needing instruction in the work ethic and guidance to function in mainstream American life. Both groups are denied prevailing wages and rights because they are told that they are "employable," yet their labor is not work but charity, repayment of some debt, or punishment.

The Connecting Issues work group (since disbanded) emerged out of the Critical Resistance Conference on the prison industrial complex held at UC Berkeley in September 1998. The group undertook popular education and actions to draw the connections between sweatshop labor, prison labor, and workfare issues, and to link the movements against these interconnected systems of exploitation. In a meeting in San Francisco in October 1998, participants discussed the factors common to all of their movements, including the exploitation of all three types of workers in forced, low-wage, unsafe work for the profit of the same corporations, subsidized and supported by the government; the criminalization and scapegoating of workers in public opinion and media; the isolation and difficulty in reaching and organizing workers; the use of workers in union-busting; the neglect, nonetheless, of these workers by mainstream labor unions; and, finally, the use of divide-and-conquer tactics against them.

One participant, Ilana Berger, then–lead organizer for the workfare worker union POWER, observed that she encounters workers who have said that they were better off and making more doing workfare than they were in prison, illustrating the ease with which these groups of workers can be played against each other. For example, at a welfare-to-work training, when one man announced that he had gotten a security-guard job at $6 an hour, as opposed to $1 a day in prison, the trainer heartily congratulated him.[83] Ben Murdoch, a former prisoner now organizing to develop prison workers' unions, commented that the nature of coercion to do prison work is "not so much force, but the mentality that exploited work in prison for 23 cents per hour is a *privilege,* so you can buy toothpaste or send money back to your family."[84]

This is exactly the operative and prevailing ideology among the American public: that people should be grateful for the work they get under any conditions, that it is a privilege, that they are better off with it than without. The belief is that sweatshop workers are fortunate to have such high wages relative to the majority of starving workers in their home countries; that prisoners are privileged to be "allowed to" work so that they can pay for their own toiletries, health care, and library use; and that workfare workers are lucky to have the opportunity to "repay their debts" to society and "learn a trade" at the same time.

If immigrants have been cast as disposable workers, then workfare workers are at best being seen as recyclable workers, particularly if the proposed rotation system of workfare assignments is instituted. The main challenges, then, are finding ways to prevent immigrant, workfare, and unionized workers from being pitted against each other, and to give these workers a way out of being recycled in a permanent low-wage job pool.

A new contract negotiated by Hotel Employees and Restaurant Employees (HERE) Local 11 of Los Angeles in January 1998 makes positive steps in these directions. Historically, the hotel industry has been notorious for exploiting immigrant workers. Corporations such as Marriott International have captured the labor of welfare workers at tremendous profits. The new HERE contract seeks to address some of these employer tactics through a few key provisions. First, a new clause states that workfare employees are entitled to all of the rights and working conditions of the union contract. Second, union workers will not be displaced by "workfare" employees. Third, immigrant workers whose work authorization expires will have a 12-month guarantee of reinstatement with full seniority after they have corrected any immigration problems, or an additional 12 months if they are rehired for the next available opening.

James Elmendorf, community outreach director for HERE Local 11, says that many hotels quickly agreed to the clauses covering workfare employees, perhaps because most hotels were not employing large numbers of them. The union had devised this clause more as a preemptive strike against the looming threat of welfare-to-work programs. The clause protecting immigrant workers held up some hotels from signing the contract, however, because the hotels have used the intimidation of immigrants, firing or threatening to fire them, as such a powerful union-busting tactic.[85]

Resisting efforts to pit immigrant and workfare workers against each other will be particularly challenging, as we can expect to see private and state employers alike increasingly employing these tactics. A critical ingredient will be for workers to recognize this phenomenon, as POWER members joining an action against INS raids in San Francisco did on International Workers' Day, May 1, 1998. In addition, each of these groups of workers is mobilizing internally around its specific concerns and strengths. James Elmendorf says that HERE Local 11 has drawn on the strength of many members' histories as political radicals in their home countries and their courage to survive the strife and escape from these embattled regions. Local 11 is one of the most militant, predominantly immigrant unions in Los Angeles.[86]

Berger sees POWER members identifying and connecting more as workers rather than as welfare recipients, helping to overcome internalized racism and divisive identity politics.[87] Berger observes that POWER's mission to organize low- and no-wage workers is critical to a labor movement that has largely ignored the employment needs and rights of nontraditional workers. Berger remarks incisively, "As long as contingent workers or alternative workers remain unorganized, it will severely impact all workers, and we will not get at the heart of the problem in this economy."[88]

In many ways, the parallel struggles of workfare or welfare workers and immigrant workers illustrate how organized labor will need to shift to meet the needs of the growing numbers of contingent workers. POWER has not only focused on gaining recognition, rights, and protections as workers but has fought for services making permanent, living-wage jobs viable for members. For example, after a year-and-a-half-long fight, POWER forced the DHS to provide city-bus passes to workfare workers (many of whom clean those same buses) so they can travel around the city. As Steve Williams of POWER notes, this victory has far-reaching impacts for all workfare workers, allowing people with disabilities to travel to medical appointments, enabling those workers assigned to language-specific work sites (primarily Latino workers) to have greater choices of where they live, and making it possible for women workers to have access to services for themselves and their children.[89]

Immigrant and workfare workers are identified both in public policy and in popular opinion as "employable," as if this were an indictment or sentence to hard labor. Indeed, official definitions could be interpreted to define "employable" not only as capable of working but as suitable to be made or "suffered" to work. As Williams comments, the prevailing belief and practice is that you are assumed employable until proven otherwise. The burden is on the potential workers to provide proof of disability or other intervening circumstances. Berger emphasizes that, contrary to public opinion, workfare workers want to work, but demand decent, living-wage jobs. Likewise, immigrant workers seek viable work with full rights and protections, as well as recognition of the work they do. At the core, the struggle that all of these workers share is to disabuse the American public and US employers of the belief that employing them in service work resembling servitude is an act of justice or charity.

1 "INS Raid," *All Things Considered,* hosts Linda Wertheimer and Robert Siegel, National Public Radio, April 3, 1997.

2 "INS Raid," NPR, April 3, 1997.

3 "INS Raid," NPR, April 3, 1997.

4 "INS Raid," NPR, April 3, 1997.

5 Neil Demause, "Are There No Workhouses?," *In These Times* 21: 5 (January 20, 1997), p. 6.

6 Danielle Gordon, "INS Aims at Businesses, Hits Mexicans," *Chicago Reporter* 26: 4 (July/August 1997), p. 6.

7 Demause, "Are There No Workhouses?," p. 6.

8 Ezell co-authored Proposition 187. Richard Louv, "Western INS Chief Seeks Job Program for Americans," *San Diego Union Tribune,* December 8, 1995, p. A-3.

9 Louv, "INS Chief Seeks Job Program."

10 "INS Raid," NPR, April 3, 1997.

11 "INS Raid," NPR, April 3, 1997.

12 Interview with Emma Harris, May 7, 1999.

13 Interview with Steve Williams, February 1998.

14 Williams interview, February 1998.

15 Aurelio Rojas, "Lifeline or Dead-End?," *San Francisco Chronicle*, February 16, 1998, p. A-1.

16 Statement of Michael Josephers, Civil Service Commission Hearings, San Francisco, October 19, 1998.

17 Michael Josephers statement.

18 Statement of Steve Williams, Civil Service Commission Hearings, San Francisco, October 19, 1998.

19 Steve Williams statement.

20 Interview with Steve Williams, San Francisco, March 2, 1999.

21 POWER member testimony, San Francisco Department of Human Services Public Dialogue, March 7, 1998.

22 Department of Human Services, "Facts About Department of Social Services Fiscal Year 1994–95," report.

23 Steve Williams interview.

24 Louis Uchitelle, "Welfare Recipients Taking Jobs Often Held by the Working Poor," *New York Times*, April 1, 1997, p. 1.

25 Rojas, "Lifeline or Dead-End?," p. A-1.

26 Karen Carillo, "Welfare Warfare," *Third Force* 4: 6, February 28, 1997, p. 10.

27 Uchitelle, "Welfare Recipients Taking Jobs."

28 Louis Uchitelle, "Maryland Order Limits Hiring of People in Workfare Programs," *New York Times*, July 1, 1997, p. A-15.

29 Uchitelle, "Welfare Recipients Taking Jobs."

30 Mae Saulter, "A Partnership Success: JOBS and Marriott in New Orleans," *Children Today* 2: 24 (March 22, 1997), p. 31.

31 Ed Watkins, "Be Wary of Welfare-to-Work in the Hotel Industry," editorial, *Lodging Hospitality* 11: 563 (November 1997), p. 2.

32 Erin J. Aubry, "Welfare's Phantom Workers: Coalition Challenges Unfair Workfare," *LA Weekly*, February 13–19, 1998.

33 Nicholas Timmins, "Off to Work We Go: The Social Contract Has Been Rewritten," *Financial Times*, January 10, 1998, p. 1.

34 Sarah Deutsch, *No Separate Refuge: Culture, Class and Gender on an Anglo-Hispanic Frontier in the American Southwest* (New York: Oxford University Press, 1987), cited in Mary Romero, *Maid in the U.S.A.* (New York: Routledge, 1992); George Sanchez, "Go After the Women: Americanization and the Mexican Immigrant Women, 1915–1929," in Ellen Dubois and Vicki Ruiz, *Unequal Sisters* (New York: Routledge, 1990), pp. 250–63.

35 Sanchez in *Unequal Sisters,* p. 256, citing California Comission of Immigration and Housing, "Primer for Foreign-Speaking Women, Part II," Mrs. Amanda Matthews Chase (Sacramento, 1918), p. 3.

36 Sanchez in *Unequal Sisters,* 257.

37 Deutsch, *No Separate Refuge,* cited in Romero, *Maid in the U.S.A.,* p. 84.

38 Mario Garcia, "Americanization and the Mexican Immigrant," p. 72.

39 Sau-ling C. Wong, "Diverted Mothering: Representations of Caregivers of Color in the Age of 'Multiculturalism,'" in *Mothering: Ideology, Experience and Agency,* eds. Evelyn Nakano Glenn, Grace Chang, and Linda Rennie Forcey (New York: Routledge, 1994), p. 70.

40 Patrick McDonell, "Domestic Worker Given Back Pay in Rare Win," *Los Angeles Times,* June 1, 1997, p. 1.

41 Interview with Mulyono, July 28, 1997.

42 Interview with Christina Riegos, July 28, 1997.

43 *Brennan v. Partida* (492 F. 2d 709), 5th Cir., 1974. Interview with Michelle Yu, Los Angeles, California, July 1997.

44 Plaintiff's Trial Brief, *Yuni Mulyono, Plaintiff, v. Lina Nilam, et al., Defendants,* Superior Court of the State of California for the County of Los Angeles (Case No. TC 008 897), May 19, 1997, p. 7.

45 Declaration of John T. Affeldt.

46 Reporter's partial transcript, *Yuni Mulyono, Plaintiff, v. Lina Nilam et al., Defendants,* Superior Court of the State of California for the County of Los Angeles, p. 6; Judge Morgan cited the case *Patel v. Quality Inn South* (846 F. 2d 700), 11th Cir., 1988, which established that undocumented workers are entitled to recover wages under the Fair Labor Standards Act (FLSA) for work done. Legal precedent regarding the employment rights of undocumented workers has been articulated in key cases such as *Patel* and *Sure-Tan v. National Labor Relations Board* (467 U.S. 883), 1984, which established that undocumented workers are covered by the National Labor Relations Act (NLRA). My aim in this book is to present the realities that immigrant workers face in their struggles for human and worker rights, rather than the legal precedent informing these struggles, because too often there is no connection between the two. For a good review of some of these cases, see William R. Tamayo with Maria L. Blanco, "The Effects of Immigration Status on Employment Litigation," presented at the National Employment Lawyers Association Convention, June 1996; available from the U.S. Equal Employment Opportunity Commission, 415-356-5100.

47   Reporter's partial transcript, *Mulyono v. Nilam* et al.

48   Mulyono interview.

49   Romero, *Maid in the U.S.A.*, p. 163.

50   Rosanna Hertz, *More Equal Than Others: Women and Men in Dual-Career Marriages* (Berkeley, CA: University of California Press, 1986), p. 183.

51   Casey McKeever and Maurice Emsellem, "California's Failure to Apply the Minimum Wage to CalWORKs Work Activities," Western Center on Law and Poverty, National Employment Law Project, April 1998; letter from John Fraser, US Department of Labor, to chairwoman Dion Louise Aroner, State Assembly Committee on Human Services, regarding California Draft policy on welfare-to-work activities and the Fair Labor Standards Act, March 30, 1998.

52   CDSS All-County Letter No. 98-32, May 7, 1998.

53   Interviews with Muneer I. Ahmad, staff attorney, Asian Pacific American Legal Center, Los Angeles, May 7, 1998, and Amy Schur, Association of Community Organizations for Reform Now of Los Angeles, April 14, 1998; for more information, contact Muneer I. Ahmad at APALC, 1010 South Flower Street, Suite 302, Los Angeles, CA 90015, 213-748-2022; or Amy Schur at ACORN, 1010 South Flower Street, Suite 215, Los Angeles, CA 90015, 213-747-4211.

54   Lawrence Mishel and John Schmitt, "Cutting Wages by Cutting Welfare: The Impact of Reform on the Low-Wage Labor Market," briefing paper, Economic Policy Institute, September 1995, p. 2.

55   Mishel and Schmitt, "Cutting Wages," p. 2.

56   Uchitelle, "Welfare Recipients Taking Jobs."

57   Uchitelle, "Welfare Recipients Taking Jobs." Another study, done by the Preamble Center for Public Policy, documents the scarcity of jobs, and particularly living-wage jobs, which will only be exacerbated by welfare "reform" policies that do not provide for the viable creation of new jobs. Mark Weisbrot, "Welfare Reform: The Jobs Aren't There," Preamble Center for Public Policy, December 10, 1997.

58   Workshop on the prison industrial complex and unemployment, Critical Resistance Conference, UC Berkeley, September 27, 1998.

59   "INS Agents Arrest Seven in San Francisco," press release, United States Department of Justice, Immigration and Naturalization Service, San Francisco District Office, March 19, 1998.

60   "INS Agents Arrest Seven in San Francisco," INS press release.

61   "INS Arrests 10 Working Illegally for Napa Stone Products Manufacturer," press release, United States Department of Justice, Immigration and Naturalization Service, San Francisco District Office, January 12, 1998.

62   National INS Raid Task Force of the National Network for Immigrant and Refugee Rights (NNIRR), *Portrait of Injustice: The Impact of Immigration Raids on Families, Workers, and Communities,* October 1998, p. 15; available through the NNIRR at 510-465-1984 or nnirr@igc.apc.org.

63   In August 1997, then-governor Wilson signed the California Work Opportunity and Responsibility to Kids Act (CalWORKs), establishing CalWORKs as California's TANF block-grant program. Under this law, participants are restricted to a lifetime five-year limit for receipt of aid, beginning January 1, 1998. Adult recipients must engage in "work activities" and find work within 18 months of enrolling in the program if they are new applicants or within 24 months of signing the "welfare-to-work" contracts if they are current welfare recipients. Equal Rights Advocates, "From War on Poverty to War on Welfare: The Impact of Welfare Reform on the Lives of Immigrant Women," April 1999, p. 3.

64   "Workers Say Firm Aided Big INS Bust," *San Francisco Chronicle,* January 18, 1997.

65   NNIRR, *Portrait of Injustice,* p. 34.

66   "Workers Say Firm Aided Big INS Bust."

67   NNIRR, *Portrait of Injustice,* pp. 34–35.

68   INS Revised Operations Instruction 287.3a, cited in NNIRR, *Portrait of Injustice,* p. 60.

69   Interview with Muzaffar Chishti, co-counsel for Montero, Attorney, Union of Needletrades, Industrial, and Textile Employees (UNITE!) Immigration Project, June 3, 1998.

70   *Gloria Esperanza Montero v. Immigration and Naturalization Service,* U.S. Court of Appeals, 2nd Cir., August 28, 1997.

71   Muzaffar Chishti interview.

72   *Montero v. INS,* 1997.

73   *Montero v. INS,* 1997.

74   Muzaffar Chishti interview.

75   A new Memorandum of Understanding (MOU) between the Department of Labor's Employment Standards Administration (ESA) and the Immigration and Naturalization Service (INS) was established on November 23, 1998, with the goals of clarifying the roles of the two agencies and allaying fears that might prevent immigrant workers from filing complaints against employers. NNIRR issued a statement recognizing this effort but calling for outreach and public education on the new MOU's repercussions. Contact NNIRR for more information: 510-465-1984 or nnirr@igc.apc.org.

76   Statement by Mike Wishnie in the Enforcement in the Workplace workshop, at the Challenge for Human Rights: Confronting Immigration Law

Enforcement Today. Conference organized by NNIRR and the National Employment Law Project (NELP), June 5–7, 1998, Los Angeles.

77 Lena Sun and Peter Goodman, "Poultry Firm to Help INS Monitor Workers," *Washington Post*, October 23, 1998, p. A-18.

78 Sun and Goodman, "Poultry Firm to Help INS."

79 Sun and Goodman, "Poultry Firm to Help INS."

80 NNIRR, *Portrait of Injustice,* p. 33.

81 Personal communication with Sasha Kokha, Oakland, California, May 1999.

82 Aubry, "Welfare's Phantom Workers."

83 Statement by Ilana Berger in the PIC and Unemployment workshop, Critical Resistance Conference, UC Berkeley, September 25–27, 1998.

84 Statement by Ben Murdoch in Prisons: The New Slavery workshop, Critical Resistance Conference, 1998.

85 Interview with James Elmendorf, February 1998.

86 Interview with James Elmendorf, February 1998.

87 Berger statement, Critical Resistance Conference.

88 Interview with Ilana Berger, March 16, 1999.

89 Interview with Steve Williams, March 22, 1999.

Artwork from *Super Domestica: En: El Caso de las Trabajadoras Explotadas* (Los Angeles: CHIRLA) by Kelvin Manzanares. See page 203.

Gatekeeping
and Housekeeping

It is the weekend before the elections, and immigration, the source of much national angst in years past has disappeared from the election debate.... [T]here seems to be a growing consensus among lawmakers that too much control of immigration is not good—for politicians, who recognize that immigrants' votes could be pivotal in some races; for business and the economy, because valued employees have had to return home ... or even for the government itself, since control is expensive and time consuming.

—"Once Divisive, Immigration Is a Muted Issue,"
New York Times, November 1, 1998[1]

Reports of the death of the immigration issue are greatly exaggerated. The very visible signs of the US government, employers, and, more frequently than ever before, common citizens waging war on immigrants on every front—ideological and physical—are daunting. At the US-Mexico border, we see some of the most "advanced" technologies, paralleling only those in the finance industries and the military, used for the surveillance and apprehension of immigrants. Apparently, the technology has rendered some Border Patrol agents "bored" because their jobs entail that they "sit on an X" every quarter mile to survey the border. Some agents, who refer to themselves as "human scarecrows," are paid an average yearly salary of $34,000 plus overtime for this work.[2]

Even more frightening is the growing phenomenon of citizen vigilante groups such as Concerned Citizens of Cochise County (CCCC) in Arizona, which has lobbied with government officials to control the "slow-motion invasion" of illegal immigrants. In April 1999, the CCCC asked Arizona Governor Jane Hull to send the Arizona Army National Guard to defend the border in the area. One member personally took it upon himself to detain 27 "illegals" on his ranch while he called the US Border Patrol. The threats, if not gunshots, are flying all over the county. One ranch owner who patrols his 22,000-acre property with a group of friends, all armed, said, "If this was any other country besides the United States, they'd have troops on the line and there'd be bloodshed." Larry Vance, cochair of the CCCC, keeps a pistol handy on his coffee table and climbs a 30-foot-tall tower in his backyard each night to look for "two-legged coyotes that are illegal to shoot." Vance's father said, "It's time for US leaders to tell their southern neighbor, 'Either you do something about it, or we're going to.' "[3]

Why is it that when we hear people making comments of this sort, threatening to take the law into their own hands, it is always members of this type of vigilante group, looking to round up "illegals" like animals? It is never a group of "concerned citizens" hoping to pressure lawmakers to reform its foreign policy and trade agreements or crack down on exploitative employers, or trailblazers who want to take it upon themselves personally to pay their household workers a decent wage. As I have already argued, professional women must take a stand for household workers' rights and be prepared to dig deep into their households' pockets to support this in practice.

Recently, I came across an appalling syndicated "women's column" in which a freelance writer lamented her trials and tribulations in "keeping good household help."

> I've had dozens of cleaning ladies and one cleaning gentleman. Alas, all of them eventually left. As anyone who's ever done it knows, housework can be mind numbing. Why scrub and sweep when it's only going to get dirty again? There's a high burnout rate

because cleaning people tend to feel that no matter what they charge, they are underpaid, undervalued and overworked. Unless they are highly self-motivated or love the smell of ammonia in the morning, they often find employment in another field.[4]

This exercise in narcissism is offered for entertainment purposes, we are to believe, or perhaps to garner sympathies from fellow employers of overpaid, overvalued, and underworked "household help," which the author urges us to send her via e-mail at among_friends@ hotmail.com.[5] We can only hope that her mailbox will be flooded with household-worker sympathizers directing her to wake up and smell the ammonia herself. The CCCC members and the "women's" columnist probably share little else but a profound ignorance and a fierce grip on what they perceive to be threatened: property, in the case of the former, and privilege, in the case of the latter—two good old American values. These form the core of what immigrant women workers face in the struggles for their rights. I offer these two news items as examples to remind us that there are developments each day posing new challenges or revisiting age-old obstacles for immigrant women workers and their families. Having said that, let me present some significant victories for immigrant women workers, while tempering this information with enduring challenges to this progress.

In the introduction to *Alien Nation,* Peter Brimelow presents a summary of his assertions. He writes:

> In this book, I show that the immigration resulting from current public policy
>
> 1. is dramatically larger, less skilled and more divergent from the American majority than anything that was anticipated or desired
> 2. is probably not beneficial economically—and is certainly not necessary
> 3. is attended by a wide and increasing range of negative consequences, from the physical environment to the political
> 4. is bringing about an ethnic and racial transformation in America without precedent in the history of the world—an aston-

ishing social experiment launched with no particular reason to expect success.[6]

On the contrary, in this book, I have shown how immigration and welfare policies are fashioned and implemented such that the resulting immigration is exactly as "anticipated" and "desired," creating a reserve of those lacking the resources or alternatives to do anything but accept low-wage employment without rights or protections. Second, I have examined how this labor immigration is, indeed, extremely "beneficial economically" and otherwise to the state, to corporations, and to individual household employers, and, in fact, critical to the functioning of transnational capital. Third, we have seen how immigrants have been used as scapegoats for the environmental and political "negative consequences" imagined to be their creation but which are in reality caused by their employers. Finally, in this chapter, I will present some of the social transformations brought about by efforts to attack and exploit immigrants and people of color through initiatives such as Proposition 187. In some cases, the impacts were more devastating than anticipated, and in others more positive than the likes of Peter Brimelow and Pete Wilson could ever have intended.

Even in the face of one anti-immigrant measure after another, including California's Propositions 187, 209 (which dismantled affirmative action), and 227 (which ended bilingual education in the public schools), immigrants persevere and do indeed organize themselves. As Lucia Hwang observes, "[U]nions in the [San Francisco] Bay area are finally courting immigrant workers" because they are the fastest-growing segment of the state's workforce and will outnumber native-born workers by the year 2000.[7] Luisa Blue, organizing director for SEIU (Service Employees International Union) Local 790, adds that with only 13 percent of the country's workforce unionized presently, unions will have to recruit 300,000 new members each year just to maintain their present representation. Moreover, there is growing recognition that unions cannot expect to just absorb immigrant workers into their ranks but must respond to the particular needs of these workers. As one organizer who pulled together a soccer league to reach and organize Latino roofers said, "We're in new times, which calls for a new way of thinking and a new union culture."[8]

In the last decade, mainstream organized labor has begun to understand the potential power of immigrant women and women-of-color low-wage workers in particular, and it has been testing a strategy to target these groups to reinforce waning membership. On February 25, 1999, Los Angeles County's home-care workers' union, SEIU Local 434B, saw this effort pay off, winning the largest union election in modern US history. The workers voted almost ten to one to join SEIU, expanding the membership by 74,000 workers, which surpasses even the 1941 vote by Ford's River Rouge plant workers to join the United Auto Workers.[9]

David Rolf, then–deputy general manager of Local 434B and a leading force behind the election's success, says that the victory came 12 years after SEIU began organizing workers in Los Angeles. That was when the union realized its first battle was to identify an official employer with whom the workers could engage in collective bargaining. After winning the creation of the public authority in Los Angeles County in 1997, the union began a massive organizing drive. This involved phone banks, direct mail, precinct walks, and canvassing, with organizers knocking on the doors of 30,000 workers between March and November 1998 to get cards signed petitioning for the election.

SEIU President Andy Stern said that the election symbolized the beginning of giving the "labor movement a face that's the face of today's work force.... If this labor movement is going to see a resurgence it will bring in the hundreds of thousands of women and immigrant service sector workers who were left behind after the great industrial organization."[10] Stern's comment, portraying immigrant women and women of color as neglected or "left behind," strikes me as somewhat patronizing, underestimating these women as a new force for organized labor to contend with, not just to incorporate. In contrast, Rolf clearly recognized at the outset the work that would be necessary to reach and organize this force as "the backbone of the new, low-wage service sector economy."[11]

While the victory for Local 434B is indeed a landmark and great cause for celebration, other developments present reminders that these hard-won gains are in constant threat of attack from employers, politicians, and others seeking to exploit low-wage workers. In one particularly alarming case, the United Domestic Workers (UDW), an affiliate group of the American Federation of State, County, and Municipal Employees (AFSCME), lobbied in 1998 to use state welfare-to-work program funds to train and employ welfare recipients as home-care workers. California state senators Peace and Alpert took up the idea and introduced a bill to establish a three- to five-year pilot project in seven California counties to screen and train CalWORKs recipients to work as in-home support-service (IHSS) providers or home-care workers.[12] The text of the bill states:

> Under welfare reform, an expected 500,000 adults receiving CalWORKs cash aid will have to find jobs in the next five years. In many parts of the state, recipient advocates and county officials are concerned about the ability of the job market to absorb all these individuals. To assist in moving CalWORKs recipients to work, counties receive funding allocations that they can use for a variety of training and support services.[13]

Ostensibly, one goal of the measure is to increase the wages of all IHSS providers (home-care workers), but when you read the fine print, you see that the proposed raise is 50 cents per hour, in contrast to the union's and several California cities' much higher goals of living wages. Furthermore, the bill text reveals that 13 counties have contracts with private agencies to provide IHSS workers to clients and that these contractors' employees are not paid the wages governed by state IHSS law but determined by individual contractors or the employees' union. Not surprisingly, UDW represents agency employees in most of these 13 counties, and thus stands to benefit from such a pilot program. This bill alerts us to how readily the state, employers, and, in this case, a body that claims to be a labor organization will jump at the opportunity to capture federal and state money at the expense of disenfranchised workers under the guise of "welfare reform" and even worker advocacy.

Such proposals immediately conjure images of INS raids and deportations of immigrant home-care workers, allegedly engineered to make room for the 500,000 CalWORKs recipients who will need to find jobs that have not been created. Thus, welfare workers will once again be pitted against low-wage immigrant workers who predominate in the home-care industry. Moreover, these welfare workers will be presumed to be qualified to care for other poor people who are elderly and/or disabled and cannot find other "affordable" care except courtesy of Uncle Sam's exploitation of alleged "welfare queens."

In *When Work Disappears,* sociologist William Julius Wilson blames demagogues for creating or exacerbating racial divisions:

> In a time of heightened economic insecurities, the poisonous racial rhetoric of certain highly visible spokespersons has increased racial tensions and channeled frustrations in ways that severely divide the racial groups. During hard economic times, people become more receptive to simplistic ideological messages that deflect attention away from the real and complex source of their problems. Instead of associating their problems with economic and political changes, these divisive messages encourage them to turn on each other—race against race.[14]

I suggest that it is not so much the demagogues but employers and politicians who employ a multiplicity of tactics to divide worker against worker, exploiting the American public's receptiveness to simplistic rhetoric and "solutions" to deflect attention away from the true problems, their causes, and their perpetuation. When subjected to this rhetoric and these tactics, people will indeed turn on each other, race against race, in many instances. We see ample evidence of employers and politicians trying to achieve just this goal, but often meeting with resistance.

For example, at the Oaks Club in Emeryville, California, manager and owner Bryan Cadhina attempted to pit different ethnic groups against each other by stepping up enforcement of an English-only rule just as the Hotel Employees and Restaurant Employees Union (HERE) Local 2850 was negotiating a contract with his workers. In a series of actions in the spring of 1998, more than 80 union members and supporters from several community organizations protested the policy, chanting *"Escucha, escucha! Estamos en la lucha!"* ("Listen ! Listen! We are in the struggle!") and "Talking union is our right! We are HERE and ready to fight!" By April 1999, after a yearlong fight the union succeeded in pressuring management to withdraw the English-only policy from the union contract proposal.

Wei-ling Huber, lead organizer for the campaign at Oaks, said that management was particularly persistent in this case, while in other cases she has seen employers who try to institute English-only policies eventually give up. In many cases, it is impractical to enforce the policy when the staff is predominantly non-English-speaking or has limited English proficiency and even the supervisors are bilingual. In this case, Huber explained, the policy had already existed for almost two years, but employers began enforcing it more vigorously because they believed that it would be an effective way to divide the workers. They believed that they could exploit the typical divisions between "front of the house" and "back of the house" workers. Tensions between waitstaff and cooks are common, and at Oaks the "front" waitstaff was approximately one-third Chinese and over one-third Eritrean with a few Latinos, while the "back" kitchen staff was all Chinese.

Management thought it could exacerbate these existing tensions by interjecting a racial dimension to the conflict through the English-only issue, but the strategy backfired. As Huber said, it actually united the workers "around the principle that the union should not give employers more ways to mess with us." Management buckled when it saw that every racial and ethnic group of workers participated at the actions, along with a strong showing from the Asian-American community, including customers, the Asian press, and labor, civil, and immigrants' rights groups.[15]

Legal precedent on the English-only issue currently is based on *Garcia v. Spun Steak Co.,* in which the court allowed the employers' English-only rule on the premise that it did not impose hardship or create an atmosphere of hostility or intimidation for one group based on their national origin. Ironically, the employer's stated rationale for the English-only policy in the *Garcia* case was two-fold: to promote racial harmony among the workers and thereby to increase productivity. The actual uses of English-only policies in the workplace belie this rationale so commonly used by employers. At the Oaks Club, while the employer did indeed increase productivity and profit by capitalizing on the staff's Asian-language skills to serve the Asian clientele, the employer's attempts to promote racial conflict through this policy were readily transparent.

In *Alien Nation,* Peter Brimelow devotes two entire chapters to the alleged negative economic consequences of immigration, attempting to deliver the "simplistic ideological message" (to borrow from William Julius Wilson) that immigration is bad for black Americans. Brimelow laments the plight of blacks who predominated in domestic work in New York in the 1830s before being almost entirely supplanted by Irish immigrants 20 years later. Brimelow goes on to mourn blacks' loss of skilled jobs in the steel, logging, and lumber industries to immigrants, and posits that "immigration from Europe after the Civil War is often said to have fatally retarded the economic integration of the freed slaves."[16] He concludes that the steady growth of black unemployment rates is undoubtedly related to the "opening of the immigration floodgates ... which is why it is to current policy, and not to critics of immigration, that the charge of 'racism' might best be applied."[17]

Thus, it is out of a profound sense of concern for his African-American fellow citizens and lust for racial justice that Brimelow opposes immigration. For the same reasons, he would probably support the recent initiatives to arrest and deport undocumented workers and replace them with "American" workers. Never mind that these programs, like the 1995 experiment in Dallas, Operation Jobs, did not accomplish anything beyond securing the cooperation of employers in trapping undocumented workers in secured rooms to facilitate their arrests. Employers were promised replacement workers from "linkage agencies," such as the Salvation Army and Dallas Police Department, which were to supply applicants from among welfare recipients, ex-offenders, and refugees. A 1997 study by the University of Texas at Austin's Department of Government and the

Tomas Rivera Institute showed that these linkage agencies provided only about 200 replacement workers for the 1,515 undocumented workers removed. One hundred sixty of these went to one single employer.[18] The program's poor performance in supplying "American" workers exposes the faulty premise of such initiatives: that undocumented workers "steal" these low-paying, arduous, hazardous jobs that other workers would choose if only they had the chance to compete with greedy, backstabbing immigrants for them. While INS Commissioner Doris Meissner would like to institute programs modeled after the Operation Jobs and Virginia's Jobs for Virginia's Workers programs across the nation to "free up jobs and wages for America's legal workers," I suggest that it is America's so-called illegal workers who are in need of freedom, not the jobs.

Immigrant workers, workers of color, and all low-wage workers will have to form alliances and formulate integrated organizing strategies to counter these employer and government tactics, which are becoming ever more sophisticated, covert, and coordinated. This will entail dialogue and cooperation among the low-wage, contingent workers who have been pitted against each other at every turn. Such alliances have been growing, for example, around the proposed living-wage ordinance in San Francisco, which would require companies contracting with San Francisco to pay workers at a "living wage," instead of the federal minimum of $5.15 an hour. Representatives from traditional labor unions, alternative worker associations, immigrants' rights groups, welfare rights groups, and nonprofit organizations spoke at hearings on the ordinance before two members of the San Francisco Board of Supervisors in the spring of 1999.

One Salvadoran man who works at a rental-car agency at the San Francisco airport spoke about the hardships he and his family have endured since coming to this country, living on wages of $3.65 to $5.77 an hour:

> I am sad because I am working so hard and my kids are missing me and asking why are you working so hard and we still have such a hard time.… It is hard to be a parent, raise a family—we should be able to do it without working two jobs.… My company has a

slogan: "We try harder." This company tries harder to make sure that they squeeze every drop out of us so we suffer as much as possible.[19]

A young boy, Jonathan Perez, whose parents both work as janitors, also testified: "My mom has to live with friends and my dad in a one-bedroom apartment. When I go to school, I'm thinking, how is my mom? I haven't seen her in a week. She says she is working all the time."[20] Similarly, a woman from *Mujeres Unidas y Activas* (MUA) of San Francisco said:

> A lot of us provide care to elderly people, work more than 40 hours a week and in many cases, after rent, we only have two or three hundred dollars to pay for food, clothing, and other needs for our kids. Today I had to leave work to testify and that meant that my kids will go with less. I would like the living wage to pass so I could at least have one full day to spend with them.[21]

What each of these testimonies shares is the hope and struggle to sustain families, not just to survive as super-exploited workers. Ultimately, this may be what will join immigrant workers, welfare workers, and other contingent workers together.

As Steve Williams of People Organized to Win Employment Rights (POWER) said, "The Living Wage Coalition is striving to cover as broad a base of workers as possible in San Francisco. In Los Angeles and Oakland, it has been very limited, but here we have made a big push to protect as many low-wage workers as possible, and we are seeing a real budding movement across many sectors of low- and no-wage workers." POWER has fought to make sure that both CalWORKs and General Assistance (GA) workfare workers will be covered under the living-wage ordinance if it passes.[22] In May 1999, POWER had its first meetings with CalWORKs's welfare-to-work participants who are facing the end of the time limits to fulfill work requirements. Efforts to reach and include these workers, many of whom are women with children, have posed new challenges for the organizing team at POWER, including having to make provisions for child care and translation at meetings. As groups like POWER strive to organize alternative workers, new organizing methods will have to be created to address the specific needs and concerns and encompass the strengths of immigrant women and women-of-color service workers.

The work of two groups of domestic workers, MUA in San Francisco and the Domestic Workers Association (DWA) of CHIRLA (Coalition for Humane Immigrant Rights of Los Angeles), both primarily Latina in membership, offers some good models for nontraditional labor and community organizing among immigrant women and women of color. Sociologist Pierrette Hondagneu-Sotelo and the late Cristina Riegos, then–director of the DWA of CHIRLA, observed that while the structure of domestic work poses certain obstacles to organizing, these can be addressed through new tactics that draw on the strength of women's connections around gender as well as around worker occupation identity. For example, it is not practical to ask individual members to risk their jobs when the workers do not share a common employer. Taking legal action against a current employer can be too costly and risky. Thus, DWA members focus on "expressive or cultural events, with self-help seminars and consciousness-raising" around common issues they face, such as negotiating hours, wages, and conditions in a contract with employers and sexual harassment on the job.[23]

Members of DWA see all of the women in the group as leaders, rather than selecting individual spokeswomen, and rely on all members to do outreach in their daily lives and within their direct communities. This approach is critical, given that workers do not gather at one work site. Moreover, it is highly effective, as demonstrated by one woman, who insisted *"no tengo mucha que ver con la política"* ("I don't have much to do with politics"), yet could mobilize 100 people for a community meeting or event on short notice.[24] As one member and organizer of DWA, Libertad Rivera, put it: "I do not want to be held up [as a leader]. If I fall, I hope that they [the other members] can catch me. I want the liberty to cry also."[25]

At a conference in Los Angeles in June 1998 on developing strategies to fight against immigration "law enforcement" abuses, several members of DWA and MUA testified in a workshop, "Organizing the Undocumented."[26] Rivera, who also organizes single mothers from Posada, reported on the struggles shared by DWA members:

> For years we have not been respected by employers, by our fami-
> lies, our husbands and children.... We educate people to tell em-
> ployers that they don't need to know whether you are
> undocumented or not. Once an employer asked me if I had pa-
> pers. I said, "All I know is I am human. What about you?" We try
> to let employers know that we are also mothers, we also have
> families. Some employers try to pretend that we don't have a life
> outside of working for them.[27]

DWA produced a comic book, *Super Domestica en: El Caso de las
Trabajadoras Explotadas,* depicting the story of Veronica, a domestic
worker asked by her employer to stay late at the last minute to assist
with a dinner party.[28] When Veronica explains that her children are
waiting for her and that she must attend to her family, her "patrona"
threatens that many people would like her job. This scenario appealed to many domestic workers facing this and similar problems
with abusive employers, and the comic book offered strategies to
negotiate with employers toward resolution. As Rivera said, "I may
be working for a lawyer, but I am still a professional, teaching your
children. Besides, there are more of us [domestic workers] than abusive politicians."[29]

Rosa Montana from MUA also spoke of her organization's work
to counter the ongoing attacks on immigrants and their families,
such as phone banking to reach voters on issues like Proposition
227, the antibilingual education initiative, or engaging in popular education on what to do when an INS raid occurs. Montana addressed
the particular challenges they face in organizing as women, mothers,
partners, and community members:

> We dance, we cry, we laugh. What we are doing is raising aware-
> ness in our communities. We also learn how to fight and to
> change our family lifestyle, [which] is very critical.... Our hus-
> bands don't want us to do our political work. We also have the-
> ater, and through theater we inform our communities.[30]

Another member of MUA added that her organization uses
self-esteem-building workshops and leadership trainings to develop

ways to deal with husbands who are unsupportive of their political activity and to "counter machismo among our sons and husbands, because we definitely need support from them and from the community."[31] Another member explained that almost everyone in the group has children, so they always provide child care for meetings and actions: "One goal is that the children should not have to go work, so we have a system of rotation, have licensed care providers and also a member of MUA doing child care." On the other hand, one member spoke to the importance of doing their political work around their children: "Our own children understand a lot about issues from watching us doing theater, doing outreach. We are models. They are learning from us."[32]

The recent success of the home-care workers' union election also offers important ideas to consider in organizing immigrant women workers, particularly those in care work. David Rolf said that during the campaign planning in 1998, the union polled approximately 400 workers and found that certain patterns seemed to emerge along the lines of gender, racial/ethnic, and immigration status. Members of one group, called the "pro-union" group, identified strongly as workers and believed that the solution to their problems was collective action. Those who fell into this group were largely African-American workers and included fewer workers who were providers for their own family members. Members of another group, the "proworker" group, also saw themselves as workers but did not believe in collective action. Members of a third group, the "proclient" group, were most concerned with the question, "Will this be good for the clients?" When they framed the issues in terms of how they would enhance the quality of care for the clients, support for the union increased dramatically within this group, which was predominantly composed of Latina immigrants.[33]

Thus, Rolf designed the campaign highlighting three priorities: a living wage, health benefits for workers, and improved quality of care for clients. Rolf says that emphasizing quality of care even helped to overcome the ambivalence about unions among some immigrants who had experienced unions in their home countries to be arms of the ruling party or government. The quality-of-care focus also garnered the support of the senior and disabled communities, which had been critical allies in the struggles for the Public Authority as well.

But workers' concern for clients proved to be a double-edged sword, challenging as well as boosting organizing efforts. Rolf says that among Asian immigrant workers, particularly those caring for their own family members, the tendency not to identify as workers was very high. One Korean woman expressed her belief that her IHSS paycheck was like a welfare check. She felt that being paid to take care of not only her own parents but other people's parents was "a scam." Similarly, in the initial polling groups, Armenian immigrants did not usually identify as IHSS or home-care workers until pressed. One Armenian woman said, "Aren't the streets paved with gold here? I was taking care of my mother in Yerevan and wasn't getting paid." In contrast, Rolf says, Latina workers held the quality-of-care ethic strongly but still could "talk like a worker, not a saint, and care about Mom and Dad but also be angry about low wages."[34]

Without jumping to any sweeping conclusions about race/ethnicity and correlations with worker identity, Rolf utilized these survey results to plan a highly effective strategy for organizing home-care workers around different concerns that appealed to them. Beyond this, what we can learn from the statements by these two immigrant women is that the rhetoric presenting work as charity, so often used by statespeople and employers these days, is potentially very threatening. While in the case of these women, this rhetoric may have only been consistent with their attitudes as women caring for their own family members, the danger is that it may carry wide appeal to immigrant women transplanted from societies where women, whether individually or collectively, do care for their children and elders to a society where privileged people, whether men or women, by and large do not.

I encountered other, more explicit demonstrations of how effective the racist, anti-immigrant media messages have been within communities of color and immigrant communities. I interviewed one woman, Patricia Tejada, who had fled El Salvador in the late 1980s without her husband or children and worked for four years as a domestic worker to save enough money to bring her family into the country. She now does child care during the week, housecleaning on weekends, and "occasional baby-sitting" on weeknights. Her son attends high school and her daughter works as a waitress while taking vocational classes in computers. When I asked Tejada if she had ever had any experience with government agencies, receiving benefits or social services, she responded that she felt proud that she had never had to ask for welfare, preferring to work harder instead. Still, she said that she wished she could talk to the president and tell him to "walk in our shoes."[35]

I interviewed Tejada's friend, also a refugee from El Salvador working in child care and housecleaning, and she responded similarly. When I asked the two women, "I know that you do not want to receive benefits yourself, but what do you think about Proposition 187? Is it okay for people to receive benefits if they need them?" they responded with some compassion but also scorn reflecting their exposure to the dominant media images of immigrants as welfare abusers. One said, "It might be better if those who needed it—for one family, they could receive three years, because now a lot of people are using it for 15 years." When her friend responded, "There are exceptions, like people who are older or sick, children's medicine," she added, "Yes, and prenatal." Suddenly her son interjected, "It's like you say here in your article," pointing to a magazine article I had brought with a political cartoon depicting a pregnant woman carrying an American flag while floating in an inner tube featuring the words "US or bust." When I explained that the article and cartoon were trying to expose what the government and media want to make us believe, he insisted: "When we were coming over, I saw lots of pregnant women coming over to have babies and get welfare right away. I see it on Spanish TV also ... you know, especially the Mexicans." I suggested that maybe this was because the media chose to focus on those cases, but he did not seem convinced. His 20-year-old sister, who had helped to translate during the interview, added: "Yes. They always show the bad things."[36]

Much like the views expressed by the immigrant and refugee women I interviewed prior to the introduction of Proposition 187 (see chapter 1), these statements are disturbing, as they reflect the broad power of the media and politicians in spreading their racist, sexist, nativist messages to people of color and others who might otherwise ally themselves with or have some empathy for the immigrants' rights movement. This is not to argue that these people are deluded and self-hating or need to be politicized around feminist and immigrants' rights issues, but to observe that these ideologies—for example, the rhetoric of work as charity and of immigrants as "welfare queens"—are so strong and so prevalent in US society that many people of color and immigrants fall prey to them as well. Ultimately, it reflects that the effect of these policies and media images is not only to produce workers who are more easily exploitable but to reproduce the racist, sexist, classist, imperialist ideologies upon which this exploitation is founded. In other words, these legislative and ideological attacks serve not only to capture immigrant workers as super-exploitable service workers but to recruit immigrants, refugees, and people of color as gatekeepers.

This raises a broader question of how immigrants can most effectively fight against the continuing onslaught of anti-immigrant media images and legislation. Immigrants and allies will have to work on many levels to challenge exploitative employer and government tactics and the oppressive ideologies that lie at their core and fuel their success. For example, even opponents of Proposition 187 did a disservice to immigrant workers by continuing to frame the debate much as the measure's proponents did, in terms of resources. Rather than expanding the debate to advocate the rights of immigrant workers, opponents often brought the cost-benefit approach to a level that would appeal directly to the self-interests of individual "citizens."

For example, the primary strategy used to oppose the initiative was to highlight the administrative costs that would be involved in implementing the law. Opponents also emphasized that California would lose $15 billion in federal funding if the law passed because its provisions would violate federal privacy law. In all of these discussions, the point that such a law would violate human and civil rights, at great costs to the dignity and safety of undocumented adults and children, was secondary to the point that California "taxpayers" (read: citizens) would suffer from the loss of federal funds. Another common approach of opponents of Proposition 187 was to emphasize the cost-efficiency of providing preventive health care through immunizations and prenatal care, thus perpetuating the disregard for the health of immigrants in favor of concern for their alleged "costs" or, as the case may be, "savings" to society.

Opponents also framed the argument against denying immigrants health care in expedient terms, suggesting that this denial would threaten public health—but not general public health, just that of "consumers." One pamphlet distributed by the group Taxpayers Against 187 said, "Denying basic medical attention and immunizations to millions of people, many of whom handle our food supply every day, would spread costly and preventable, communicable diseases throughout California."[37] This line of reasoning is particularly perverse, since it recognizes that undocumented immigrants provide labor in food preparation and service, yet in the same breath voices more concern for the health of those being served than for the servers handling "our" food. While it vaguely acknowledges the contribution of immigrants' labor, it dismisses wholesale these immigrants' worker or human rights.

Finally, some opponents of Proposition 187 advanced a particularly unfortunate argument, suggesting that illegal immigration is indeed a problem, but that this initiative would not provide the solution. Such rhetoric only served to pit the undocumented against documented immigrants and to divide the immigrants' rights community. Moreover, it obscured how US lawmakers and employers actively invite and support what they then choose to call and condemn as "illegal immigration."

On July 30, 1999, the *Oakland Tribune* reported: "Proposition 187, the controversial 1994 ballot measure that denied social services to California's undocumented immigrants, essentially died Thursday." Some might even say that the measure died quietly, as the ending to this five-year battle over Proposition 187 was almost anticlimactic, receiving very little media coverage. The *Oakland Tribune* reported dismissively that the measure had never been implemented, as if this meant that it had never had an impact. Immigrants and the immigrant rights community know better. In a 1995 report, *Hate Unleashed,* CHIRLA assembled and analyzed 229 stories shared by callers to the CHIRLA hotline. These included cases of discrimination, denial of services, civil-rights violations, hate speech, and hate crimes related to Proposition 187. All of the calls were recorded on intake forms, referred to attorneys, and verified in follow-up interviews.[38]

The general findings of the CHIRLA study were what many had anticipated Proposition 187 would bring:

- Discrimination in businesses against Latinos escalated after 187 passed. Latinos have been sent to the back of the bus, insulted at business establishments, and interrogated about their rights to live and work in their own neighborhoods.
- Hate speech and crimes against Latinos increased by 23.5 percent in 1994, according to the Los Angeles County Human Relations Commission.
- Abuse and discrimination by law enforcement officials against Latinos has increased, including police subjecting Latinos to unreasonable searches, insulting them with racial slurs, and demanding immigration papers without cause.
- More than 60 percent of the cases of civil-rights violations, discrimination, hate speech, and hate crimes investigated for the report involved citizens or legal permanent residents.
- As expected, all people of color, particularly Latinos, were subjected to increased "suspicion" and persecution as a result of 187.
- Finally, in follow-up calls made months after these incidents, surveyors found that the feelings of pain, outrage, and distress were long lasting for the victims.[39]

Even though many had expected that people of color in general would be "victimized because of skin color or accent … few were prepared for the pervasive discrimination and suspicion that actually followed."[40] The actual testimony is perhaps most compelling: In October 1995, one woman reported that a man cut in front of her while she was waiting to pick up food stamps at a check-cashing business. When she complained, the employee told her, "Shut up, stupid," throwing the coupons for the woman's food stamps in the trash. When she protested, he said, "Shut up, motherfucker. You people don't have a right to ask [for food stamps]. That's all you know how to do," and told her that he did not have to give her the food stamps if he didn't want to. On June 1, 1995, arsonists set fire to the home of a Latino family after spray painting on the walls, "Wite [sic] power," "your family dies," and the word "Mexico" with an X through it.

In one of the worst accounts, a 54-year-old woman—a home-care nurse and a legal permanent resident—was walking near a high school in November 1994, shortly after Proposition 187 passed. A group of eight teenage boys came out of the school site and began chasing her, yelling racial slurs and pelting her with rocks. She tried to ignore them and get away but weakness from surgery and a recent heart attack prevented her from running. They followed her and became more insulting, yelling, "Get out of here Indian! Mexican! Go back to your country!" and "Fuck you, motherfucker!"[41] The woman cried to the hotline operator: "Nothing like this had ever happened to me before.... I have always been accustomed to respecting others and to being respected."[42]

Finally, these hate crimes should not be mistaken for inadvertent or unanticipated effects of the measure. Many proponents of Proposition 187 unabashedly expressed their malicious intentions with the measure. For example, Ruth Coffey, founder of Stop Immigration Now, told the *Los Angeles Times,* "I have no intention of being the object of 'conquest,' peaceful or otherwise, by Latinos, Asians, Blacks, Arabs or any other group of individuals who have claimed my country."[43] Ronald Prince, another backer of Proposition 187, dubbed the Save Our State (SOS) initiative, said to a gathering in Orange County, "You are the posse and SOS is the rope."[44]

The quiet demise of Proposition 187 through a series of political maneuvers suited many politicians and employers quite well, as it enabled them to "have their cake and eat it too." For example, Gray Davis successfully averted political disaster by taking the stance that, while he had opposed the measure in 1984, he was also obligated to uphold the will of the people of California, 60 percent of whom had voted for it in 1994. Davis reminded Californians that during the elections, he had opposed Proposition 187 "because it pits Californians against one another, and I believe it hits hardest at children, who are truly innocent in all of this."[45] But when he inherited this political land mine from his opponent, Pete Wilson, whose grand finale in office was to appeal Judge Pfaelzer's ruling striking it down, Davis sidestepped the dilemma by relegating the issue to mediation. As Genethia Hayes, then–executive director of the Greater Los Angeles Southern Christian Leadership Conference, said, "We are disappointed in the governor's decisions. This is a way for him not to really have to make a tough decision, and making tough decisions is why we worked so hard to get him elected."[46]

The staff in Davis's office was trained to explain that the governor really had no other choice, that while he personally opposed the measure (before the elections), as governor he was obligated to enforce it. Furthermore, his staff explained, we could rest assured that Judge Pfaelzer's ruling regarding the unconstitutionality of many provisions would carry great weight. Yet in a press conference on April 15, 1999, Davis noted that "a great many things have transpired over the last five years that affect the legal status of Proposition 187," including the passage of the welfare "reform" law and the immigration law changes of 1996. Davis said, "These many laws effectively put into federal law many of the provisions of Proposition 187, particularly as they relate to the denial of welfare and health services other than emergency medical care."[47] In my view, Davis's statement effectively put into the hands of Proposition 187 supporters a great many arguments to lend legitimacy and viability to their efforts to salvage the measure.

Many immigrants' rights advocates feel that Davis copped out by emphasizing that the federal immigration law of 1996 had already formalized many of the restrictions on immigrants' rights contained in Proposition 187. Similarly, much of the debate surrounding Proposition 187 was focused on the measure's unconstitutionality because it conflicted with federal authority over immigration matters. This focus was misplaced and served to distract attention from the other ways that Proposition 187 raised serious constitutional questions regarding the rights of immigrants, including and especially the undocumented. For example, one of the principles that was largely lost in discussions around Proposition 187 is the idea raised in *Plyler v. Doe,* a 1982 US Supreme Court case dealing with similar issues: that undocumented immigrants are people, entitled to equal protection under the law regardless of their immigration status. Justice William Brennan, citing a number of related cases dating back to 1886, wrote the opinion for the majority, asserting:

> Whatever his status under the immigration laws, an alien is surely a "person" in any ordinary sense of that term. Aliens, even aliens whose presence in this country is unlawful, have long been recognized as "persons" guaranteed due process of law by the 5th and 14th Amendments.[48]

The *Plyler* case involved a 1975 Texas statute that authorized local school districts to deny enrollment in public schools and withheld the use of state funds for the education of children who were not "legally admitted" into the United States. The district of Tyler, Texas, did not implement this law and continued to admit undocumented children until 1977, when the school board adopted a policy charging undocumented children $1,000 in annual tuition to attend school. Michael McAndrews, coordinator of a church project in Tyler assisting Mexican Americans, met with Superintendent Plyler to raise concerns about how such a policy would be implemented. He asked, "Who will decide who can come?... [T]he principals ... have no idea who's undocumented and who's not." Although Plyler assured McAndrews that letters would be sent to the parents of children who would be excluded, no letters went out and McAndrews's fears indeed materialized. He reported:

> On the first day of school, some children were refused. They were children whose parents couldn't speak English and were dressed poorly. There was no rhyme or reason as to who got in and who didn't. One family had two children in and two out just because the kids were in different schools.[49]

A temporary injunction was placed on the district's policy and the children were admitted to school until the matter was settled. In December 1977, Judge Wayne Justice of the US District Court placed a permanent injunction on the Texas law, rejecting the state's arguments that it was acting within its constitutional authority to attempt to discourage or keep out "illegal aliens" and the district's claim that it was attempting to avoid a heavy fiscal burden from increased enrollment by immigrant children. The judge observed that the increase in school enrollment was mostly by children who were legal residents, that barring undocumented children from the schools would not improve the "quality of education," and that the policy had neither "the purpose or effect of keeping illegal aliens out of the State of Texas."[50]

Judge Justice cited the expert testimony of Dr. Gilbert Cardeñas that 50 to 60 percent of current legal-alien workers were formerly "illegal aliens," and of Rolan Heston, district director of the INS in Houston, that undocumented children "can and do" live in the country for years and later adjust their status through marriage or otherwise to citizen or permanent resident. He concluded that, under current immigration laws and practices, "the illegal alien of today may well be the legal alien of tomorrow." Furthermore, he argued, these undocumented children, "[already] disadvantaged as a result of poverty, lack of English-speaking ability, and undeniable racial prejudices ... will become permanently locked into the lowest socio-economic class" if they are denied an education.[51]

Affirming the district court decision, the US Supreme Court struck down the Texas statute in 1982, arguing further that the failures of immigration law or its enforcement, and the failure to prohibit the employment of undocumented immigrants, has resulted in "the creation of a substantial 'shadow population' of illegal migrants." Justice Brennan warned:

> This situation raises the specter of a permanent caste of undocumented resident aliens, encouraged by some to remain here as a source of cheap labor, but nevertheless denied the benefits that our society makes available to citizens and lawful residents. The existence of such an underclass presents most difficult problems for a nation that prides itself on adherence to principles of equality under the law.

Brennan went on to point out the innocence of the children as "special members of this underclass" and the unfairness of imposing such hardships and penalties on those who had no control over their presence in the country, their immigration status, or their parents' conduct. He also argued that, although public education is not a "right" guaranteed under the Constitution, it is "necessary to prepare citizens to participate effectively and intelligently in our open political system," to be "self-reliant and self-sufficient," and that it is "the primary vehicle for transmitting the values on which our society rests." Finally, Brennan wrote:

> We cannot ignore the significant social costs borne by our nation when select groups are denied the means to absorb the values and skills upon which our social order rests. Paradoxically, by depriving the children of any disfavored group of an education, we foreclose the means by which that group might raise the level of esteem in which it is held by the majority.[52]

Here is where I depart from Brennan, although I share his ultimate conclusions regarding immigrant access to education as one of many social services to which they are entitled. My assessment of the value of American public education, and its benefits for immigrant children in particular, is far less sanguine, as I believe that the purposes or ultimate functions of schools are far less lofty than what Brennan presents. Schools function primarily to reproduce economic inequalities and social hierarchies, to channel children and young adults into their "proper place" in the industrial order, and to socialize them to accept this position. In the case of immigrant children, that place is at the periphery, as "outsiders," or at the bottom, as low-wage service workers.

Brennan's reasoning is also tinged with the cost-benefit approach that we must go beyond in questions of immigrant-women-worker rights and, ultimately, human rights. Brennan wrote:

> It is difficult to understand precisely what the state hopes to achieve by promoting the creation and perpetuation of a subclass of illiterates within our boundaries, surely adding to the problems and costs of unemployment, welfare, and crime. It is thus clear

that whatever savings might be achieved by denying these children an education, they are wholly insubstantial in light of the costs involved to these children, the state, and the nation.[53]

Although Brennan puts a finer polish on the cost-benefit approach here, the focus on the "bottom line" is still readily apparent. Brennan emphasizes the perceived or projected social costs of the presence of immigrants in the United States, particularly their unregulated or unsupervised presence—that is, without the guidance of education providing proper values and skills. He still neglects to see the unfair costs to immigrant workers in hardships suffered, hate violence endured, and labor stolen from them. Brennan declines to view undocumented adults as he sees their children: as innocent and as deserving of protections and basic entitlements.

In some ways, the opinion written by Judge Justice for the US district court was more incisive, focusing on the plight of the immigrant workers who were these schoolchildren's parents, and in whose footsteps these children would most likely follow. Justice asserted that US government policies resulted in "the existence of a large number of employed illegal aliens, such as the parents of plaintiffs in this case, whose presence is tolerated, whose employment is perhaps even welcomed, but who are virtually defenseless against any abuse, exploitation, or callous neglect to which the state or the state's natural citizens and business organizations may wish to subject them."[54]

Both the opinion in the *Plyler* decision and much of the anti–Proposition 187 rhetoric revolved around the idea that it would be too "costly" to the United States to deny immigrant children the "means to absorb" American values, skills, or basic public goods. This points to the contradiction that belies Proposition 187 and similar exclusionary measures. Restrictionists assert that immigrants pose a menace to US society and American culture because they are "unassimilable," yet they attempt to deny immigrants access to the resources and avenues that would enable them to "assimilate." Efforts to exclude undocumented immigrants from school are particularly ironic, given that schools function mostly to socialize and discipline the workforce, specifically to train low-wage, menial laborers for industrial society. Perhaps proponents of such restrictionist measures do not want immigrant children to be molded into this brand of worker but another category entirely of super-exploitable worker—those with no access to language or other skills and, most of all, no access to a status even remotely resembling citizenship that might allow them the safety to organize.

Immigrant community and labor organizing have thrived despite the populist and legislative attacks, hate crimes, and countless injuries endured by immigrants on a daily basis. In fact, in some cases, these assaults have served to galvanize people of color and immigrant communities rather than to suppress them. As one observer put it,

> [Proposition 187] inadvertently triggered the political awakening of many Latinos who saw themselves, regardless of their citizenship status, as being targets. In Los Angeles, with its emerging Latino majority, Proposition 187 inspired one of the largest protest demonstrations ever—activism that eventually translated into growing Latino political participation.[55]

Proposition 187 is widely seen as having stirred unprecedented numbers of immigrants to become citizens and register to vote, increasing the Latino and Asian presence and power in the electorate. Frank Sharry, executive director of the National Immigration Forum, observed, "Pete Wilson brought out the angry white male in California and used immigration as a hot-button issue to get reelected. That brought out the angry new citizen in record numbers to vote and punish the Republican Party."[56]

Thus, while the intended effect and, to a large extent, the result of these attacks on immigrants by lawmakers and common "citizens" have been to teach or allow racism and sanction violence, they have also inspired action and forged unity among the targets of these attacks. At the same time that restrictionist efforts breed hatred against immigrants and people of color, they also breed renewed commitment among these communities to pull together, to survive, and to fight back. Ironically, immigrant activists are emerging as exactly the radicals that their foes have feared. US Representative Dana Rohrabacher, a Republican from Huntington Beach, California, said shortly before the passage of Proposition 187, "Unlawful immigrants [will] represent the liberal/left foot soldiers in the next decade."[57] This comment gives new meaning to the term "unlawful" when viewed in the context of fighting laws such as Proposition 187.

Immigrant women workers pose a formidable force in today's labor movement. James Elmendorf of HERE Local 11 said that he commonly sees workers who are initially reluctant to strike come to the realization that they have survived poverty, hunger, war, persecution, and dangerous journeys to escape these conditions in their home countries. They have little to fear and much to gain in fighting against the daily assaults on their lives, families, and rights here.[58] As Roy Mendoza of United Food and Commercial Workers, whose membership is 80 percent undocumented, says, "The big lie is that [people] are afraid. Yeah, they're afraid, but they'll fight a lot harder than you think."[59]

In the fall of 1994, Maribel Delgado, then a third-year law student at UC Berkeley's Boalt Law School, spoke out against Proposition 187. As a child, Delgado had come to California with her mother as an undocumented immigrant. Her attendance at California public schools, which was completely lawful under the prevailing constitutional protections and legal precedent, could be estimated to have cost the state approximately $40,000. When Delgado reached the age of 18, she was awarded a scholarship to attend Stanford University and became a legal permanent resident.

Delgado and her mother had been recruited by an American family who hired her mother to work for them as a housekeeper and nanny. The family gave them a bedroom, $35 a week, and fake documents. Delgado attended school while her mother cleaned house and cared for the American family's children around the clock, six days a week, for almost 10 years. When the Delgados wanted to apply for amnesty, they asked the family to sign an affidavit attesting that they had lived with them for years, but the family refused, afraid that they would be caught employing an "illegal." Yet when Delgado was a junior at Stanford, the family's daughter called her to ask if she knew anyone undocumented who could cook and clean for her. Delgado asked why the person had to be undocumented, and the daughter replied that documented people "make better money in other jobs." Delgado said:

> I was shocked, even though I shouldn't have been. I realized she thought of me as a commodity.... We're not puppets that can be taken out of a bag.... In the end, people just want to use other people and just snuff them out when they don't need them anymore.[60]

Delgado's analysis captures perfectly the prevailing mentality of employers of immigrants, both documented and undocumented. This ideology is particularly insidious as it operates in the minds of countless employers in the privacy of their own homes, and clearly is passed on from one generation of US citizens to the next. Delgado's insights were echoed by many of the women I interviewed for this book, including one woman whose employer extended this mentality to lethal proportions.

Alma Zaragosa, a member of CHIRLA's DWA, provided home health care for an elderly man living in a wealthy suburb of Los Angeles. She had been employed by the man's daughter to care for him for about a year when the daughter instructed Zaragosa to give her father a double dose of all of his medications, including sleeping pills, pain killers, and antihallucinogens. The daughter pressured her for two weeks, screaming, "You do it!" and once even moved toward Zaragosa to punch her. Zaragosa said, "She wanted me to kill him." For two weeks, Zaragosa continued to work under these terrorizing conditions, caring for the man until he died. Zaragosa's employer fired her immediately, refused to pay her for the last two weeks' work, and told her to leave the man's home in the hills right away, at two o'clock in the morning.[61]

Since that episode, Zaragosa has done mostly child care, although occasionally she does home-care work. Eventually, she would like to pursue training beyond a CNA degree. Zaragosa has done much of the media and outreach work for the DWA in local churches and parks since 1992. She does this work as a volunteer in addition to her full-time child-care work in the hope that these cases will get the national media attention that they deserve and that the association will grow in membership. It is truly remarkable that so many women like Zaragosa and the Delgados persevere with intelligence, integrity, courage, and compassion when they encounter none of these qualities in their employers and instead meet with merciless exploitation and ignorance. These women's perseverance serves as their greatest weapon in their struggles against employers and the anti-immigrant attacks that they encounter on a daily basis. It is ironic that immigrant women who provide our society with the most intimate care services are treated as if they are invisible, or at best disposable. Immigrant women will not tolerate being condemned to do the caring and the dirty work for other people, only to be dumped like toxic waste when their services are no longer needed.

1   Mirta Ojito, "Once Divisive, Immigration Is Muted Issue," *New York Times,* November 1, 1998, national ed., p. 28.

2   "Border Patrol Turns 75," *Migration News* (May 1999), prod. University of California, Davis; available via Internet on the *Migration News* home page, http://migration.ucdavis.edu. To subscribe, send your e-mail address to: *Migration News,* <migrant@primal.ucdavis.edu>. See also José Palafox, "Militarizing the Border," *CovertAction Quarterly* 56 (Spring 1996), pp. 14–19, and *New World Border,* Rollin' Deep Productions, prod. Casey Peek and Jose Palafox, 1997, videocassette; available from NNIRR, 510-465-1984.

3   Mark Shaffer and Dennis Wagner, "Bordering on Madness," *San Francisco Chronicle,* May 10, 1999.

4   Tad Bartimus, "Time to Make a Clean Break with Another Cleaning Lady," "Among Friends" column, *San Jose Mercury News,* May 23, 1999, p. 11-G. Respond to Bartimus at among_friends@hotmail.com or c/o The Women Syndicate, Box 728, Puunene, HI 96784.

5   Bartimus, "Time to Make a Clean Break."

6   Peter Brimelow, *Alien Nation: Common Sense About America's Immigration Disaster* (New York: Random House, 1995), p. 9. I am grateful to Brimelow for serving as my foil, and I credit him for this tactic of making backhanded references to one's intellectual adversaries.

7   Lucia Hwang, "Border Crossing," *San Francisco Bay Guardian,* April 28, 1999, p. 23; see also David Bacon, "Changing Demographics—A Promise of Survival," *Dollars and Sense* 225 (September/October 1999), pp. 42–48, on the centrality of immigrant workers to today's labor organizing and leadership.

8   Hwang, "Border Crossing," p. 23.

9   Nancy Cleeland, "Home-Care Workers' Vote for Union a Landmark for Labor," *Los Angeles Times,* February 26, 1999, pp. A-1, A-20; Steven Greenhouse, "In Biggest Drive Since 1937, Union Gains Victory," *New York Times,* February 26 1999, pp. A-1, A-15.

10 Frank Swoboda, "A Healthy Sign for Organized Labor," *Washington Post,* February 27, 1999, p. E-1.

11 Greenhouse, "Union Gains Victory."

12 CalWORKs (California Work Opportunity and Responsibility to Kids Act) is California's implementation of the federal welfare-reform mandates, imposing work requirements and time limits on recipients. It is funded through a combination of federal TANF block grants and required state matching grants.

13 SB1955.

14 William Julius Wilson, *When Work Disappears* (New York: Knopf, 1996), p. 192.

15 Interview with Wei-ling Huber, May 15, 1999.

16 Brimelow, *Alien Nation,* pp. 173–75.

17 Brimelow, *Alien Nation,* p. 175.

18 "INS Worksite Raids Pit Immigrant Workers Against Welfare Recipients," *National Employment Law Project NELP Update* (Spring 1998), p. 1.

19 Testimony of Teamsters Union member at Living Wage Ordinance hearings before the San Francisco Board of Supervisors, San Francisco City Hall, March 6, 1999.

20 Testimony of Jonathan Perez at Living Wage Ordinance hearings before the San Francisco Board of Supervisors, San Francisco City Hall, March 6, 1999.

21 Testimony of Mujeres Unidas y Activas member at Living Wage Ordinance hearings, San Francisco City Hall, March 6, 1999.

22 Interview with Steve Williams, March 22, 1999.

23 Interview with Victor Narro and Libertad Rivera of Domestic Workers Association, February 16, 1998; DWA has also had success in assisting in legal action against abusive employers, such as in Yuni Mulyono's case (discussed in chapter 4), and against employment agencies, such as the Betty Blue Agency, which had been charging inordinate placement fees to women seeking housekeeping jobs through the agency. See also Victor Narro, "Home Is Where the Union Is," *Third Force* 5: 6 (January/February 1998), pp. 18–21.

24 Cristina Riegos and Pierrette Hondagneu-Sotelo, "Sin Organizacion, No Hay Solucion: Latina Domestic Workers and Non-traditional Labor Strategies," *Latino Studies Journal* (Fall 1997), pp. 19–23.

25 Challenge for Human Rights: Confronting Immigration Law Enforcement Today conference, Los Angeles, June 5–7, 1998, sponsored by the National Network for Immigrant and Refugee Rights and the National Employment Law Project.

26 Challenge for Human Rights conference.

27 Challenge for Human Rights conference.

28 *Super Domestica en: El Caso de las Trabajadoras Explotadas* ["Super Domestic in: The Case of the Exploited Workers"], produced by CHIRLA. Artist Kelvin Manzanares. Available through CHIRLA. Contact number: 213-353-1345. See illustration on page 190.

29 Challenge for Human Rights conference.

30 Testimony of Rosa Montana, Challenge for Human Rights conference.

31 Testimony of MUA member, Challenge for Human Rights conference.

32 Testimony of MUA member, Challenge for Human Rights conference.

33 The polling was done by a polling firm, the Feldman Group, Inc.; interview with David Rolf, April 12, 1999.

34 Rolf interview.

35 Interview with Patricia Tejada (pseudonym) and family, and Amalia Hernandez (pseudonym), February 16, 1998.

36 Interview with Patricia Tejada and family, and Amalia Hernandez. Ironically, one Mexican woman I interviewed (chapter 1) believed that migration for the purpose of welfare use was particularly common among Central Americans.

37 Pamphlet produced by Taxpayers Against 187.

38 The Spanish-language hotline was established shortly before the November 1994 elections. Coalition for Humane Immigrant Rights of Los Angeles (CHIRLA), *Hate Unleashed: Los Angeles in the Aftermath of 187,* November 1995.

39 CHIRLA, *Hate Unleashed,* p. 16.

40 CHIRLA, *Hate Unleashed,* p. 13.

41 CHIRLA, *Hate Unleashed,* p. 13.

42 CHIRLA, *Hate Unleashed,* p. 16.

43 CHIRLA, *Hate Unleashed,* p. 7.

44 Leo Chavez, *Shadowed Lives: Undocumented Immigrants in American Society* (Fort Worth, Texas: Harcourt Brace College Publishers, 1998), p. 192.

45 "Governor Davis' Statement on Proposition 187 as Delivered," press release, April 15, 1999.

46 Don Terry, "California Governor Ducked Immigrant Feud, Some Say," *New York Times,* April 17, 1999, pp. A-1, A-10.

47 "Governor Davis' Statement on Proposition 187."

48 457 U.S. 202, 210; 102 S. Ct. 2382, 2391; 1982; citing *Shaughnessy v. Mezei,* 1953; *Wong Wing v. United States,* 1896; *Yick Wo v. Hopkins,* 1886.

49 Fred W. Friendly and Martha J.H. Elliott, *The Constitution: That Delicate Balance* (New York: Random House, 1984), p. 241.

50 458 F. Supp. 568, 575 (1978).

51 458 F. Supp. 568, 575 (1978), p. 577.

52 *Wisconsin v. Yoder,* 406 U.S. 205, at 221. 457 U.S. 202, 221; 102 S. Ct. 2382, 2397.

53 457 U.S. 202, 229; 102 S. Ct. 2382, 2401.

54 458 F. Supp., at 585.

55 Patrick J. McDonnell, "Davis Won't Appeal Prop. 187 Ruling," *Los Angeles Times,* August 6, 1999. See Elizabeth Martínez, *De Colores Means All of Us: Latina Views for a Multi-Colored Century* (Cambridge: South End Press, 1998).

56 Ojito, "Once Divisive, Immigration Is Muted Issue," p. 28.

57 Chavez, *Shadowed Lives,* p. 192.

58 Interview with James Elmendorf.

59 Statement of Roy Mendoza at Organizing Immigrant Workers: Defending the Rights to Organize conference, organized by Labor Immigrant Organizing Network (LION), Oakland, CA, January 23, 1999.

60 Marcos Breton, "State Economy Lures Immigrants, Some Say," *Sacramento Bee,* October 23, 1994, p. A-30.

61 Interview with Alma Zaragosa (pseudonym), February 15, 1998.

Index

caregivers, 14, 35
Caring Capacity versus Carrying Capacity (Eisenstadt and Thorup), 23
Casa San Miguel nursing home, 93–97, 99, 114
Catholic Community Services, 66
Census Bureau, 5, 26, 29
Center for US-Mexican Studies, 5
Central America, 38
charity, 168, 181, 184, 207
Chavez, Leo, 12
Cherne, Leo, 43
Chicanas, 170–71
child care, 69, 125, 218–19; in African-American communities, 78; living wage and, 201; *Mujeres Unidas y Activas* (MUA) and, 204; women as preferred labor source for, 5; working-class mothers and, 55–56, 57–58
children, 1, 5, 11; denial of benefits to, 113; discouragement of women from having, 12; education and, 214–15; paternity of, 9; poverty and, 81; public assistance to, 71–74; undocumented, 213. *See also* citizenship
Children Today (government publication), 164–65
China, 123, 124, 128
Chinese Exclusion Act (1882), 24
Chinese immigrants, 23–24, 56, 198
Chishti, Muzaffar, 176
"citizen" groups, 14
Citizens' Commission for Justice, 94, 114
citizenship, 12, 15, 83; access to benefits of, 46, 216; of children, 25, 26, 31, 64, 68, 213; denial of,

82; economic, 146; "true" citizens, 2
civil rights, 7, 207
Civil Rights Act (1964), 97
class, 26, 36, 48
Clinton, Bill, 7–8, 165
Cloward, Richard, 70
Coalition for Humane Immigrant Rights of Los Angeles (CHIRLA), 169, 202, 209, 218
Coalition for Immigrant and Refugee Rights and Services (CIRRS), 56, 67
Coffey, Ruth, 210
Coles, Tony, 166
colonialism, internal, 101–2
Commission for Filipina Migrant Workers (Britain), 138
Commission on Immigration Reform, 108
Committee on Economic Security, 72
community service, 171
Comprehensive Adult Student Assessment System (CASAS), 67–68
Concerned Citizens of Cochise County (CCCC), 192, 193
Congress, 59–61, 64
Connecting Issues work group, 181
Conner, Roger, 28, 29
consumption patterns, 33
contraception, 11
Cornelius, Wayne, 5
cost-benefit approach, 30–31, 207–8, 214–15
Crispin, Mayee, 131–32
Cruz, Merceditas, 142

About
Grace Chang

Grace Chang is a long-time immigrant rights and welfare rights advocate, writer, and researcher active in the San Francisco Bay area. Her work has appeared in *Socialist Review, Radical America,* and several anthologies, including *Dragon Ladies: Asian American Feminists Breathe Fire* (South End Press, 1997). She is a co-editor of *Mothering: Ideology, Experience, and Agency* (Routledge, 1994) and has contributed to *American Families: A Multicultural Reader* (Routledge, 1999), *Reading Between the Lines: Toward an Understanding of Current Social Problems* (Mayfield, 1998), and *Race, Class, and Gender: An Anthology* (Wadsworth, 1998).

About
Mimi Abramovitz

Mimi Abramovitz teaches social policy at Hunter School of Social Work and the Graduate Center of the City of New York. She is the author of *Regulating the Lives of Women: Social Welfare Policy from Colonial Times to the Present* (South End Press, rev. ed. 1996) and *Under Attack, Fighting Back: Women and Welfare in the United States* (Monthly Review Press, rev. ed. 2000).

About
South End Press

South End Press is a nonprofit, collectively run book publisher with more than 200 titles in print. Since our founding in 1977, we have tried to meet the needs of readers who are exploring, or are already committed to, the politics of radical social change. Our goal is to publish books that encourage critical thinking and constructive action on the key political, cultural, social, economic, and ecological issues shaping life in the United States and in the world. In this way, we hope to give expression to a wide diversity of democratic social movements and to provide an alternative to the products of corporate publishing.

Through the Institute for Social and Cultural Change, South End Press works with other political media projects—Alternative Radio; Speakout, a speakers' bureau; and Z magazine—to expand access to information and critical analysis.

To order books, please send a check or money order to: South End Press, 7 Brookline Street, #1, Cambridge, MA 02139-4146. To order by credit card, call 1-800-533-8478. Please include $3.50 for postage and handling for the first book and 50 cents for each additional book. Write or e-mail southend@igc.org for a free catalog, or visit our web site, http://www.lbbs.org/sep/sep.htm.

Related Titles
from South End Press

*Regulating the Lives of Women: Social Welfare Policy
from Colonial Times to the Present* (Updated Edition)
By Mimi Abramovitz
0-89608-551-1 $22

*Dangerous Intersections: Feminist Perspectives on Population,
Environment, and Development*
Edited by Jael Silliman and Ynestra King
0-89608-597-X $20

De Colores Means All of Us: Latina Views for a Multi-Colored Century
By Elizabeth Martínez
0-89608-583-X $18

Dragon Ladies: Asian American Feminists Breathe Fire
Edited by Sonia Shah
0-89608-575-9 $17

*Race, Gender, and Work: A Multi-Cultural Economic History
of Women in the United States* (Updated Edition)
By Teresa Amott and Julie Matthaei
0-89608-537-6 $21

See previous page for ordering information.